Evolutionary Playwork and Reflec...

Play is a crucial component in the development of all children. In this comprehensive and accessible text, Bob Hughes explores the complexities of children's play, its meaning and purpose, and argues that adult-free play is essential for the psychological well-being of the child.

The book is divided into three main sections. The first examines the fundamentals of evolutionary playwork, from creating the right play environment to issues of safety and participation. Second, the book explores the key theoretical concepts underlying playwork. Finally, the book offers new models to help playworkers develop their own professional practice. Throughout the text, the author brings his arguments to life with vivid reflections on a lifetime's experience of play and playwork.

Evolutionary Playwork and Reflective Analytic Practice is the first book of its kind, and represents essential reading for all playwork students, practitioners and researchers. It also incorporates dedicated material for parents looking to better understand and enhance the development of their children.

Bob Hughes MA, has been a theoretical and applied playworker for 30 years. He has been the National Co-ordinator of PlayEducation, an independent playwork agency providing training and research services since 1982.

Evolutionary Playwork and Reflective Analytic Practice

Bob Hughes

London and New York

First published 2001
by Routledge
11 New Fetter Lane, London EC4P 4EE

Simultaneously published in the USA and Canada
by Routledge
29 West 35th Street, New York, NY 10001

Routledge is an imprint of the Taylor & Francis Group

Typeset in Times New Roman by Wearset, Boldon, Tyne and
Wear
Printed and bound in Great Britain by TJ International Ltd,
Padstow, Cornwall

British Library Cataloguing in Publication Data
A catalogue record for this book is available from the British
Library

Library of Congress Cataloging in Publication Data
Hughes, Bob, 1944–
    Evolutionary playwork and reflective analytic practice / Bob Hughes.
        p. cm.
    Includes bibliographical references and index.
    1. Play. 2. Recreation centers. 3. Child development. I. Title.
GV182.9 .H84 2001
155.4′18—dc21

                                        2001018066

ISBN 0-415-25166-4 (pbk.)
ISBN 0-415-25165-6 (hbk.)

To Bob, Jean, Thomas and Finnian

Contents

Figures

Acknowledgements

This book would not have seen the light of day without the help and support of numerous people. My deepest gratitude goes out to them.

To my sons Rob and Maf who read an early draft of the manuscript and reassured me that I wasn't too far away from what they remembered. To Gordon Sturrock whose incredible generosity in making time available to read drafts, correct grammar and debate issues was typical – even when he was under considerable pressures himself, he kept me sane. To Steve Chown, who read the main draft and who offered me advice and ideas about changes and inclusions. To Mel Potter, who was always available to solve my computer crises and who translated my visual ideas and doodles into the original computer graphics. To Annie who tolerated and supported me over the three-year period it took to plan and write. And to my grandsons Thomas and Finnian. Liz, Domi and Maggie and all the children I have been honoured to work with over the years, for convincing me that however poorly I may have written them, the fundamental ideas contained within the text are accurate.

I also gratefully acknowledge that the following organisations have granted me permission to reproduce the following:

- Chapter Two – 'Evolutionary Play', an earlier version of which was presented as a keynote speech at 'Issues Affecting Play Today', a conference hosted by the Families, Children and Young People's Team of Watford Council, November, 1998.
- RAP Example 1. 'Built Environmental Effects on Instinctive and Intuitive Play Outcomes – Some Reflections', originally presented as a paper at the 11th IPA World Conference, June 1990.
- RAP Example 5. Four examples of RAP from research undertaken in Northern Ireland, which first appeared in my MA in Playwork Development Studies dissertation for Anglia Polytechnic University.
- RAP Example 6. 'Playwork, Philosophy and Practice – A Personal View', which was first presented as a paper at PlayWales Conference, Cardiff, 1999.
- Various references and passages drawn from *Play Environments: A Ques-*

tion of Quality and *A Playworker's Taxonomy of Play Types*, first published in London by PLAYLINK, 1996.

I would also like to take this opportunity to thank Stephen Rennie and Peter K. Smith for reviewing the manuscript, my editor Simon Whitmore, for his helpful advice and ideas, and the following for their advice, guidance and frequent inspiration: Sandra Melville, Mike and Sue Greenaway and family, Jess Milne, Mick Conway, Ian Chamberlain, Wendy Roberts @ UCCANA @ APU, Mary, Joe and Maeve McKee, Belfast Travellers Sites Project, Tony Chilton, Marianne Manello, Keith Cranwell, Pat Petrie, Perry Else, Paul Eyre, Jackie Hopfinger, Sakine, Maria Almy, Becky Harrison, George Gawlinski, Cath Gordon, Paul Hogan, Joe Frost, James Talbot, Bridget Handscomb, Parvez Iqbal, Jimi Jolley, Anna Logan, Hazel Maguire, Joan McGrath, Angela Stallard, Gary Moore, Tessa Hall, Gary Pennington, Robin Moore, Nilda Cosco, Maureen Palmer, Michelle Virdi, Pete Rawlinson, Joe, Janet and Gavin Blake, Jo Seccombe, Sam and Isobel Murray, Chris Taylor, Robert Fishwick, the staff at the following libraries: University of Cambridge Library, Department of Experimental Psychology, University of Cambridge, Scientific Periodicals, University of Cambridge, The British Library and Queen's University, Belfast, and Jackie Woolcott, Danielle and Louise (and Frank of course), Suzanne Wright-Crain and Itoku Tsukamoto.

Introduction

- A boy, perhaps nine years of age is playing right beside me, using small farm animals in a pen. He is moving them about and making mooing and other animal noises. He is in immersion and seems oblivious of everything around him. Suddenly the general noise level drops and he looks up. Then he lays down and begins the imaginative narrative again. Now he is bringing it out into the centre of the room, still making mooing and other noises. He is transporting the whole thing to the sand-play area. Eventually he lays in the sand-pit himself with the animals, burying them in the sand.

- Joe had been singing the praises of playwork to a friend. The discussion had been about trusting children. He had said, 'Playwork teaches us that, if children are playing near water, don't be too protective by hanging onto their coat collars. Stay close, if you are worried, but trust the child to be aware of the dangers and take the necessary precautions.' The friend took notice of playwork's wise words. And the next time he took his child to the lake in the park, instead of hanging onto her coat collar as he normally did, he let her play freely close to the water's edge. Trusting her, but at the same time keeping a close eye on her. Obviously not close enough – she fell in!!!!

What is happening in these two events? What are they telling us? That children play with toys and get so absorbed that they make non-human noises and are oblivious to the world around them? That there is something called playwork that gives parents bad advice about risks, encouraging them to let their children fall into water?

The first, every one of us will recognise. We have all played and if we are young enough may still be able to evoke that strange dissociation from reality that is imaginative play. And if we try we may still be able to recall endless play memories of events, other children, pets, places and feelings that we filed away as children.

These memories and their accompanying feelings provide us now as adults with the only real link we have of the particular kind of experience that is play. Where, as children, we navigated a seething children's reality populated by the interplay between our evolving minds and bodies and the world we were growing up in. An interplay so powerful, so internalised, so highly personal and intimate that years later we are able to recount detail of such clarity that we would be hard pressed to remember about events that happened last week or even yesterday.

And thinking about playing we may revive moments of wincing embarrassment, of real pain or nerve jangling fear as we explored and experimented and sometimes overstepped the previous limits of our experience.

The second may be less familiar but may have no less powerful resonances although for very different reasons. As adults, as parents we want our children to play too. We want to let them out, to experience the fun and challenge we remember. But for many of us the fear of traffic, strangers and even other children, means that they either end up playing where we can see them or when we can supervise them.

One problem about this, as the second example tries to illustrate, is that when we *are* there we become a controlling influence on what they are able to do. We supervise and we protect. We often over-supervise and over-protect. As if we are not only frightened of traffic and strangers but afraid of everything when it comes to our children. In one sense it may be with good cause, but in another we may simply be delaying the inevitable.

It is a natural expression of the bond between parent and child that we do not want our children to come to harm, to experience pain or fear. But herein lies a dilemma. Should we adults be there at all when children play, and if the answer is yes, how long do we expect this to go on for? Until our children are ten, fifteen, twenty-five?

And what impact might this level of adult supervision be having? Is it possible that the supervision described in the example, rather than protecting the child, actually had the effect of disabling her, and that the reason she fell into the water was not because she had not been supervised enough, but that she had been supervised too much in the past?

Is the lesson in that example, that we must make it possible for our children to take more risks rather than less? That to be able to navigate the world with the minimum of harm and injury throughout life, they must experience and learn to deal with the real world as early in their lives as possible? Is that part of what play is for?

These are difficult and vexed questions for us all. They appear to query the ability of parents to look after their own children's development. They certainly highlight a gulf between the experiences many of us had when we were children and those we are prepared to tolerate for our own children.

And yet these same questions imply a genuine concern for children. That perhaps playing – whether in an imaginative narrative, or in close proximity to a dangerous element – is such a vitally important ingredient of childhood, that it is essential that children experience it even if it does put them at risk of harm and injury. That without play they will certainly come to harm.

From where do these notions come? The answer is, from something called playwork.

Playwork

Supervised and organised spaces for children's play have been around for years. Until the late 1960s the adults who supervised and organised them were known as 'playleaders', and there were hundreds of them around the UK and elsewhere.

However, at the beginning of the 1970s there began to evolve a new generation of playleaders who called themselves playworkers who, uncomfortable with simply supervising, organising and socialising – what I would call 'domesticating' – the children in their charge, began increasingly to turn to the scientific literature to underpin their practice. What they found there caused a revolution in their thinking and formed the embryo of what I am calling 'evolutionary playwork'.

Prior to this paradigm shift, playleaders had depended upon their intuition, common sense and job description to guide what they did and how they did it. Suddenly playworkers discovered an Aladdin's cave of concepts, ideas, outcomes and mechanisms that they believed would be translated from the biological literature into principles and practice that would provide a service which although less civically biased might be of infinitely more value and relevance to the children, and be intuitively recognised by them as such.

For the past twenty-five years, the struggle to promote that idea has continued.

The theory of play

What did playworkers find in the literature? Their initial discovery was that, for many years, natural scientists – psychologists, ethologists, ethnologists, evolutionists, ecologists and primatologists – and others including historians, writers, clinicians, architects, educationalists and sociologists, had been studying play in humans and in non-humans; that there were a vast array of data, and that whilst some (for example, Schlosberg, 1947) were arguing that as play could not even be properly defined, it could hardly be a manageable topic for scientific research, others were pondering its possible centrality in evolution (Bruner, 1976: 13–14).

Every playworker interested in the scientific study of play had their favourite influences. For some it was the psychologists, Lorenz, Fagan, Sylva and Bruner. For others it was the work of evolutionary ecologists like Clutton-Brock, ethologists like Hinde, anthropologists like Bateson, or primatologists like Lowick-Goodall whose work at the Gombe Stream Reserve went on to fascinate television viewers for over twenty years. But choices were more preferences of style and accessibility. Many playworkers were not university graduates and found the scientific method daunting and convoluted.

What these texts demonstrated was that, as diverse as play was, it was virtually universal among mammals; its diversity and duration was linked to phylogeny and immaturity, and that its complexity, in any given species, was viewed as an indicator of evolutionary development. Bruner (1972) for example, analyses the behaviour of different species as less to do with their evolved manual morphology and more to do with the nature of the programme that controls the use of the hands (pp. 36–7). This notion of a 'programme' becomes increasingly central to the evolving idea of playwork as it moves from its genesis to the contemporary period.

For some playworkers, viewing children as the young of a species – albeit their own – rather than as 'children' was and remains a problem. However, for those who felt more able to make the compromise, they suddenly had a wealth of data about play in non-humans, which could be juxtaposed with experience from their own and other's practice, about play in humans. This made it possible to translate and transfer the practical implications gleaned from non-human studies into playwork practice and *vice versa*. (Playworkers were beginning tentatively to conclude that their experience was, in many cases, more long-term and in-depth than any scientific study of human children to date.)

Work in genetics and socio-biology also helped further to cement the development of playwork practice into the evolving literature. Reading Wilson (1975), for example, when he stated, 'Human genes have surrendered their primacy in human evolution to ... culture', I inferred that because genes were now seen to be affected by 'non-biological, superorganic factors', if playworkers were to comprehensively provide for children's evolutionary needs – which was how playwork was beginning by some to be perceived – play spaces had to be a mirror of 'culture' as well as biology.

For a period of time there was lull. The 1980s and early 1990s were comparatively quiet periods for this developing relationship, although playworkers had more than enough to contend with, attempting to unravel the implications of the various scientific works already in existence and clarify their implications for practice. This unravelling resulted in, for example, work by King on play environment criteria and the 6 X's, Battram on possibility space, Gordon on Riskogenics, and Rennie on the ethics of confrontation.

More recently, research on play which is pertinent to playwork practice has started to be published, again, particularly in the fields of evolutionary psychology and neurology. In order to provide a theoretical context for the playwork concepts explored later in the book, the outlines of this research are examined very briefly in this introduction.

Evolutionary psychology

Evolutionary psychology is a fusion of two fields, cognitive psychology and evolutionary biology. Christened, 'Evolutionary psychology' by the anthropologist, Tooby and psychologist, Cosmides (Pinker, 1997: 23), its basic premise is that the design of the mind must have evolved by a process of natural selection.

Central to evolutionary psychology is the premise that the mind, operating like a piece of computer software – a program – evolves new mental modules, as it solves the adaptive problems of survival and reproduction each organism is presented with in the environment in which it finds itself.

The role of genes in the evolution of the mind was felt to be a significant although not an exclusive factor. Evolutionary psychology accepts, for example, the work of behavioural geneticists, that environment as well as genes determines the mind and that 'genes often build different minds in response to different environments ... changing the way in which the mind causes behaviour' (Evans and Zarate, 1999: 159–60).

They continue, 'Indeed this flexibility is an important part of the way we are designed. Natural selection has programmed human development to be contingent on various environmental triggers' (ibid.: 160).

So evolutionary psychology offers a model in which a flexible mind – determined by the rigours of natural selection – triggered by various environmental factors, determines behaviour.

How does this happen? Naturally evolutionary psychologists have their own explanation but play is no stranger to genetics nor the playworker to the notion of adaptation or flexibility, so could play be at the centre of the evolutionary psychology equation? And if so, could playwork have a pivotal environmental role? There are other similarities between these two areas, too.

For example, at the beginning of the last century, Hall's theory of recapitulation 'maintains that the play of children reflects the course of evolution from prehistoric hominids to the present' (Garvey, 1977: 9), alluding to the role of genes in the recapitulation process. Several psychologists and ethologists, including Loizos (1967), Eibl-Eibesfeldt (1967, 1970) and Bruner (1972, 1974, 1976), claimed that the essence of play lies in combinatorial flexibility, requiring the restructuring of thought or action (see Sylva, 1977: 60). Hutt *et al.* (1989) linked the idea of combinatorial flexibility to innovation (p. 225), whilst Sutton-Smith (1979) viewed these 'new combinations of thought' as providing 'an increase in the cognitive alternatives available' (p. 316).

Thus, there is a possibility that it is through the medium of play – itself a characteristic of many species and determined by the process of natural selection – that the evolution of mind may be facilitated. That the play drive exists to bring the human child into contact with the various features of its environment and that then, via playful recapitulation, the mind and genes are adapted as a consequence. Is this simplistic or useful conjecture?

Sutton-Smith offers this:

> play as novel adaptation, may have developed in two stages: the first as a reinforcement of potential synaptic variability through the performance of variable antics [flexibility], and the second as a fuller imitation of the evolutionary process itself, in which the organism models its own biological character [recapitulation].
>
> (p. 229)

This suggests a relationship, if not a conspiracy, between the drive to play and the development of mind.

Neurology

Sutton-Smith, also features prominently in propositions relating to the relationship between neurology, play and playwork.

In Sutton-Smith (1997), citing the neurologist Huttenlocher, he suggests that 'the infant's brain's ability to constantly undergo physical and chemical changes as it responds to the environment is taken to suggest enormous plasticity', and that, 'Play's function . . . may be to assist the actualisation of brain potential . . .' (p. 225).

Citing Kotulak (1996), he also states that 'an over abundance of cells and synapses is produced and the brain has to use them to make itself work' (p. 223).

In fact Huttenlocher (1990, 1992), having suggested that children under ten years of age may have brains of twice the potential size of children over that age, has proposed a sensitive period for plasticity which far exceeds infancy, spanning from about eight months to eight years in length.

The playwork corollary of this is that anyone working in any way with children in early or middle-childhood cannot escape the potential importance of play in those children's lives during that time-span, given that 'children spend more time playing than any other waking activity' (PlayBoard, 1990: 8).

The role of the environment

Needless to say, the nature of environment is a vital factor in playwork, but it has also been shown to be a vital factor in plasticity too. Whilst Sutton-Smith (1997) has drawn our attention to the role of environment in the plasticity phenomenon more recently, work by Bennett *et al.* (1964), Rosenzweig (1971), Rosenzweig *et al.* (1972) and Ferchmin and Eterovic (1979) discussed the implication on brain growth of different kinds of environments, suggesting that interaction with 'enriched' environments resulted in brain growth whilst interaction with 'impoverished' environments did not.

Bruner (1972) gave a fascinating pre-emptive analysis of this later work on brain growth, when he suggested that the evolutionary backdrop to rapid brain growth after birth was related to anatomical design, stating, 'If a bigger-brained creature is to get through a smaller birth canal, there is required, of course, a smaller initial brain size and therefore, greater initial immaturity – the human brain grows from approximately 335 to 1300 cubic centimetres during development' (p. 37).

Whilst Bruner's figures may have been overtaken by more recent findings, e.g. Huttenlocher (1990), the implication of what he says is very interesting. For if, as a part of human evolution, a larger human brain becomes an outcome of natural selection, but a fully developed brain will not fit through the birth canal (Grof (1975) gives us a fascinating insight into the struggle human babies may endure during birth (pp. 95–153)) – then nature's answer is to provide enormous potential for growth prior to birth, which is only realised once birth has taken place.

I take the Sutton-Smith and Huttenlocher material to imply that it is play that is the realising medium.

Sutton-Smith (1997) encapsulates this stating, 'humans are born with more going for them than they will ever have again', (p. 225), emphasising the importance to development of the period described by Huttenlocher (1990, 1992) as 'the sensitive period'. Bjorkland and Green (1992) add to this by describing the key neonatal cognitive characteristics of children up to the age of five – i.e. during this period of massive brain growth – as 'unrealistic optimism, egocentricity and reactivity', or to put it another way, play (Sutton-Smith, 1997: p. 226).

Thus a useful relationship between play, brain growth and environment begins to materialise. Play, described by Gould (1996) as a 'flexible, quirky, unpredictable, evolutionary potential for creative responses' (p. 44), interfacing with an 'enriched' environment, facilitates plasticity and 'actualises' novel connections (Sutton-Smith, 1997).

However, later research by McEwan (1999) also emphasises the role of environment on brain development, but concludes that factors like stress can have a negative impact upon what he terms 'adaptive plasticity' (p. 118). The theme of the impact of what may constitute an example of an 'impoverished' environment has also been available in the literature over the years. Its conclusions not only highlight the serious consequences of the 'play-deprivation' caused by them, but invites environmental reflection on what the defining characteristics of 'enrichment' might be, and clinical reflection on how the effects of 'play-deprivation' might be eliminated (Suomi and Harlow, 1971; Huttenmoser and Degan-Zimmermann, 1995; Chugani, 1998).

The challenge for the playworker

The challenge posed by the literature for the playworker was and is considerable. For whilst yesterday's playleaders may not have felt strongly that they needed to be guided by the literature, today's playworkers cannot avoid it, and this development is highlighted by the almost exponential growth of playwork training in the 1980s and the subsequent development of NVQ and higher – Dip. HE, Degree and Masters – education outlets in the years that followed.

Now, not only does the prospective playworker need a better understanding of what play is, what it does and what facilitates it, s/he also has to wrestle with the enormously complex environmental and ethical issues I have alluded to above.

A further complication for the professional has arisen as the designated and supervised play space has increasingly been identified as a compensatory medium for those children, who because of a whole raft of social and environmental factors, are playing *less*, are playing *outside* less, or are only able to play in a context when there are *adults present* (Hughes, 1996b).

Playing less, as we have seen may negatively affect children's development and evolution. Playing outside less may similarly affect their development, but may also have the effect of dissociating children from the natural world, a dissociation which Orr (1993) suggests means 'that we will have cut ourselves off from the source of sanity itself' (p. 437). Playing in a continual adult context generates similar concerns, for there are numerous examples of adults making arbitrary judgements about what constitutes allowable, politically correct, safe and sanitised play (Hughes, 1999c).

From an evolutionary perspective any development that creates in children a dissociation between the present and the past, could cause enormous problems for them. Wilber (1996), discussing the evolution of human consciousness, highlights the problems that may result if human beings start, in the words of Ruse (1979) 'to control and direct their biological evolution' (p. 222).

Describing the human individual as a 'compound individual', Wilber states, 'compounded, that is, of all levels of reality that have unfolded prior to man's present stage, and capped by that present stage itself' (p. 169). Paraphrasing Hall's Theory of Recapitulation, Wilber continues, 'We begin by repeating that each stage of evolution transcends but includes its predecessor ... that each stage of human evolution, although it transcends its predecessors, must include and integrate them in a higher unity'. He finishes with a stark warning: 'Failure to do so equals neurosis' (ibid.). In other words, if adults interfere with play, if they stop children engaging in certain types of play, they may make children ill.

Thus, for the playing child the major lessons I can draw from the literature of the past thirty years are that play is critically important to human development and evolution; it takes place most effectively in a variable, enriched environment, in a context which although sometimes facilitated by human adults should not be contaminated or adulterated by a non-play agenda.

Evolutionary playwork

Darwin is quoted by Gruber (1974: 54) as saying, 'Survival depends upon the organism remaking itself'. What I interpret this to mean is that at birth human children are driven to contextualise themselves in the here and now, that playing enables this complex compound individual to begin a process of discovering who and where it is now, as a comprehensive entity with a genetic perspective of past, present and perhaps future (Hughes, 2000). Play enables children to 'ground' themselves physically and psychologically.

By translating the biological literature and integrating it into their principles and practice, those playworkers who perhaps more accurately designate themselves as evolutionary playworkers can begin more effectively to:

- enable the child as a compound individual to be in touch with what and where it is
- facilitate Wilber's transcendence via recapitulation
- inhibit the problem of neurosis, associated with 'metaphysical dissociation'.

I have called this book *Evolutionary Playwork and Reflective Analytic Practice*. 'Evolutionary Playwork', because it differs from *playwork*, as defined in Bonel and Lindon (1996) as 'managing the play environment and providing the resources which enable children's play' (p. 15), for example, by identifying and emphasising play as a powerful biological force which, I believe may only be subsumed into any particular social model at the expense of the children it is attempting to serve.

What the scientific literature says to me is that, from an evolutionary perspective, we should not view our children as having been born into a static social preconception, but rather into a developing continuum. Children play to change, thus change rather than comfortable predictability must be the overriding characteristic of the play space.

Else and Sturrock (1998) get closer, by defining playwork as 'work[ing] with children in the expansion of their potential to explore and experience through play'.

However, I would extend that to define Evolutionary Playwork as: working with children (in the expansion of their potential to explore and experience through play) in a context which both recognises and integrates their biological needs and the integrity derived from them, into their practice.

'*Reflective Analytic Practice*' I would define as: the process of deep immersion in the literature and in practical playwork experiences and the subsequent analysis and synthesis of the outcomes, to answer questions fundamental to playwork's evolutionary vision.

My reason for writing this book

In the *Origin of the Species*, Darwin (1859) states, 'In the distant future I see open fields for far more important researches. Psychology will be based on a new foundation, that of the necessary acquirement of each mental power and capacity by gradation. Light will be thrown on the origin of man and his history' (p. 488).

Whilst I would certainly never claim that Darwin was referring to texts like this as 'more important research', I would regard evolutionary playwork, at least potentially, as such, and a volume which emphasises the relationship between the biological and evolutionary nature of play and the developing practice of playwork is long overdue. Hence evolutionary playwork.

My own experience of practical playwork, as far as I can remember it, was that, although I made awful and fundamental mistakes to start with, which I regret, my practice did improve with time. Knowing what I know now – not just about practice and the field of playwork, but about the essential underpinning vision provided by the literature, which takes playwork out of the realm of clumsy social intervention and into the realm of species necessity – would not only have prevented those early errors, but would have provided me with something which has been lacking in playwork throughout its brief history – professional esteem.

Although this book may fall some way short of this objective, that is its purpose. To make practice more relevant to children's biological needs and by so doing to help those who work with children in play settings to feel that they are doing something important, *and* doing it well.

Another reason for attempting to make a connection between theory and practice, is that it is all but avoided in the more sociological analyses which have tended to dominate playwork's thinking and development to date. In my view playwork has been a discipline more distracted by politics than is healthy for any of those involved. On occasions it has seemed more interested as a profession in structures and committees than in its impact on children and on how to make that impact more conducive to children's needs.

I may be accused of being deliberately provocative, even controversial where the text moves into more politically sensitive areas. If that is the case, it has not been my intention. I am simply deeply and genuinely concerned about the way playwork apparently integrates non-play notions into its practice without first subjecting them to the rigours of its fundamental tenets.

My final reason for attempting what has turned out personally to be a gargantuan task, is to encourage a field which has ostensibly relied upon verbal tradition, to discuss and explore playwork, to ground that debate in the literature and to write about the findings and ideas that arise.

What this book is about

There is a sense in which this book is less about play than it is a plea to let children be children without any undue and unnecessary pressure to continually adapt to changing man-made (educational and economic) circumstances, for example.

Towards the end of his inspirational paper, Bruner (1972) sends us this warning from the past:

> I would only urge that in considering these deep issues of educability we keep our perspective broad and remember that the human race has a biological past from which we can read lessons for the culture of the present. We cannot adapt to everything, and in designing a way to the future we would do well to examine again what we are and what our limits are. Such a course does not mean opposition to change but, rather, using man's natural modes of adapting to render change both as intelligent and as stable as possible.
>
> (p. 706)

Like climate change, how best to address the fundamental need of human children to play is going to be one of the thorny issues of the new millennium.

Play relies on many factors to be effective; to enable us to not only conspire to change but survive it too. More than any other factor, it needs time to happen, and time is increasingly what there is a shortage of in our children's lives. So, if nothing else, this book tries to emphasise the beauty and awe of the play process and underline how vital it is to the continued existence of our species and its humanity that our children continue to be able to engage in it *when* and *how* they decide.

It is deliberately and unavoidably a highly personal perspective – deliberately, because it will hopefully act as a counterpoint to the status quo; unavoidably, because there is very little playwork material of substance save that which I have included or referred to in the text.

It is presented in the form of three distinct parts, which are graduated in complexity.

Part I – Fundamental Principles of Evolutionary Playwork contains chapters on evolutionary play, the play environment, play types, values, and methods, and provides useful new tools for assessing environments. It is aimed at the novice playworker or new parent, who is interested in learning about a view of working with children from the perspective of the child as a young organism, rather than purely as a social animal. It will be valuable in providing an alternative theoretical and practical perspective to NVQ students.

Part II – Some Advanced Evolutionary Playwork Concepts discusses the evolutionary playwork construct, stimulation theory, advanced ideas like combinatorial flexibility and calibration, democracy and participation and guidance about whether or not the play space is working. It is aimed at the more advanced student and at experienced playworkers who wish to explore the possible mechanisms and benefits of play and devise practical ways of facilitating them. It will be of particular value to Dip. HE and graduate students of playwork.

Part III – Evolutionary Playwork and Reflective Analytic Practice examines the development of reflective analytic playwork and gives some examples of the author's own playwork RAP thinking over the past decade or so. It will be of particular interest to graduate and post-graduate students of playwork.

Throughout the text there are also a number of 'Reflections', cameos which attempt to provide a warts and all moving picture, a video of some of the author's personal and professional experience. The reader should be warned that some of these Reflections contain so-called, 'industrial' language.

The book finishes with a large number of exercises used in the author's own playwork training sessions, an appendix directed at evolutionary playwork and parenting and a bibliography.

Bob Hughes
PlayEducation
Autumn 2000

Part I

Fundamental principles of evolutionary playwork

'Play, the behavioural and psychic equivalent of oxygen'

Bob Hughes 2000

Chapter 1

An introduction to evolutionary playwork

Setting the scene

Evolutionary playwork is a new and developing discipline. As yet it has no agreed theoretical or practical base. Typically there are any number of conflicting views of what it is and what it is for. Some of these, including those contained within this text, are derived from personal, long-term professional experience and reflection. Others are more political or pragmatic in their orientation.

Each of these different views has been created by a number of factors:

- the ethical base each of us uses to determine what we believe is right or wrong, good or bad, appropriate or inappropriate, and the process by which that base has evolved. For example we might have been taught ethics at school or university. Or perhaps, like me, your ethical judgements have come from an amalgam of life experiences.
- the memories and emotions that come to us when we recall playing when we were children. Was playing a good experience, was it fun, was it interesting, did we miss out on bits of experience, did we have experiences we could well have done without? Was our play narrow, structured and full of 'do not', or was it a broad experience, where we did more or less what we wanted, and where we took responsibility for whatever happened? Are our memories of playing accompanied by feelings of warmth and amazement, or varying degrees of pain and bewilderment?
- our rationale for working with children in their play time. Is our involvement for us, or for them? By 'us' I mean as individual adults and as adult society. Are we engaged in socialisation and citizenship training, are we playing out an as yet unplayed out childhood, or are we stepping out of our adult views and utilising our life experience as a resource for children? Is our motive more sinister? Do we need to control, or bully or abuse?
- the impact which the literature has had upon our perception of play and children. Over the years, a great deal has been written about play, about its importance to development, survival, well-being, self-esteem, sanity and

our evolution. Some may feel that the literature is irrelevant, too difficult or an attempt by 'professionals' to mystify and exclude people from playwork, whilst others may see it as a source of inspiration and knowledge.

Aware of each of these influences, *Evolutionary Playwork and Reflective Analytic Practice* attempts to navigate a course that puts children and their drive to play at the forefront. It does not claim to be definitive, but rather attempts to provide the reader with an authentic – although sometimes controversial – view of some of playwork's contemporary thinking.

Play leadership

Until the early 1970s, playwork as I understand it did not exist. What did exist was 'play leadership'. Play leadership had developed throughout the 1940s, 1950s and 1960s as a response to adult society's perception that there was a need for supervised play provision, both after-school and during the school holidays. This included the early development of adventure playgrounds.

Although, on the surface, this provision existed to provide children with somewhere to go and with something to do, below the surface there was an expectation that it would address areas of juvenile crime and other social and moral issues of which the young, i.e., children and adolescents, were the main focus.

By the time I was employed as a playleader on an adventure playground in 1970, play leadership was established throughout the UK as the main approach for working with children in supervised play projects.

However, quite quickly, the expectations of citizenship and crime reduction raised by play leadership's underlying philosophy began to make me and others who were new to the field feel uneasy.

Although my own play experiences had not been idyllic – I had had my fair share of bullying, beatings and lucky escapes – it had been a period of intense and diverse experience. I had learnt to survive without my carers. I had experienced privacy; I had experience of personal power; I was becoming conscious of beauty and imagination and I had not only had first-hand experience of fear and risk, but had learnt to overcome and control them to some extent.

Certainly a lot of what I experienced at play was bad, and some of it was awful, but balanced against powerful feelings of freedom, self-reliance and in my case an affinity with nature, which increasingly accompanied it, I still felt generally at ease with the ups and downs of life as a playing child.

At play, as well as skipping, dens and tag, I had experimented with sex at the age of nine, I had killed frogs and stolen apples, and I had reflected on those experiences, and begun to form a view of life, and of myself, which changed and developed me.

Play was a huge and important area of my life. An area which accessed the totality – the positives and the negatives – of interacting with other children, other species and other systems, on every level of my being, in a time and a space which was adult-free. I would not have been the 'me' I am without it.

By 'adult-free time and space', I mean just that. Although my friends and I did not avoid adults at all costs, we did tend to go where they were not. Not because we disliked or hated them particularly, but because they were always stopping us doing things, or worse still, telling us how to do them, or even worse, doing them for us.

We hid, ran, climbed and imagined invisibility, to get away from their control and, perhaps more importantly, from their perception that the world belonged to them alone; that we were at best their pet morons, and at worst, their subjects, their property, with no rights or original thoughts of our own.

Without adults, we could create our own rules, and change them to suit our circumstances. We talked for hours, making our decisions in our way, negotiating and compromising along the way. Thus we survived freezing cold winters, explored the landscape, educated ourselves, developed our own mythologies and adopted the gods and philosophies that felt relevant to the world we inhabited.

Of course there was a sense in which *that* was not reality. We had, for example, to go home to refuel and sleep and we had to go to school. But there was another sense in which it was our only *reality*, interfacing as it did with nature and the fringes of adult society, accompanied always by myths and rituals.

Coming from this perspective, I found play leadership's agenda manipulative. Certainly I wanted to facilitate the play of the children on the adventure playground where I worked, for reasons I will explain, but I wanted nothing to do with socialising them or deciding the what, why and how of playing for them, except perhaps for reasons of self-preservation – theirs and my own.

But the play leadership world seemed content to cast itself as a legitimate agent for social intervention in the child's private world. I felt that was intrusive and interrupted something of huge importance. I also believed that play leadership's objectives could have been more easily achieved, and their achievement more legitimate, in an out-of-play, school setting.

For, although I could see that training in citizenship might be necessary in order to enable children to more effectively function in what was gradually becoming a multi-cultural democracy, and that all kinds of inputs might be needed to prepare children for life in a complex and overcrowded world, it seemed the oddest of misfits, to use children's play and what might be their sole play environment in order to achieve these social objectives.

Like others at the time, I felt that children's play was best left to children. Increasingly I felt that it was the external evidence of an important biological process. That uncontaminated, unadulterated play was a human necessity and an essential, and that my primary function as a playworker was to help and support that process in as transparent and authentic a way as possible and certainly not exploit it for personal political or social ends.

Now, as I write, the reasons for this original reluctance are much clearer, but in the early 1970s they were instinctive and embryonic rather than informed. However, what was gelling was that a space dedicated to playful development could not be informed by social or political imperatives, but had to be informed by the more subtle and long-term imperatives of biology and evolutionary history.

Play is a unique experience, which, among many other things, enables us to have a view of the world which is not mediated through an adult prism, unlike home and school. At play, children are very different beings to the ones they are when under the adult's watchful glare.

I saw playing as that part of childhood which enabled each child to develop an adult-free view of who they are and of how they want to proceed. Of course it would only be a part of the total view they would have, but I saw it as the part which had the effect of counterbalancing the thrust of adult hegemony, the part which said, 'I am an individual in my own right too, I am also a unique member of our species on this planet'.

It was around 1972 when I and others began to feel uncomfortable with our play leadership designation. Increasingly I was being expected to have a professional rapport with the police, the probation and social services, and schools. And whilst on one level this was instructive and useful, on others it was creating a dilemma of considerable magnitude.

I felt increasingly that the play space – the adventure playground – I operated, was the sovereign space of the children who attended. It was their space. They needed it; the way they were using it was proof enough of that. Other children's services did not agree and assumed that because the space was operated by an adult, they would have easy access to the children, who used it. However, these same children would, in different circumstances, have been miles away in adult-free spaces, as I had been when I was a child. Their vulnerability to adult influences left me feeling uneasy.

There was nothing particularly sinister in the authorities' desire to have access to the children. Usually it was just for a chat about a stolen car, a break-in or a runaway child. It was not what these adults did that so troubled me, but that they assumed that as adults they had the right to invade the children's play space, without any preconditions or negotiations. They didn't respect the children's integrity and the children knew that. My fear was that if they got away with that unchallenged, the children would simply leave to find other spaces which, although adult-free, might also be hazardous or leave them vulnerable.

This thinking was a professional watershed for me, when a vital piece in the playwork jigsaw fell into place. I was beginning to take what I perceived as the children's plight personally, allowing my own childhood play criteria to merge with my evolving professional perspective, to create a professional practice that made sense to the child in me as well as to myself as an adult. Being able to take this dual perspective is important to 'good' playwork practice and is something which everyone in evolutionary playwork has to discover and make some sense of. I know that many have found it difficult and have preferred instead to override it with a purely adult perspective.

I wanted children to want to play in the spaces that were operated on their behalf. I wanted them to feel stimulated and interested enough to play there. However, I also wanted them not only to choose to come to the playground, but to decide what they did there and how and why they did it. The reasons I felt this so passionately are outlined below.

Because of my own childhood experiences, I still had the perception that, until relatively recently, it had been safe for children to locate what they regarded as their own ideal play places. Away from adults in general, away from the noise, dirt and danger of traffic, and from bullies and dogs. Invariably these spaces were children's private areas that were not overlooked, and often incorporated wild space, dirt and undergrowth.

Increasingly, however, these wild, private areas were becoming less and less accessible to children. Farming and industry were rendering many of them hostile and polluted. Roads and road building programmes broke them up and put children in mortal danger. Railway developments did the same. The human built environment was not being developed to accommodate the needs of children. Of course, they still played in the wild areas, but the price they paid could often be unacceptably high.

The problem was, how children could access the private, non-adulterated experiences that would enable them to form their own unique view of the world, if the spaces they needed for that were either hazardous, dangerous, or perceived as dangerous.

One solution was to make dedicated provision for play. But for such provision to be effective and authentic, it needed to mirror those private, unadulterated spaces to which children were naturally attracted as closely as possible. My view was that, although many of them contained the physical characteristics, spaces operated along play leadership lines would not meet this objective.

A new perspective had to be developed. This was the beginning of evolutionary playwork.

The rationale underpinning this embryonic notion of evolutionary playwork was not that children should be separated from their adult counterparts. But it did implicitly suggest that children should be able to do so, should they so wish, for a period of time every day. It certainly contained the germ of an idea that, to preserve children's individual and collective integrity against the almost irresistible encroachment of adults into what I saw as children's physical and psychic domain, values and practices urgently need to be developed that focused on the child's play needs rather than on the needs of adult society.

Needless to say, there would be problems attached to this child-centred view of play. One was the adult world's apparent difficulty with children having any experience of freedom of expression. Another was parents' apparent insistence that they were the sole arbiters of what their children experienced.

There were practical playwork problems too. When would a playworker intervene if there was a problem? What would a playworker do if adults came and expected entry to the play environment? What about smoking, or swearing or sexual activity? And what about physical or psychological violence? These professional dilemmas, together with the inevitable pressure from employers and other adults to impose an adult agenda on the prevailing children's culture, made me realise that there was a great deal to learn.

However, on a personal level, I felt that playworkers had a responsibility to the children they worked with to vigorously oppose such encroachments, whilst trying to remain employed and explain what they saw as the alternative view. I believed this view was only attempting to protect the child's right to play in ways and for reasons determined by the child. What that meant in practice was that in specifically dedicated spaces, in which evolutionary playwork's rationales applied, children would be free to do things, or say things, for good developmental reasons, but to which some adults might object.

Now, years later, the importance of such designated spaces for children to play in has not diminished, rather the reverse. But at least playworkers are more equipped to argue the case, albeit a still rather tenuous one. There is more evidence that play is a vitally important ingredient in the development and evolution process. There is evidence that being deprived of play has a serious affect on children. Practising playworkers are gradually learning what the criteria for 'good' play spaces are, and there are a whole range of other initiatives relating to quality taking place.

But making provision for the evolutionary essentials, particularly fire, risk and personal control are proving more difficult in litigious and pre-emptive societies, where we tend to be focused with now rather than with the future. However, as I write, significant changes are taking place and playworkers and other who are involved in playwork delivery are once again thinking what would have been the unthinkable.

Look at fires, for example

Knowing that I risk lapsing into nostalgia, in my childhood fires were things one sat by in solitude, feeding the flames, staring into the embers and watching the smoke drift; they were a focus to dance around and sing by – ritual places which facilitated rites, conversations and reflections; they were feeding places where beans were heated, spuds baked and chippatis cooked; they were places where everyone had a job – to fan the flames, feed the flames or get some water. Fires created communal areas where childhood culture was passed on and they were places to learn of life's dangers and thrills. They kept us warm and dry and gave us light in the darkness of winter nights.

We jumped them, swung over them, stood around them, rode our bikes through them, urinated on them, producing vast clouds of steam, built them into bonfires and burned rubbish on them. Sometimes they burned us too, or someone near us if our play was too immersed, or if we lost concentration, but in general they were a wonderful opportunity for self-expression and group co-operation.

The problem now is that most adults are not happy with the combination of fires and children. They seem not to trust children, they seem to think children are stupid, or worse they seem to believe that children should live for ever and should be protected from every planetary risk. The possibility that the experience of fire might be *essential* survival and developmental knowledge, seems not to enter into the calculations of those who are wracked by fear of children injuring themselves or by fear of litigation if they do.

Look at risk, for example

All children will take risks if they are not stopped from doing so. Encountering and overcoming risk is a normal part of a child's day-to-day life. However, the perceived nature of those risks will be less or more extreme depending on the previous experience and current perceptions of the child. Whether it involves jumping from a foot-high step, propelling a wheelchair at speed down a ramp, climbing a high tree or riding a bike on the parapet of a bridge, children will engage in risk. It is in the tradition of explorers and scientists that as a species we should; but all too frequently now, children are stopped from undertaking risky activities, unless they, the activities, are perceived by adults as safe. In reality they cannot be both safe and risky. If risk is to be real and not an illusion, it has to have a *real* element of potential physical harm attached to it. That means if the child does not concentrate or if the activity overstretches his or her abilities, someone could get hurt; this is essential knowledge for life.

However, this is not to confuse risk with danger or what some professionals call hazard. Risk is something children recognise. They are aware or conscious of it. It is something they know they are entering into, like consciously climbing higher, swinging faster or balancing more precariously.

Danger, on the other hand, is unassessable to a child. Pollution and poison are dangers. High tension cables are dangers. Rotting timber is a danger. Radioactivity is a danger. Dog excrement is a danger.

There is a developmental legitimacy in injuring ourselves as we attempt to stretch our limits and evolve our abilities. Lessons can be learnt. A broken arm now might save one's life later. The planet Earth is a risky habitat and children need to be aware of the risks and where they can, learn to assess, avoid or manage them.

But in a complex human environment like a city, children cannot be expected to know of dangers that may have only been in the knowledge domain for a relatively short period of time and they should be protected from such things until they are aware of their lethal nature. Then, like the rest of us, they will have to take their chances.

Evolutionary playwork embraces the proposition that experience of risk, of the elements, of rituals, of other species and systems, are some of the legitimate play expectations of human children the world over. It seeks to compensate for the loss of all or much of that experience for many children, by providing environments where those experiences and their component parts are accessible in forms which, whilst providing challenge, do not expose children to unknown dangers, fears or feelings of failure.

Evolutionary playwork constructs children as young organisms rather than as small dependant adults and creates spaces where they can playfully explore and experiment with a huge variety of sensory and emotional experiences, gaining their own version of events as they do. It tries to see children as equal to adults, as objects of respect and integrity.

Modification

However, play spaces are artificial spaces. And, although the children who use them will significantly change them by digging, building and other forms of activity, in a macro sense, they are constructed by playworkers. In order to ensure that when the children use them they are able to control what they do, it is essential that much of the 'behind the scenes' work is done when children are not actually present. This process of preparation is known as 'environmental modification' and, as the term suggests, it is about changing or modifying the play space in ways that will attract children and stimulate their play drive.

Intervention

Although 'modification' may satisfy the child's need to play in a space that is interesting and stimulating, if s/he is going to get the maximum developmental benefits from the play, s/he also needs to feel that it is an authentic play space in which s/he has control over what s/he does without undue interference from playworkers.

How, when and why playworkers engage with children is known as 'intervention'. Ensuring that intervention is appropriate, i.e. that it only takes place when it is necessary, is a matter of skilled judgement and of continual debate within playwork.

The ideas of modification and intervention are explored in greater depth in Chapter 6.

Chapter 2

Evolutionary play

Play is a very personal experience. For some it is dolls and fights, for others it is climbing and skipping. It is what children do when adults are not there or what children do when the adults that are there are perceived as honorary children.

When my five-year-old grandson Thomas catches my eye, gives me a manic stare and rushes off to dive into a pile of leaves, that is play. When, as a woman described recently to me, that as a child she would dig up worms so that she could wash them and put them back into the ground, that too was play.

Play, as Kent Palmer describes, is an 'ecstasy of variety' (Sturrock, 1997). It is the infinite expression of the human soul in communion with its universe (see also, Palmer, 1994).

It is painting, acting, experimenting and exploring. It is risking and it is death defying. It is the child at its most immersed in the fantasy of other worlds where s/he may be transported into what Winnicott called a 'potential space', to become a horse or a space alien (Ogden, 1993: 223).

Or where he imagines he is so tiny that it is possible for him to disappear between the roots of a tree or voyage into the flames of a fire.

Play is damming streams, fighting back the tide, nicking apples and making dens and caves. It is spiritual, creative, locomotor, dramatic, archetypal and precious. It crosses species boundaries and gives life to inanimate objects and voices to ideas.

Play is what happens when human children are propelled by a desire to know and understand, or by the thrill of attempting to transcend their previous limits. Except for the few, who by force of circumstance or lack of opportunity have not been able to play, it has happened to every child in the past, as it is happening to every child currently on this planet, whether that child is living in the high Andes in Peru, with Bedouins in the Sahara, in Japan, India or here in Europe.

It is one of the single most profound forces we share as a species but one most of us knows little about, although our memories of playing, what Sobel (1993) calls our 'touchstone' memories, live with us throughout our lives. It is, on the whole, what children do, and historically what children do has tended not to be particularly important to adults, as long as they do it quietly and preferably somewhere else.

It is regarded by many as trivial, as a waste of time or as a way of using up excess energy. But, as I have said, we have all done it, it has often had a profound effect on us, yet as adults we often only value it as a sanitised and adulterated experience for our own children. It certainly is an enigma.

Having said that, if play is so diverse, so personal and so universal how can it have any meaning, why should it be important? How, for example, can we pin down what it is? How can we say it even exists, let alone define why it has any relevance to us?

How do we identify what is play?

Play is a personal experience. For each of us it happens where *we* play, with *our* friends, with *our* toys. These are the things *we* consciously remember as players.

But for those who investigate play there are, even with this huge diversity, many characteristics that are as common to my play as they are to everyone else's. And it is these defining characteristics which tell us what is play and more importantly, what is not.

According to the literature, behaviour has to satisfy several of the following criteria to be play. It has to:

- be spontaneous (Patrick, 1914)
- be first-hand experience and include struggle, manipulation, exploration, discovery and practice (Bruce, 1994)
- be goalless – it is often described in terms of process rather than product (Bruner, 1972)
- be freely chosen, i.e., is a voluntary activity (Neuman, 1973)
- be personally directed by the child (Hughes, 1996b)
- be intrinsically motivated – i.e., performed by the child for no external goal or reward (Koestler, 1964)
- be where the child is in control of the content and intent (Hughes, 2000)
- contain play cues or meta-signals, like eye contacts, facial expressions and body positions that start processes of many social *and* non-social engagements (Bateson, 1955; Else and Sturrock, 1998)
- be a performance of motor patterns in novel sequences, like gallumphing, or movements out of context, like the cat that runs sideways with its tail at an odd angle (Miller, 1973)
- be repetitious, thus facilitating learning of complex skills (Connolly, 1973)
- be neophilic, i.e., attracted to the novel, new, fun, interesting (Morris, 1964, 1967)
- be non-detrimental (King, 1987)
- balance experience (Hughes, 1988).

And if it does not satisfy several of these criteria, whatever else it is, it is not play.

As we can see, play is a very complex phenomenon, where a number of conditions, that seem to be less about what the player actually does and more about how and why s/he does it, have to be satisfied.

However, the rather eccentric behaviours we call play often fly in the face of much of what are generally regarded as acceptable social or socialised adult standards. Some adults would actually call this description of what children do irresponsible, or pointless, even dangerous – for example, children being allowed, even encouraged, to have control over what they do.

Nevertheless, the literature and our own experience confirms that the potential for these behaviours exist in all of us. They seem to come from within us, they certainly are not taught or learned. It is as if the child already knows how to do them, that they are instinctive, that the child has an agenda independent of our own, almost like a research programme, where s/he is trying to find things out, moving at his or her own pace and in his or her own way.

The question then is, 'Why is behaving like this important?'

One reason is that increasingly play – the spontaneous behaviours I have referred to previously – is believed to be the outcome of a vital biological drive, in much the same way as eating and sexual activity are recognised as the results of other biological drives.

Drives, as I understand them, are like genetic rivers, whose primeval forces come from sources deep within us and, which, in flowing through us, give us the energy and focus to make attempts at satisfying our most fundamental desires for life and understanding, often in the most trying of circumstances.

The play drive may exist to guarantee, that as vulnerable and naïve young organisms, we engage with the world we live in, in a way which suits our abilities but which is also highly efficient, so that we can gradually understand and make sense of information learned through playing. Much of this is absolutely essential to our continued survival and to our development.

In other words, if play is the result of a drive, or what a BBC film about play called an 'urge', then like other drives, play has to happen, it is irresistible, it is something which, as the same film suggested, will happen later if it does not happen sooner (*Horizon*, 1998). In other words, it is something which, if it does not have an outlet, will result in physical or psychological damage or both, to those who suffer that restriction.

So, when we see a child playing with a flower, or in the dirt, or skipping or playing tag, we should remind ourselves that what we are looking at is the child-like result of a deep and irresistible urge to interact with and have knowledge of the world and everything in it.

The play drive is important because it has a vital role in the development of our ability to adapt to changing environmental and atmospheric conditions. A major reason why as a species we have not become extinct so far, is that we play.

The psychologist, Lorenz (1972), has argued that because we play, we have become what he called 'specialists in non-specialisation', meaning that as a species we have become good at a lot of things rather than expert at a few, a vital aid to our ability to adapt.

Simpson (1976) suggested that because we play we are able to adapt more easily to new physical surroundings, using the skill of calibration, whilst Suomi and Harlow (1971) argued that not playing made calibrating our physical surroundings difficult, if not impossible.

Others, including Loizos (1967), Bruner (1974), Sylva (1977), Sutton-Smith (1979) and Hutt *et al.* (1989), have written about the importance of play in terms of the flexibility it affords the player, suggesting that flexibility leads to new thought, which leads in turn to new combinations of thought, a prerequisite of the problem solving process. More recently, play has been thought to have a vital role in the human evolution process, particularly if the child is playing in what is called an 'enriched' environment (Sutton-Smith, 1997).

The potency of play to help in furthering our understanding and treatment of psychological disorders may in part be due to another of its important roles – as a mechanism in the development of our identity. Thomashow (1995) writes that play, by giving children a sense of place, a sense of self, enables them to realise that they have a unique perception of the world – their own identity.

Normally we tend to think of identity as a social concept, but as some theorists (Hart, 1979; Chilton-Pearce, 1980; Shepard, 1982; Cobb, 1993) say of middle-childhood play, 'this is the time that children establish their connections with the earth ... which is crucial to their personal identity'. This implies that identity has a biological facet too; that we have a bio-identity (p. 10).

Perhaps some mental illness is due to the impact of the loss of this bio-identity, a characteristic of humanness which, rather than being derived from social interaction, comes from the relationship we have with everything which is not human but which is a huge part of what makes us who we are.

Sobel (1993) writes, 'as we bonded with our parents in the early years, so we bonded with Mother Earth in middle-childhood' (pp. 159–60).

The psychologists, Stanley Hall (1904) and Ken Wilber (1996), develop this theme too. Hall's Recapitulation Theory suggests that play enables an essential re-enactment of the various stages of human evolution. Wilber describes what those stages might be in terms of an evolving consciousness and includes the reptilian, savage and ritualistic stages, which playworkers see on a daily basis when children are able to dig, build dens and play with fire. This is a theme I will be returning to later.

Other reasons why the behaviours we call play are important are as follows.

First, it is generally agreed by playworkers that they have an important role in the development of the following essential skills:

- motor skills
- communication skills
- social skills

- perceptual skills
- emotional skills
- problem-solving skills
- logical skills
- aesthetic skills
- creative skills
- skills of abstraction.

(See Hughes 1996b for a more comprehensive explanation of these play skills.)

This means that if we do not behave playfully, if we are play-deprived, then we may not gain these skills with the same degree of competence and effectiveness as we otherwise might.

Second, play behaviours are important because they enable children to learn many things in many ways by engaging those children in the use of the following fifteen different and essential play types:

- symbolic play
- rough and tumble play
- socio-dramatic play
- social play
- creative play
- communication play
- exploratory play
- fantasy play
- imaginative play
- locomotor play
- mastery play
- object play
- role play
- deep play
- dramatic play.

(See Appendix 1 and Hughes 1996a for a more comprehensive explanation of these play types.)

What children's use of these play types may be saying is that there is a direct relationship between the various play types they enter into and the development of their ability to symbolise, to create, to imagine, to communicate and so on.

I am convinced that, in the longer term, the ideas underpinning playwork will become part of some form of mainstream social policy perception, somewhere. However – and I share this analysis with other playwork colleagues – contemporary society is just not in the right mode to seriously consider some of what playwork is offering at the present time. It is a problem of the interface between a 'magician' and a 'non-magician' system (Palmer, 1994). And governments seem happiest listening to pragmatic individuals who hold views that fit into their prepared policy jigsaws, and one can hardly blame them for that.

The implications of playwork on society are huge and similar to those which accompanied the alleviation of the impact of urban violence on children in the United States, where Perry (1995) concluded that 'nothing less than a transformation of culture, including radical changes in child-rearing practices is required' (p. 140).

Third, these behaviours are becoming an important consideration in the diagnosis and treatment of serious conditions like Attention Deficit Disorder (ADD) and Attention Deficit Hyperactivity Disorder (ADHD). Huge numbers of children world-wide are currently having to look to a bleak future on life-long medication because of these disorders.

This is a vital new area of knowledge which is being pioneered in this country by playworkers like Sturrock, Else, Rennie and Taylor, based on the premise that free-play has a vitally important role both in the diagnosis of psychological disorders and in their treatment. This is in line with the work of eminent investigators from other disciplines like Stanislav Grof, Melanie Kline, the Freuds and Gustav Jung.

Finally, play is important because as a species we say it is, by allocating it the status of a 'human right' as enshrined in Article 31 of the UN Convention of the Rights of the Child which states, 'State parties recognise the right of the child to engage in play [which is] appropriate to the age of the child . . .'

This fairly recent development is more important than perhaps we give it credit. As a playworker I have become used to that glazed look on most adults' faces when I say what I do. But the UN, even with all of the world's current and future problems to contend with, have given play the time of day, concluding that it is a vitally important experience for the world's current and future generations of children and giving it the status of a human right.

Conclusion

Evolutionary play is important for numerous reasons.

- It is important for our sanity and for our psychological well-being.
- It enables us literally to keep our feet on the ground by helping us to discover who we are, to form an identity, in particular a bio-identity.
- It enables us to access infinite information through the use of fifteen play types.
- It facilitates calibration, non-specialisation and problem-solving skills.
- It is a human right. The right to play is enshrined in Article 31 of the UN Convention of the Rights of the Child.
- There is scientific evidence that indicates that play is a vital ingredient in the creation of survival and development skills.
- Finally, play is increasingly implicated as a mechanism in the continued evolution of our species. This has huge implications for our future social, educational, economic and planning policies, which I believe we ignore at our peril.

Chapter 3

The evolutionary playwork environment

Every play environment can be different and still satisfy important basic design ideas. Ideally an evolutionary playwork environment would provide at least:

- outdoor and indoor space
- access to elements – fire, earth, air and water
- access to height, depth, motion, balance, co-ordination
- access to creative experiences like music, inventions, discovery and arts
- access to mastery experiences like building, planting, digging and damming
- access to other species and systems, like farm species, rocks and sand
- compensatory alternatives and choices like new foods, music, views, noises, and perspectives
- landscaped areas with flowers, fruits and berries.

The words 'access to' could be replaced by the words 'opportunity for'. What I will continually stress is that evolutionary playwork is never about compulsion or coercion, it is not even about encouragement. If the experiences or props provided are appropriate to the needs of the children, they will be driven to engage in them spontaneously and without any adult prompting. As soon as children are invited to, 'Come and join in', or asked, 'Will you do it for me?', the child's play is being adulterated and s/he may not be engaging in the experience for intrinsic motives. It is absolutely crucial that we understand that the playworker's role is never to lead play but rather to facilitate it.

The new playworker's first experience of this kind of environment might be a wall of sound, or a chaotic tangle of activity. Play tends to be noisy and messy. If it is not there is probably something wrong. That is not to say that children do not relish seclusion and privacy, because they do, but a great deal of play is about vigorous interaction, either with the physical environment, or with other children, or both.

Dependency

For young children play is a new and exciting experience and it is nearly always accompanied by squeals and shrieks of laughter which are contagious and often uncontrollable. They are into everything and will expect the playworker to watch, to help, even to take part. Obviously s/he will, but s/he must remember the play-worker's facilitative function and resist becoming part of the gang, or someone on whom the children may become dependent. It is very easy for them to become dependent on the playworker. It is equally easy for the playworker to become dependent on them. If the playworker does the thinking then they as children do not have to. As a consequence the playworker may start to feel needed and so a cycle of dependency starts to evolve between playworker and children.

There is a sense in which the evolutionary play environment is managed wild-ness. But the wildness will not really manifest itself whilst the playworker is a prominent feature of the space. S/he must withdraw, but keep an eye on the chil-dren. The playworker's participation in their world must be minimal or s/he will become a source of the contamination that playworkers call 'adulteration' (Else and Sturrock, 1998: 25–6).

Peripheral vision

Perhaps one of the playworker's most important skills is their highly developed peripheral vision. There are many things children will not do if they think they are being watched. Although scanning the play space with eyes and ears is a vitally important defence against injury and insecurity, it is essential that the playworker learns to be sensitised to what s/he needs to see and hear. At the same time it is essential that s/he does not overtly stare either at individuals or groups as they play. Hence, peripheral vision. The skill of staring in one direc-tion whilst keeping children elsewhere in view, ensures that they are safe from excessive unpleasant attention from other children and secure from external threats, but are not being overtly overlooked or monitored, whilst they engage in what is, after all, their private behaviour.

Moving in and out of the play state

Feeling safe and secure, even when engaged in risky activity, is essential for children at play. Safety and security makes it possible for children to relax, to switch off or moderate their natural vigilance, enough to make engagement in fantasy or imagination possible.

Immersion

Interruption by child or adult destroys the process of the child becoming immersed in fantasy that is so much a part of the dream-like state which is play.

Alternatively, when they have been deeply immersed in play, I have known times when children have been deaf to calls, shouts, even whistles, and oblivious to taps on the shoulder. One group of relatively older boys, who had never been to the seaside, at one play project I worked on, got so 'lost' in play in our large sand pit – building tunnels and castles, and making rivers from the water stand pipe – that it took me several minutes to make the appropriate 'sensitive' contact with them and let them know that we were closing.

Knowledge of immersion is a very important part of the playworker's tool kit too. When children are engaged in particularly potent play narratives, i.e., when they are deeply immersed in an imaginative experience, either with other children or alone, they are in another place – an immersed reality – with other people or things we cannot even imagine. It is vital if closing time is approaching that adequate time is given to bringing these children back to 'now'. For the child who is immersed it can be both painful and disappointing to be 'juddered' out of the play state. The best approach is to facilitate a natural, gentle transition, first using soft cues, like a quiet voice or a gentle touch, only gradually building up to louder or firmer cues, if necessary. Using whistles, or shouting at closing time, hurrying children out of the door, forgetting what some of the children may be going home too, is not good playwork practice.

The visual environment

Play environments can be visually very different. Adventure playgrounds, probably the most advanced play environments to be developed so far, are a good case in point. In their early days, as Junk Playgrounds, they were more like children's allotments; whereas, in the UK in the 1950s and 1960s, they were more like children's settlements, with dens, shops, small farms and fire and water-play.

In the late 1960s and 1970s large structures began to predominate on adventure playgrounds. Huge flags appeared, massive swings, slides, towers and walkways constructed by playworkers and children, took root and altered the skyline of many towns and city districts.

Resource Centres

However, from the mid to late 1970s evolutionary playwork environments also saw some other important visual changes. For example, until then, what a play space looked like had depended upon the use of materials like timber, paint and boxes, which had often been scrounged from parents, local businesses and factories. The development of the Play Resource Centre meant that a whole new range of creative play materials were made more accessible, particularly to the huge number of small community play organisations springing up around the country.

Community artists

Community artists were also making their presence felt by the mid 1970s, creating attractive murals on bleak playground walls and depicting cartoon, political, industrial and cultural scenes on gable ends. Community artists also gave the play world the 'inflatable', arguably the most important piece of interactive community sculpture ever conceived. However, these inflatables were not the bouncy castles that came later and were just pale imitations of what had existed originally. Action Space, an inflatables company based in London and Sheffield, for example, produced the most incredible inflatable structures. In 1976–7, they created a huge internal maze, made from different coloured plastic, that an adult could actually walk inside. It was inflated with a pump and kept inflated using a network of valves, not unlike the valves in the heart, but these were huge. It was possible to crawl through them with the pressure of the inflated air in one's face. Not only did this maze contain a network of enormous tubes, it also had a number of dead-end cubes people could sit and rest in. It ended in an inflated 'big top', where there were huge figures children could dive on and wrestle with. It had everything – thrills, mystery, fear (of getting lost), colour (lights playing on the plastic), sound (the squeals of the children, mixed in with music) and laughter, as they all bumped into each other. I spent many hours crawling about inside this thing, playing my own version of calibrating the weird world it created and enjoying the laughs and excitement of the social interaction the maze stimulated (see page 42).

Legislation

Legislation – in particular Health and Safety legislation – also had an impact on the visual nature of play space, as did the playwork field itself in this context. The publication of *Towards a Safer Adventure Playground* (NPFA, 1980) had a massive impact in professionalising playwork, but at the same time, it had the effect of inhibiting some of the visual inventiveness and creativity that, until then, had been the hallmark of the unique interaction between specific playworkers and specific children.

Innovative play environments

Now, many of the play spaces I visit have all but lost this spontaneous and original visual identity. They still look like play spaces I would recognise from years ago. They have not moved on in any visual sense. That saddens me. Thirty years on, play spaces should not still be modelling themselves on the examples of the 1970s, frozen in time, ossified by a perception that 'they had it right then'.

Certainly flags can be exciting, as can structures, allotments, landscaping, planting, painting and decorating, building, loose parts and so on. But perhaps most exciting of all, is that none of it has to be to be permanent. It can and should be changing on a daily basis – not only to create a visually interesting space but to generate energy and stimulate action. That is a problem with too many of our contemporary play spaces, they are fixed, permanent, inflexible and unchanging.

The unpredictable space

One effect of evolutionary playwork is that it is intended to enable children to be adaptable, to be infinitely flexible, at every conceivable level of being. Nothing is set in stone. Preconception of outcome is anti-play, process is everything. Going to an environment that is always the same, never evolving, never subject to major modification, even destruction, sends out adulterating messages of security and inertia, that many children will perceive as boring.

Of course, there will be times and places when stability and predictability will be more important than those of change. If, for example, the area in which the playworker works has a high level of damaged children, who as a result of extreme poverty, deprivation, abuse, racism or sectarianism, need a sanctuary or an oasis to gather their thoughts and sort out how they feel and who they are, then they will need predictability and consistency. That is a different priority and modification has to be a tentative process, because the playworker is more engaged at the therapeutic end of playwork.

But for most UK children, faced with the pressures of the adult agenda – with preconceptions of youth culture/consumerism, citizenship, the national curriculum and parental obsession with low-quality safety rather than high-quality risk – the play space must address the biological bottom line that predictability, although comforting, is also unreal. Human society may be a 'global village', we might be able to communicate in seconds by e-mail and whatever is invented in the future, we may feel the dominant species in a predominantly human landscape, but we still live on a piece of matter in the middle of space, which can be the subject of internal or external change at any moment. Children need to develop the skills both to survive that context and survive any changes that will inevitably occur. Play helps them to do that.

Children need experience of things, events and concepts to even be aware that these things exist. Knowledge of the idea of impermanence, for example, is vitally important to children, if they are going to interact with their environment in ways that will enable the skills of adaptability and flexibility to evolve. In responding to this need, by creating a temporary, transitory play space, which children can engage with in an infinite number of ways, the playworker facilities in the children an awareness of the transitory nature of everything that they can feel comfortable with.

Visual stimulation

A play space should also be visually stimulating. It must also be subject to regular visual change or it will become stagnant. For example, one playground I visited had had the same murals on the walls of its play building for over ten years. Colours had moved on, techniques had evolved, the images were antiquated. The whole thing sent a message which was, 'do nothing' – quite the reverse of the message it should have been sending out, 'consider doing everything'.

The play space has to speak the truth to children. It has to say, 'you are a visitor to this life, you are passing through', but in saying it, it also has to facilitate optimism. Not the false optimism that says, 'if you jog, eat the right food, wear this type of clothing, etc., etc., you will live forever', but the optimism that says, 'even though this is a journey, which ends inevitably in death – whatever that means – a playful life can be an incredible and exciting experience which human beings have enjoyed and have returned to, since the birth of our species.' If that was not the case, play would have disappeared from our behavioural repertoire millions of years ago. The problem is that the play spaces we create have to be up to that challenge. A swing and a slide and a roundabout set in tarmac just will not do.

Three case studies

The best way to get some idea of the possibilities of a particular space is to look at it and imagine using it from the perspective of a child. Can I hide in it? Can I run in it? Can I light a fire or build or make a mess or a noise in it? If I cannot then the space is already restricting my locomotor, mastery, creative and imaginative choices.

Among the provisions I have operated over my thirty plus years as a playworker, are three adventure playgrounds. Although some of my practice, particularly in the early days, would probably be considered below standard now – I certainly think some of it was – it may be useful here to provide some insights into how I made certain visual and other choices about the appropriateness of certain environments and the modifications I undertook to improve the space for the children who came.

As much as possible I will use the IMEE protocol for reflective practice I described in Hughes (1996b) as a guide. The IMEE protocol is a simple reflective tool that enables playworkers to organise their analysis of the quality of play environments against their own **intuitive** judgements of what a 'good' play environment should be like; against their childhood **memories** of 'good' play environments; against their **experience** of what 'good' play environments are from their professional practice and what they have deduced about 'good' play environments from the **evidence** in the scientific literature.

Because these case studies are only intended to throw light on playwork thinking rather than on past municipal priorities, some of their physical description will only approximate their reality. There are many examples just like these all over the world.

Playground A

Playground A was developed out of an initiative by the local Round Table and District Council following a proselytising visit by Drummond Abernethy, one of the founders of adventure playgrounds in the UK, who was then Director of the Children and Youth Department of the National Playing Fields Association.

The space, one-third of an acre of chain-link fenced land, had been landscaped with horseshoe-shaped mounding on three sides of a flat area and contained two wooden sheds. I was given the job of 'playleader' shortly before it opened.

Intuition

My first feeling, my intuition, was that it was a beautiful space and a wonderful environment for playing. It had a small coppice at one end, and the fence was intertwined with hawthorn and elder, which created an enclosure, a secret space, the sanctuary, rather than the enclave. It felt safe too. Not necessarily safe from injury, but safe from things children would not know, or would not understand. Here, children could and did immerse themselves in the pursuit of playing. Here butterflies and hide and seek could act to balance the realities of bullies and some of the negativity of some children's home lives. It felt good to me, and that had to be the first test for the creation of a space, which interfaced play and childhood with playwork.

Memory

The main sound, notwithstanding traffic and the odd industrial noise, was the wind through the trees. And it created a feeling of isolation, of separateness, that I remembered from my own childhood ranging, a feeling of almost being out of one's depth, but where security was within running distance.

It had great cover for games in the bushes and trees. Building dens was a possibility. The feeling of invisibility, of moving about without being seen was provided by the bushes too. It had a public area in front of the landscaping and a secluded area behind it. The public part would be good for activity that would need some supervision. For example, heavy building, climbing and swinging at height, contact games (like mad football, off ground touch and war), fire play and some of the den building. Most of the hanging out behaviour and water and mastery play would probably also take place under the public gaze. There are some things children seem to prefer to do under the scrutiny of their mates, it is more display than play.

Any other building would be undertaken in the wooded area and on the blind side of the landscaping. This would give children the privacy they required both from other children and from me, although I would always be 'about'.

Experience

Playground A turned out to be a very diverse and popular environment for the local (and sometimes, the not so local) children. The wooded area was popular for building, but I had not banked on little children, unable to build and only beginning to become adept at tool use, hammering copper nails into the trees and killing many of them over the years – here a protective sleeve would have helped. The blind side of the landscaping was a popular location for building and games. I played hide and seek there many times myself as a playworker, balancing on the chain link fence masked by a hawthorn or immature ash, to get away from the children. Not only feeling very smug that they could not find me, but experiencing the excitement of the chase that I thought I had lost years before.

Any prospective playworker should be warned, however, that if the children like you at all, and you get involved in 'catch' type games, it will often be you they try to catch first. This is not only exhausting but impractical when you have to be free to react to whatever arises. One game is fine, but a whole afternoon may mean that you are not available if you are needed by other children.

I had half expected the blind side to be used as a toilet too. It was occasionally, but we had toilets nearby and it was only rarely that a child was 'taken short'. However, the blind side did need clearing of rubbish from time to time. This was partly due to the proximity of the local rubbish tip, which was next door, but more due to the effects of time and weather on frail dens that meant that furniture, mattresses and plywood, sometimes with nails in, had to be cleared from the area to keep it both hygienic and hazard free.

The public area was initially used as an active space – except in bad weather and during the winter when we went to an adjacent building. In the early days the space provided our main focus for dens, fires, water-play and general games, like tag. But gradually, as we constructed a network of towers, bridges, walkways, swings, a slide and an aerial runway, known there as 'the death slide', the children were able to access different and more complex experiences that incorporated height and motion – like high tag (chase played 'at height'), and swinging games – and which enabled those at different developmental stages to engage in graduated risk and incrementally challenge themselves to go further. This area was constantly evolving and growing in complexity and provided a third dimension to the playground – a second tier, an 'off-ground' playground, a play space on legs!

The barrel

We had a good relationship with our local community and got a great deal of 'scrounged' materials from them. On one occasion we visited a local chemical plant, to see if they had anything interesting for us. They had a plastic reactor which they had used to make the basics of perfume, which they said we could have. I suppose this would normally have been graciously refused by most play-workers, but I had previously been a chemist and was confident that I could make the reactor safe to use, although I had no idea how it would be employed.

Standing on its end, the reactor was about 7 feet tall, 3 or 4 feet in diameter and it had a hole in one end. We took it back to the playground, half filled it with water from a stand pipe with a hose, and washed it out for some days. When there was no trace of perfume, i.e., when we could not smell it anymore, we cut a hole in the other end and placed the reactor on its side. The first thing the children did was roll it and compared to them, it was huge. Needless to say, it did not take them long to compute that it would be more fun to roll it down the hill-side provided by the landscaping, than along the flat. And it did not take much longer to work out that it would be even more fun to be inside it when it rolled.

What followed was a piece of pure invention. The children deduced that if, say, six of them got inside it, on top of the landscaping and aimed it down the hill, by rocking it increasingly violently, it would eventually roll down the hill with them inside it, pressed against the sides. This provided thrills and spills for weeks for hundreds of children and as far as I know was the earliest – and in my view the best – example of the 'puny' play barrels that came later, that even one child would be hard pressed to get inside. It was used so much that it eventually wore out.

Evidence

Although I intend to explore the literature in more depth in Part II, I can say here that on reflection, a huge amount of what the literature forecasts should happen when children are engaged in play, did happen on this playground. Here is one example.

Locomotor play has an important role in the development of our skills of hand–eye co-ordination, balance and so on. However, at that time, I could never have predicted both the skill and grace which even the most ungainly, clumsy children would exercise on the whole variety of swings we built at Playground A. One gibbet swing, for example, required children to launch themselves into a wide arc, which at its extreme, came close to a tall and very solid structure. The children showed skill on this swing that would have warmed an instructor at the Moscow State Circus. Their acrobatic skills were amazing, their judgement incredible. They could gauge avoiding the structure's uprights by centimetres, when to have collided with it would probably have meant serious injury. They were so brave. And although the drive to engage in this form of deep play is probably irresistible, they were often very young. It was a privilege to know that this was possible – not taught, not cajoled, not for reward, not out of fear, not really for fun – it was more than that. It was a kind of ecstasy, a natural exuber-ance, because they wanted to experience it. Certainly that was how it looked to me.

Playground A was an example of a 'good' evolutionary play space.

Playground B

It is not my intention to offend anyone who was associated with it, but Playground B was a dreadful place.

Like so many playgrounds in the UK, its siting was a classic demonstration of the appalling status many adults in power give children and play. Although it was not on or next to a rubbish tip – a not unusual siting for children's spaces – it was far too small, like many play environments today, and only occupied the space that would have accommodated, say, two small houses.

It also attracted a large number of local children, who then became frustrated when they could not even exercise their most basic need to run about.

The local population, although economically varied, typically contained some 'hard' families whose children used the playground. The children and adults from these families could be violent and the workers were constantly suffering the 'what if' anxiety and were frequently pelted with stones and earth whenever they left the playground to go home.

The playground consisted of a fenced rectangle of grass and a shed. There was no planting, landscaping, indoor accommodation or space to do creative work. And there was little room outside to modify the site and make it more interesting. In addition, when I arrived, the other playworkers were 'at war' with a large group of the local children and their parents.

Intuition

After Playground A, my heart sinks when I think of B. It was tiny and boring. My first reaction was, what is this playground here to do? What do adults expect to happen here? It was minimal, it had no point(s) of interest and nowhere to get another perspective. The children were constantly overlooked by adults, always in strong light and always exposed to the weather. There were no natural features. It was a bleak place that only served to reinforce any preconceptions the children may have felt that adults had of them. I judged that the children would have been better off with nothing, rather than with this. It was a bad site and location. How could children be expected to have an attraction to such a place? Unless of course, they were damaged children, who might see the playground as a focus for their aggression, projecting that damage either onto the playground's physical fabric or onto the playworkers.

Whenever I see a play space, like this one, now – a grudging reaction to parental or political pressures to do something for children, however inappropriate it may turn out to be – I realise how far playwork has yet to go both in terms of developing and articulating its own knowledge base, and in terms of changing public perceptions. I have noticed even with 'good' playworkers, how great is the qualitative chasm between what they experienced as children themselves and what they are prepared to accept for the children they serve. Playground B was such a space. Managed by good, well-meaning professionals and parents, typical of many voluntary committees, and yet incapable of addressing the fundamental needs of those local children. Many of the children, without a convincing demonstration of commitment to them, would never view their childhood as a period to cherish and to draw from throughout their lives.

Memory

My own childhood experiences of such spaces were limited.

The playground at my school had been barren too, devoid of any natural features that I can recall now, although it was on a slope, which made for great games of attack and defence and incredible ice slides in the winter. But the school day gave that particular space a momentum and a structure, which it did not have after school – then it was dead space. The green outside my friends' houses on our council estate was also barren, but it carries powerful memories into the present for me. We could have been overlooked, but then the great majority of mums and dads would have been out at work, and so would have had little impact on what we did. My strongest memory there, probably at around eight or nine years of age, is of fixing metal bolts to the heads of arrows we had made from elder or beech saplings and, using bows we had also made, firing them vertically into the air, dodging them as they hurtled back to earth.

However, if this had been the only space we had access to, and if there had been adults there supervising me, particularly if they had been adults who showed fear – as we must have on Playground B – who talked differently, and who traditionally had been the butt of attack for many summers, it would have been a very different experience for my friends and I.

That is not to argue against playwork or playworkers when they are needed – when there is no viable or appropriate alternative – quite the reverse. Rather it is intended to emphasise the need for careful consideration of what kind of provision it should be when it is made. Thought must be given to where provision is to be placed, how it will be operated and by whom. Importantly, consideration should also be given to whether it will represent – in the minds of the local children – a lasting recognition by adults of the children's fundamental needs and rights, or an imposition on their space, or worse still, a theft of that space and a colonisation of it by adults.

As a child, I had been lucky and would probably not have benefited greatly from access to playworkers or play spaces – although this would be far less the case for children growing up in the countryside now. But then, the lack of traffic and open access to fields and streams meant that we had endless choices and opportunities to range and engage with a whole spectrum of diverse flora and fauna. (Although, even then, we had our fair share of hostility from local landowners.) But for the children who used Playground B, no such choices were available. They were trapped by traffic and territorial demarcation, and pressurised by a lack of adult-free space. And as a response to the experiential deficits these conditions caused, Playground B was just an adulterated and, in my view, irrelevant solution.

Experience

Thinking of this playground now still fills me with anxiety. For even though I am convinced that 'good' playwork can make a significant contribution to children's development and to their potential to evolve, I would still have to ask, in this particular context, if the children experienced a net gain or a net loss from our intervention. And, on the whole, the answer must have been the latter. It was not that we did anything that was particularly bad practice, rather that we could not do anything that was particularly good practice either, although we tried. It had just been too bad for too long.

However, as we will see with the next example, it is possible to turn a bad situation around, if the time and experience is there to develop an appropriate strategy. But at Playground B, I still believe that nothing would have worked. Everything was wrong. I remember many incidents, but two stand out.

1   Playground B was included in the 'round' of summer playschemes, which would now be called playdays. On these occasions, as well as being able to use the normal site, the children also had the use of an inflatable, which the playworkers were expected to supervise. The inflatable was not a bouncy castle, but more a large mattress with no sides, which, when inflated was about a metre and a half high – quite a fall-height for the small children who might be expecting to use it, along with their sisters and brothers. Access to these inflatables always brought out a variety of different behaviours in children. Most of them were relatively benign, but some of them inevitably became wild and dangerous. On this occasion, twenty to thirty children at a time, boys, girls, three-year-olds and eleven-year-olds, invaded the inflatable, wildly drop-kicking each other. One could be forgiven for asking why we did not separate them by gender, or by age? That, however, would not have been possible. As the thing became inflated, the children just mobbed it. We had no control and were only able to contain the situation and engage in some damage limitation. Instead of serving the children, we had simply been reduced to providing an outlet for their aggression. We should not have even had the inflatable in such a supercharged atmosphere – it was a wonder that children had not been seriously hurt – but that was not our decision!

2   The other incident involved another imposed visit by the same inflatable. On this occasion, only little children were playing on it and they were having a nice, gentle moment. Nice and gentle, that was, until a group of several of the local parents came along. One, who was heavily pregnant at the time, decided that she wanted to have a go on the inflatable, too. She gave us no warning and no permission was asked or granted. She just threw herself onto the inflatable, oblivious of the children already playing there. As she landed – she must have been quite heavy – the inflatable caved in and the little children all fell and

rolled into the dent she had made. And as she bounced back out, they flew in all directions. Luckily again, no child was seriously damaged, but they had been badly frightened. What would we have told the child who might have been injured, or its parents, or my employers or managers? In the real world, at this cutting edge, whose fault would that have been? Playground B should either not have been there, or if it had to be, it should have been enabled to operate in a way which was much more sensitive to its social context. Unfortunately, the mixture of playworker naïveté and inexperience, and the apparent management ignorance and disinterest that existed at that time, more or less guaranteed a painful failure for everyone involved.

Evidence

I could have considered the work of the American architect and educationalist, respectively, Talbot and Frost (1989). They recommend the application of certain classical design ideas to enhance and contextualise children's play spaces. Using, for example, changes of scale, the suggestion of other beings, archetypal images, placeness, line quality and shape, sensuality, novelty, mystery, brilliance, the juxtaposition of opposites, and so on, they believe that the spaces so adapted will both stimulate and facilitate play of all kinds. Whilst I agree that spaces containing these characteristics will provide children with interesting and sometimes fantastic experiences, I am also aware that the reality of size, resources and support for many play spaces renders their consideration somewhat unrealistic. Playground B would have been too small to make any significant physical change to it, even if it had had the necessary finance and support, which it did not.

I could have invoked the lessons of Nicholson's Theory of Loose Parts (1971), in which is stated: 'In any environment, both the degree of inventiveness and creativity, and the possibility of discovery, are directly proportional to the number and kind of variables in it' (p. 30).

It would not have made any difference to the effectiveness of this playground. The children were, by the time I arrived, using the play space to exorcise their domestic angst and any attempt to introduce interesting and stimulating features would only have resulted in their subsequent destruction by fire or other means.

And even if I had known what I now know about the therapeutic potential of playwork, as described in Else and Sturrock (1998), Rennie (1997), and Taylor *et al.*, (1999), in hindsight, I still do not feel Playground B would have provided much of benefit to its constituency.

Compensation

Although it is now widely agreed that one of the functions of play projects, playgrounds, play environments and play spaces is to compensate, that is, to address the play deficits that local children are experiencing, on Playground B at that time we did not know about compensation. Thus, no analysis of the children's local 'play' situation was ever undertaken. If it had been, we may have discovered that the playground's users, the local children, were perhaps generally play-deprived, or that they were emitting hyperactive play cues, or were caught up in a cycle of debilitating violence or abuse, or were only engaging in a limited number of play types which were biasing their experience, and we could have done something to redress this.

Superficially, compensating for play deficits means providing children with play experiences they might otherwise not have, like giving them access to creative materials, or taking them out on trips. But in the context of evolutionary playwork, compensation also means designing a large part of the operation and development of a play space around the assessed play deficits in the local area, deficits which have been arrived at as the result of an audit or a diagnosis (see Chapter 6).

Compensation is a way of ensuring that children have access to those ingredients of the play experience they need for their development as biological organisms, but which they may not have because of the nature of their living or cultural environment. One of the problems with Playground B, for example, was that it was too small and as a consequence it was frequently overcrowded, making it impossible for children to play games or experience solitude or talk quietly with their friends. It was also always frenetic and laden with layers of anxiety which may have been generated over generations. Quality compensation, because it addresses assessed deficits, should help children to feel better, more at ease, less anxious, more balanced and contented and certainly less angry.

On Playground A, I had been used to a high level of valuation by my managers. They never claimed to be experts, but always made sure that I was properly resourced, and they were interested in the children and in the work we did with them. Playground B, on the other hand 'felt' like a nuisance and a begrudged drain on resources. Perhaps it was viewed as a space intended simply to contain and entertain the local child population? Certainly no interest was taken in the work we did that I ever saw, and as the incidents with the inflatable demonstrate, the playworkers had little or no strategic say, even though they bore the brunt of any violence or abuse that resulted. Like so many playgrounds I have known of, Playground B was the victim of a policy which was manifested in long periods of denial of its existence, interspersed with brief periods of uninformed imposition from above. It was not a happy experience.

Playground C

My introduction to the users of Playground C was being called a 'motherfucker', having sand and stones thrown at me, being spat at and having my car kicked. However, although this is certainly an accurate reflection of my early experience there, it is not a fair indicator of the real humour and character of the local children, or for that matter, of the adults of the area.

Every play space is different, and every play space population is different. At Playground A, most of the children came from white, working-class families who were part of the London overspill programme. Many of them had lived in cramped, impoverished housing, with no access to gardens or secure open spaces. Their main play needs, as I perceived them then, were to be able to navigate an unusual volume of space, particularly three-dimensional space, and gradually to be able to integrate themselves into what was a new and very strange rural environment, which would probably necessitate interactions with domestic species, wild flora and fauna, darkness and stars. At the playground we tried to address some of the implications of these needs by creating a space which had, on the whole, a fairly relaxed and welcoming ambience, where the children felt ownership and belonging and where, above all, they could express the diversity of their newly stimulated drive to play, in as many formats as resources and reasonable safety would allow.

Playground B, on the other hand, had a mixed white population with a high proportion of children who had experienced instability, insecurity and prejudice, together with a whole raft of other socio-economic and health problems. None of us was prepared for the ways this context would manifest itself and the levels of violence and aggression that would result. This was one reason why this particular play space proved to be unsuccessful.

Playground C was different again. The major group of users were first or second generation children either from Pakistan or Kashmir. I was told that many of the children's parents and relatives had come from very rural parts prior to coming to the UK. Most of the children who came were from a Muslim background. Initially, most of the users were also male.

Other groups, although smaller in number, also contributed significantly to Playground C's diversity. There were families from eastern Europe, Italy and India; a large representation from the Caribbean; and a small number of white British and Irish families and local Travellers' families.

At that time, the area was economically quite disadvantaged, its housing stock was run down and some of it overcrowded, and there was a drugs issue, although nothing serious by today's standards. There were also race issues, which, because of mixed population, were very complex. There were also religious and cultural issues, particularly around how parents viewed the playground and the concept of play in general. Needless to say, like Playground B, Playground C had had a long and quite turbulent history.

As a playworker, who by then knew a lot more about the practice and theory of playwork than I had at Playground A, this seemed an ideal place for me to practice, and to see which theories would stand the test of a real play space. I was beginning to feel that the children on this playground, unlike those on B, would at least get my best shot, however far short of the ideal that turned out to be.

Three days after I started, however, there was a 'riot', an alleged sexual assault by a user against another playworker, there was some criminal damage, and several of the users were arrested by the police – whom I had not called – and the playground was closed. The reasons for these events are complex and attempting to unpack them probably unproductive. My perception is that they were the inevitable culmination of a period of what I can only describe as inappropriate input at several levels.

Whatever the reasons, Playground C had gone through a period of considerable turbulence. The children seemed very unstable and untrusting and this manifested itself in some anti-everything behaviour, which came to a head around the time of my arrival. I was just left reeling and wondering, what was going on?

In order to clarify the situation I talked to a lot of people, including many of the children, workers from the local multi-cultural centre, youth and community workers, teachers, my own colleagues and managers, and parents and councillors. I suggested that we should close the playground for three months, whilst I tried to develop and implement a playwork strategy, which hopefully, with their help and support, would salvage the situation.

However, before I could do anything, I needed to gather some intelligence about the children's context. I had only been there for a week and knew little about the general area the children lived in, or more importantly about their play patterns, or how they interacted with one another and their play environment.

Initially I did two things. First I made myself frequently visible in the general area of the playground, particularly when children were going to and from school. I went to the local shops, I said hello to everyone I met, and I did that for several weeks and for several hours of every day. Initially I was met with blank faces, but gradually people started to say 'Hello' and were as friendly as people who do not know each other can be. The children knew I was from the playground and did not appear to hold a grudge, not in the street context anyway.

The second thing I did – because I assumed that children might still want to use the outside area of the playground, even though we were closed – was put some water in the playground's little paddling pool and leave a few bits and pieces around that could be played with – some paper, a pencil and so on. I did this every evening. Then, every morning I looked for evidence of use of the area and materials. I was aware that leaving even a small amount of water in the pool all night did represent a risk, but judged it to be so tiny and that the chances of anyone getting hurt were almost non-existent. This proved to be the case.

What the first part of this strategy told me was, although I had been the object of a number of frightening incidents, these were not remotely representative of the general atmosphere in the area, except in periods of high tension. It also served as a reminder that I knew little or nothing about growing up either in an inner-city area, or in a predominantly Muslim community. And although every community I had worked in had had its fair share of life's problems, this situation was very foreign to me, and that needed to be rectified.

The second part told me that a range of children of different ages were still using the outside play area in the evenings. I would find grass floating in the water in the morning, chalk drawings and graffiti of different levels of maturity were on the walls, heavy pieces of wood had been moved, children had been seen on the roof, and the play materials had been used. I also noticed new cigarette ends, evidence of joints being smoked and, on one occasion, I found a hypodermic needle. So some children and presumably adolescents and adults still viewed the playground, or at least its outside area, as a place to go.

The area, in daylight at least, was reasonably friendly and not at all threatening. Children liked and still used the play space, and from this I deduced that the main barrier to a successful re-launch of the playground would be me and how I dealt with the situation.

One thing I also did early on was go to the playground in the evenings and appear in the outside area. Without a word, I would put more materials out and go back inside. Initially this meant that I again became the focus of their attention, and doors and windows were banged and abuse hurled, but gradually any children who were there ignored me as much as I ignored them and an unofficial truce was declared. My reason for doing this was to demonstrate to children that I was there to serve, rather than to intervene. That as a playworker, my presence was to enable their play, not to invade their space.

Suffice it to say that at the end of three months we re-opened with two assistants from the local Muslim community, one male, one female, and the children's behaviour was transformed.

Language

I have a theory about why this was. Although almost all of the children spoke English, for many of them Urdu was their mother tongue. And although most of these Urdu speakers could communicate fluently using English, there seemed to be some circumstances – particularly those in which emotions were involved – where English appeared an inadequate medium for communicating how the children felt. In fact during arguments, the use of English seemed to be almost counterproductive, inhibiting expression and causing further frustration.

To better understand the significance of this, I tried to put myself in their place, in the place of a child from a displaced minority population, where almost everyone else in the family only spoke Urdu. In this context, Urdu would be used to do most of the important and deep communicating, like expressing emotions and articulating other deeper ideas like religious and political concepts. From this I interpreted that children might find it difficult, even impossible to communicate deeper feelings in English. For one reason they did not use it all the time and may never have used it when dealing with emotions or relationships at home. And for another, I had noticed that the form of English they spoke did not appear to carry the range of intonation and emphasis so essential to communicating accurately those things that matter, whereas their use of Urdu did appear to. What this told me was that more than anything else, these children desperately needed access to Urdu-speaking playworkers who were cognisant of their circumstances, and who could help me to provide an appropriately playful context with which the children could engage.

If this analysis was accurate, imagine the relief any of us would have felt, at having access to someone – in this case two playworkers from their own community – to communicate with who could understand both the language and the context in which it was being used, and who would confirm that they did understand, and would respond to what was being said with equality and understanding.

Intuition

Unlike Playgrounds A and B, I had mixed feelings about the appropriateness of Playground C. Although it had its faults, for example the outside area was quite hard and brutal, its indoor accommodation was good. There was a lot of space, a large hall, two smaller rooms, a kitchen and toilets. Upstairs there was an office. And although the echo in the hall could move one close to insanity on busy winter days when all doors were closed, the sense of space, with high ceilings and huge ground area was probably a luxury to us all, especially those children who lived in cramped accommodation. The two smaller rooms made it easy to separate experiences, when that was felt to be necessary, i.e. if some children wanted to be quiet or alone, whilst others wanted to engage in their customary mayhem. The middle small room was used mainly for sitting, conversation, music, dancing, table-football, pool (which I hated for the trouble and angst it caused) and small board games. The small room next to the kitchen was normally used as a creative and artistic space and everything the children produced was displayed there, if that was OK with them. I did this to demonstrate a sense of valuation of everything the children did, without being judgemental.

However, the outside area was a different matter entirely. It had previously been a builder's yard, and although it was a good size (about half the size of Playground A, and at least five times the size of Playground B), there were still immovable traces of its previous life everywhere, which were quite hazardous. In the centre of the outdoor area was a concrete mound that had been built to cover up the concrete base of a crane, and everywhere, only a few inches below the ground, was builder's rubble and slabs of concrete. (It reminded me of some of the early playgrounds in London and other cities, where digging often uncovered old cellars and the remains of bombed-out buildings.)

The playground was also close to sheltered accommodation for elderly people and the relationship between these elderly people and the children was not good. However, the playground was not near the road, it was well fenced, and although it did not have any natural features, it did have landscaping and vegetation. In short, I felt it had limited possibilities, but these had resource implications.

Memory

As a child I would have felt at home in this space. There were places to hide and climb and lose yourself. There was water, albeit in the form of a small concrete paddling pool. There was indoor and outdoor space, lots of diversity of experience, there was space for fires and building and the whole area had a feeling of enclosure, that it was hidden and private. Behind the outdoor area there was at least one mature horse chestnut tree, whose purple blossom in spring was an amazing visual display.

The biggest advantage of the space was its size. It provided the children with room to run about in after a day cooped up in school. Its biggest disadvantage was its proximity to the adolescents and adults who used the small park and community centre close to the playground, and who might have intimidated or bullied children as they came to the playground.

Experience

Although the playground's positioning was ideal in one sense – it was away from traffic, convenient for the children's homes and near a shop – in another, it was awful. Its proximity to the elderly residents' accommodation, for example, was one constant headache, as it was to an area constantly in use by older boys in a community that had a well established male pecking order.

To effectively facilitate 'adult-free' play, play provision ideally needs to be separated from other forms of adult provision, from housing, sheltered accommodation and factories and offices. If it is not, there is constant irritation. Balls go through windows – some innocently, some not so – children climb over walls, they may shout things that feel, sound or could be insulting to others They use physical gestures that intimidate the uninitiated. Older children are often out late at night, and may keep people awake and make them feel vulnerable.

Although I never had the impression that the playground's proximity to housing was a problem – these were also the children's own homes, after all – I often thought that if I had been expected to play in such cramped, overlooked and potentially explosive surroundings, my future almost certainly would have taken even more negative turns than it did!

Having said that, as a play space, it would score perhaps 6/10, given its context. It had plenty of space, and although its history put limits on den and structure building, we were able to make the most important sensory and elemental experiences accessible to the children who came.

Fire play was a very popular, although vexed activity. Many of the children had little or no experience of real fire – a very common phenomenon in this centrally heated time – and I believed strongly that they should have the opportunity to know the dangers and benefits of fire as early in their lives as possible – if only to ensure that their first experience of it would not be at the top of the stairs, when they were trying to get out of a burning house. Apart from the odd blister, which normally came from touching a piece of hot wood, or picking up a surround brick before it had cooled, there were very few accidents. I only allowed as many fires as there were fire buckets, and that limited the number of fires and ensured that there was always the wherewithal to put the fire out, as well as to light them. Fire play acted as the catalyst for one other memorable development.

Initially, it was rare to see any of the children's parents at the playground. This is not unusual, in my experience. But it was unheard of to see a mother from the Pakistani/Kashmiri community in the outside play area, at that time. Until one day, that is, when the mother of some of the regular users, came, lit a fire and prepared and cooked chapatis in the open air.

With a mother in traditional dress doing familiar things, and with Urdu being spoken, for a moment the playground seemed totally focused on one important aspect of the area, and on many of the issues crucial to all of the children, about culture, identity, choices and future possibilities. Issues which could never have been addressed in that way, if the playground had not been there.

The paddling pool was vital to the success of the external environment. For many of the children, a visit to the seaside or a river was a rarity, and water, in its many forms, like every other element – earth, fire, air – is a vital 'interactor' for the playing child. (We are evolved from sea-dwelling creatures and I imagine that, deep within our genes, is the source of that part of the play drive that forces us to search out water. This notion was first alluded to by Haeckel when he proposed that every animal re-lives its evolutionary past during its embryonic development (Jones, 1993)). However, it was Hall (1906) who proposed that children recapitulate their evolutionary past when they play. In every play setting I have operated or assisted on, water, in the form of bombs, pails, hoses, puddles, pools, streams, etc., has always been a major play feature. The paddling pool meant that hot children could immerse themselves in cool water, it could be sat in, floated on, played with and used as a prop for all sorts of imaginary scenarios. A stream would probably have been better, meandering across the outside area, with little waterfalls and pools, but the pool was very effective in its own way.

Because of the concrete and mounding it was possible to get up relatively high, thus flying balloons and using the windmills was a possibility, so to a limited extent, the element air was also catered for. What did prove difficult was access to the element earth.

If the builder's yard rubble ensured that digging holes necessary for building structures – swings, towers, walkways – and dens was going to be difficult, growing things was almost impossible. Our solution was to buy several tons of topsoil and move it bodily with the help of the children, from the gate where it had been dumped to another part of the site, to construct a garden. Most of the children who came to the playground did not have gardens and many appeared unsure of what a garden could be used for! When all the earth had been moved, we planted fruit trees, shrubs and vegetables.

This experiment was a partial success, and gave the children access to tactile, visual and mastery experiences that they otherwise would not have had. But there was an important playwork lesson here too. If the playworker does create such a focus, s/he should try not to make it mean too much personally, certainly s/he should not keep saying to the children how important this garden or whatever, is to him or her. For although, most of the time the garden will just be that, a garden – where things grow and children play – if things go wrong (and they will) the garden, or whatever other focus the playworker has created, may become a way of applying pressure on or of attacking him or her. Luckily I had expected this and accepted that there would be times when to get at me or the other workers, some of the children would pull things up and destroy them, sometimes when we were closed and sometimes before our very eyes! My solution was to view the garden as just another experiment, and to buy more plants than we needed and simply replace what was destroyed. The garden was never intended to be perceived as an imposition. Rather, it was intended to give the children access to alternatives and choices that would otherwise have been absent from their lives. From that perspective, it had to have the effect of providing a balancing mechanism to other, more de-sensitising experiences freely available in the local area. Therefore it was essential that we did not see the garden as something that had to be defended. Quite quickly the children got bored and left the garden alone.

Evidence

I return to Talbot and Frost (1989) and Nicholson (1972) for a brief final critique of Playground C. The underlying message in both of these excellent articles is that the ideal play environment, whatever else it is, must be a place that is conducive to playing. That is, it must be a space where children not only feel secure and stimulated, but one in which important aspects of their drive to play can be freely expressed. This may seem obvious, but in many of the play contexts I have known over the years, playing has been the last consideration of designers, managers or sometimes, even playworkers!

In the case of construction and mastery, this was not really possible in Playground C. In most other aspects the outside area was certainly above a qualitative bottom line, but as with spaces too small to be able to play games that involve a lot of running, because of its builder's yard history, Playground C's impact on digging and building was inhibitive and frustrating.

It is my experience that if an environment is recognised by children to contain the ambience and props for play, the play drive begins to take over and their behaviour changes. They stop being the result of whatever socialising forces they have been subjected to and instead become those embryonic engineers, architects, builders, cave dwellers, hunters and gatherers that Nicholson (1972) and others have alluded to.

The researcher Eibl-Eibesfeldt (1967, 1970) even described the play of the young as 'scientific research', whilst the educational psychologist G. Stanley Hall (1904) called the expression of these different roles 'recapitulation'. While there is little hard scientific evidence that this 'transformation' as Schwartzman (1978) calls it, is developmentally significant or has an impact on individual evolution, the fact that all children, except those who are stopped from doing it, seem to undergo this change when the environment is appropriate, is enough reason to continue to facilitate it. More research needs to be done in this area.

Playground C's impact on the local children was very positive, particularly after the addition of the two local playworkers. Attendances rose, violence all but disappeared and small children and girls started to attend in increasing numbers. There were odd clashes along the way, but these were more a consequence of cultural 'crossed wires' than of significant problems. Most importantly the playground gave the children the opportunity to experience a wider context, one that I hope said that there was a world out there to explore and experience that was not all racist and threatening by any means. Working at Playground C was one of the most enriching experiences I have ever had.

Reflections 1

Playground A was the first Adventure Playground I worked on. Next to the playground itself was a small cottage, known to all the kids as 'The Cottage'. On one occasion we invited a children's TV celebrity to visit us. It was a typical November Saturday afternoon – grey, misty and damp. The area around 'The Cottage' was a sea of mud. This, the first of the Reflections, attempts to contextualise evolutionary playwork by providing a picture of the surprises, diversity, fantasies, humour and depth of relationship the playworker shares with the children who attend play projects. The ages of the children referred to range from three years to eighteen years. It also alludes to the physical conditions many children and playworkers are expected to function under, whether as in this case, mud, or as in many others, violence and lack of resources. This Reflection also attempts to convey some of the affect that hangs over play spaces like sunlight or stormclouds. Several of the children mentioned, although resilient and apparently happy, were so damaged that their lives were already disaster areas. I appreciate that using stories is not the normal way one would communicate complex ideas in an academic work but in playwork, anecdotes, like the one that follows, have become a respected medium both in training and in sharing ideas and understanding. This is beginning to diminish slowly as theory and evidence gradually evolve, but these Reflections are examples of a verbal tradition which has sustained playwork over many years.

One interesting feature is the playworker's role as a facilitative adult who, having organised the event, is constantly observing its impact upon the children.

Reflection: the coming of the Queen

It must have been the dulcet tones of Handel's *Water Music* suddenly emanating from the murky interior of the 'Cottage' which seemed to interrupt the total bemusement which had, until then, so completely taken over her composure. The lined-up reception party hadn't helped.

Piggy had a massively snotty nose. Sid had recently fallen headlong into the sea of mud that passed for our road and was still dripping brown slime down his front. Sid's sister Judy was nervously wringing the bottom of her dress in her hands and showing her knickers because of it.

The rest were standing as curious onlookers, fags glowing in the winter Saturday afternoon dying light, clouds of warm breath vapour in the cold. We hadn't seen a real celebrity before.

For once the street lamp worked and threw a feeble orange tint over the proceedings as the sun sank over the rubbish dump, known to all as the 'Tip'.

The man accompanying her had tried to make her exit from their car as clean as possible but it was impossible. Like the rest of us she christened her patent leather high heels in the liquid mud that came down from the Tip at this time of the year.

We stepped forward and thanked her for coming. Perhaps, had she known what was in store, she wouldn't have made the effort, but it was nice that she had.

Until then, the kids had watched her every day on the television as she told stories, and played games with television children and saw birthday kids in her magic mirror.

'And I can see Raymond, and Jessica, and I can see Derek and Pauline and Josephine.' And, on and on, until finally she said, '. . . and I can see you, and you'. I always waited to see if she got caught in a nightmare tape loop and spent the rest of the day saying 'and you, and you, and you,' when I caught the odd tea time performance with my own kids, but that was as rare as it was magic.

Now it was our turn to see her in real life. A person from the 'Children's Programmes' was up at the Venture.

The music went up a 'Warp,' then faltered and mutated into 'Crackling Rose' originally by Neil Diamond, but we had the Woolworths nearly lookalike version – a hundred hits for 3/6d.

I must have heard this particular tune thirty hated times a day since John had proudly contributed it to our meagre but otherwise quality record collection – Budgie, Santana, Yes – including *The Yes Album* and *Fragile* – Emerson Lake and Palmer, really early Genesis with Peter Gabriel – although Slade, T Rex and Gary Glitter had also crept in. Records all chosen and paid for by the kids.

'Come in,' we said. 'Come and have some tea.'

She ducked in through the low front door into the murk beyond. It was like that pub in *Star Wars* at first, full of strange beings and light-reflecting eyes.

Her eyes soon grew accustomed to the light, dim due to coloured bulbs and to the glass bricks which had replaced the windows after so many break-ins. 'This is great,' she said, as she noticed the Saturday afternoon chess session between Duncan and Manuel, who had once been a Spanish champion. Kids crowded around. They were not intrusive, but they still tried to touch her. Real and live and here.

'Miss, come and see my picture, come and see what we did . . . I like your dress Miss . . . Is that your old man out there? . . . Have you got any kids? . . . Are they yours on the telly? . . . I think you're really pretty Miss . . . Have you got your magic mirror with you? Miss, Miss, Miss, Miss.'

She was carried on a sea of children, all talking, all watching, into the Bar, where mugs of tea, coffee, lemon tea, biscuits, crisps and sweets were offered and accepted and refused and normally spilt.

We showed her around – where the radio station was, where we made jewellery and other things, where kids painted and acted and dressed up and played every game under the sun. It was like a pub with no beer, but better. Darts, dominoes, cards, science games, word games, nature games. But mostly talking and going in and out of groups and in and out again.

She stayed a couple of hours. A long time for someone with no resistance to the pressure of children, the noise, the constant requests, the tripping up, the kicks up the arse that we all know are part of the normal day's work, but hard if your kids are normally only programmed to go out at 4.30 in the afternoon. I couldn't say what she thought. She seemed to like it. We wrote saying thanks and she wrote back.

Later, though, I couldn't help giggling insanely when I thought of her next looking in her magic mirror and seeing the leering snot-covered faces of Piggy and Sid looking back at her.

Reflection: flint, arrowheads and Roman coins

I can still remember this vividly. The combination of believable lies and self-fulfilling prophesy created a very powerful medium for my fertile childhood imagination. Morris's (1964) notion of neophilia which is cited through the entire text of this work suggests that children are stimulated to play by the new, the novel, the attractive and the interesting. This Reflection attempts to encapsulate what that means to children experiencing play in adult-free space and demonstrates that children create their own neophilic context using imagination and fantasy, ranging and the choice of diverse spaces for their play environments. Whilst it is not always possible to replicate this in a supervised space, playworkers should strive to create neophilic foci for the children using the space. It will ensure their continued interest in, and enthusiasm for the space.

The good playworker will recognise that much of what s/he observes taking place is in the realm of fantasy or imaginative play and that reality rules, whether in relation to physical behaviour, language or perceptions, do not apply.

'If you hit the flint right, with other flints, you can make arrowheads.' It was the 'boss' speaking, and we were on our way up to the Valley. The Valley was a deep trench cut out of the chalk, by a fast running stream, and it was a place we'd have pissing competitions; go rabbiting with ferrets, and pan for gold. It was also the place where there were huge pieces of flint.

We were walking along the railway bank, close to where the stream went under the railway lines – one of many secret places we knew. This one, where in the pool below redthroats and sticklebacks drifted in and out of the summer's watery shadows, was where we played our own version of chicken. We were very familiar with the railway. We hunted slow-worms in the summer here too, and raced them in the stream. We listened like Indian scouts, with our ears to the rails to be forewarned of approaching trains, leaving pennies to be flattened by them on the lines as they passed. But chicken was best.

As the trains came out from the shadows of the road bridge, belching steam and smoke and making an horrendous noise, the idea was that you poked your head up through the sleepers and keep it there as the train approached. It wouldn't hit you or anything, but it was a real test of nerve, watching this charging mass of steel and flame hurtling at you.

On this occasion, the 'boss' was telling us how he'd 'found' a Roman coin embedded in a piece of flint and that we might find one too. He was very convincing. Either that or we were incredibly gullible, because for years we broke open flints to see if there were coins inside, especially in the Valley.

At the top of the Valley were fields which regularly flooded in winter and on cold, moonlit, afterschool evenings, we'd go there to slide. It was our own ice rink, just me and my friends, with the cry of the pheasants for company. The Valley itself was a jumble of elder and hazel, and half fallen willows with roots exposed to the water and the weather. It invited enquiring children to hunt for treasure, especially those Roman coins.

The Valley had a diverse landscape, that included two waterfalls with deep pools at their base, sinky sands, a hollowed out tree trunk, thousands of rabbit burrows, and steep banks where the stream deposited sandy beaches. A pipe carrying gas or water traversed the gully, providing us with death defying opportunities for balancing and war games. In springtime the Valley's banks were awash with violets and peggals, and in the summer, the fields through which it passed became the backdrop for bale dens and just hiding in the uncut wheat, staring up at the clouds.

The 'boss' told many lies like the one about the Roman coin. But even though they left me longing and unsatisfied, they provided a fantasy focus for many harsh, freezing wet days when it was as much as we could do to stay warm and dry until we could go home again.

Reflection: the Action Space inflatable

Just now and again, you find yourself having one of those experiences that even in your wildest dream you could not have imagined. This was one of those. These days children's bouncy castles are everywhere, and boringly predictable in the limits of what they offer. But when inflatables were being developed by some very creative people, they were the stuff that fantasies were made of, and not only for the kids. One year an inflatable group from London came to do some work where I was based. It turned out to be two of the most innocent and playful days I had had for years.

Any 'good' play space should satisfy numerous playwork criteria simultan-

eously but this one was outstanding. Not only did it enable children to engage in action that was spontaneous, goalless and intrinsically motivated, it was full of play cues and neophilic spaces, where immersion in motor, communication and social experiences were virtually unavoidable.

I'd left Playground A about a year and a half previously and it seemed like forever. I'd tried my hand at being a playwork reporter and enjoyed it. Now I was working as a Community Development Officer (Play).

I wanted to do something unusual for the kids in the City that Christmas – a kind of 'happening'. Though I got into a row with 'Entertainments' who ran things like Pantos at Christmas and assumed that 'happenings' should also fall under their orbit, I had invited a group of people to come up to the City from London to put an event on. It turned out to be one of the most extraordinary experiences I've ever had.

Nowadays, everyone has been on an inflatable. You will find them at the seaside and at all the other 'leisure' events where children have to pay to play. But at that time, inflatables were quite new, and were sometimes very spectacular.

The group were called Action Space. I suppose they were strictly Community Artists. They had vibrancy, expertise, political empathy and were very talented and creative.

I knew we were getting an inflatable but I was totally unprepared for what transpired.

The one they brought consisted of a number of large plastic cubes which were joined together by a network of tubes in the form of a maze. The maze ended in a large sphere which itself contained a couple of huge inflated human figures.

When air was passed through the whole thing, a series of valves inside the tubes operated, and it inflated. You went in it, rather than on it, crawling along the maze of tubes on your hands and knees, although it was nearly possible to stand up, as the thing was so big.

The whole inflatable was made from different coloured lengths of plastic material, which themselves filled the interior with diffused coloured light. We played other films, lights and a stroboscope onto the inflatable's surfaces, added music via a disco and changed the level of the floor on which the inflatable was placed by putting mattresses and mats underneath it. This turned an initially disorientating experience into one that became quite fantastic.

I was so pleased that I'd asked Action Space to come early. Not only did it give us the time to properly construct the experience, it gave us 'big people' the chance to have a go, too!

Two other playworkers, Frank and Jackie King, had come to help, and with several other helpers and the Action Space team we set about exploring the possibilities which the experience offered.

It wasn't long before giggles and squeaks and startles and quiet conversations began all over the structure, which covered the floor area of quite a large gym hall. Because it was a maze, it was possible not only to *feel* lost, but to actually *get* lost. Various parts of the structure were made from dark, thick material, at these points there was no light and the interior was completely dark.

The valves which worked to keep the thing inflated were star-shaped. They closed when the air pressure on both sides of them equalised. When it decreased or increased on one side or the other, air pressure simply forced air through them until equilibrium was regained.

It wasn't just air which passed through them, of course – we could too!

I've never had so much fun. There we were, playing tag on our hands and knees, bumping and crashing and falling, as the level of the floor changed in the gloom, sweating from the warm air and exertion, coming round corners only to bump into someone from whom you had tried to escape, or hide from, and almost shouting with the surprise and exuberance of it all.

Every so often you would find yourself entering one of the cubes. In them, exhausted players caught their breath and watched the lights and films that were playing backwards on the surface of the cube. And always the backdrop of sound of 'the infant school party' as horrors and fears were played against laughter and surprise.

There was something very safe and secret about that environment. It was in all senses a 'play' environment. As long as you were not really stupid, messing with fire or deliberately hurting people, you could do almost anything, and what was more important, none of it mattered, nothing was 'the right way or the wrong way'.

The variation in range and level of stimulation was immense. Every sense was stimulated, intuitive facets like imagination were exercised, rational skills like co-operation and relationships pursued. It was another world.

The day had started with a group of adults, many of whom were strangers. It had finished in an uproarious Indian restaurant session between people who now had a special bond – they had played together.

For the following two days, children from all over the City came to try out our experience. We had to charge them to come in because even then play was seen as something which at worst, should break even and at best should actually make money – a philosophy which, in my opinion, is quite unethical and which is now more or less out of control. We charged 2p, not a lot of money but more than some children had with them. Naturally we let them in anyway.

The days were filled with the same sounds and faces as we had ourselves experienced the day before, and we couldn't get the little sods out either – that was just like the day before too!

I suppose several hundred children of all ages used that experience over that two-day period. There were scuffed knees, some kids got lost (who didn't?), and there was bit of claustrophobia too, primarily in the shape of a TV reporter, who I'd guess to this day hasn't forgotten the experience.

You actually had to enter the inflatable through one of the valves, and once in, the sensory transformation of worlds was dramatic. Suddenly you were in a world where being a child, whether that was because of size, or lack of precon-ception, or whatever, was actually an advantage.

In this situation a playworker simply becomes a child, that's what a lot of the work is about. But the reporter seemed to be unable to do this, and being an adult in a confined, noisy, hot and sweaty environment, full of high speed kids playing mad games, was more than she could take.

I sympathised, but it did say a lot about the inflexibility of adulthood, for many adults anyway, that this kind of *Alice Through The Looking Glass* experience, although available, was either not accessed, or not accessible to a lot of adults.

It was a wonderful three days. I remember driving back to Cambridge taking Frank and Jackie and myself home for Christmas and how 'up' we were feeling. Not just because we had been instrumental in making what had been an unusual and fun experience available to lots of children, but equally because we had been our own childhood characters for a while, reminding ourselves who we really were – that adults are big kids, not that kids are small adults. There is a whole world of difference between those two perceptions.

Reflection: caves

This Reflection focuses on children's capacity to incorporate mythical or spir-itual elements into their play narratives. Offerings and sacrifices are not an uncommon feature of play in the wild with children in middle-childhood – perhaps a particularly powerful recapitulative period. These manifestations of symbolic play highlight a need early in life to put an interpretation onto the notion of the 'middle of nowhere' that helps children to cope with the fear and powerlessness implicit in such a realisation.

The little river cut through the landscape like a gently glistening thread of light. Its banks were sometimes reed covered and they were overgrown with dog-rose and sloe bushes. From time to time they fell straight into the water which was sometimes deep and fast moving. On other occasions they formed steep barriers between sandy, water-lapped beaches and the green meadows beyond.

We were aiming for a smaller beach which led to a flat earth shelf before the bank rose away. It was winter, and the moon was rising as we moved across the field, although school had only finished an hour or so before.

The air was like cold liquid, you could see your breath, and when you pissed, you were, for a while, engulfed in a cloud of condensation. We talked with quiet enthusiasm about the day and looked forward to getting our work done before we had to go home to tea.

The river bank was made of solid white clay. The river sang over small stones in the darkness below. We gathered our things together on the ledge, and the diggers began to dig. One for the 'leader', one for the others to have a go in, and one for me, the priest.

The clay and inevitable flints were worked loose by borrowed shovels, nail bars, hammers and screwdrivers. Some of the others filled buckets and dumped the minings into the river. The stones hit with a loud 'plop' while the clay made translucent white clouds as it was taken by the water.

Slowly, our caves began to take shape. The 'leader's' was high and deep, held together by the density of the clay. It burrowed six feet into the bank, and when it was finished, it had candle recesses, mats, shelves and a sack over the entrance for privacy. The 'others'' cave didn't quite fit the number of those who might need to use it, even though some of them would spend much of their time with the 'leader', working out plans and other things that needed doing, and this caused some friction, but it would be resolved tomorrow, if we dug another one.

I sat close by, watching. Although we weren't that far from the road, it was like we were miles away from everywhere. We heard owls over the frosty landscape and cock-pheasants. We knew every inch of the river, the fish, the birds' nests, the best trees to climb, where to light a fire. The kids weren't digging my cave because they had to, it wasn't like that. It just happened.

On nights like this, when it was quiet and frosty and clear, the moon and stars were painted on the blackness, just out of reach. I always knew the Plough, but that was all. The rest I just looked at and loved. The outline of leafless willows moved gently against the light of far away street lamps.

Mine was finished. It wasn't deep like the 'leader's', but it was more ornate, and it had plenty of room for me and, as I was the only person allowed into it, that was OK. At the back they had even built an altar out of bricks and stones, and placed candles on top of it. The doorway was made out of a brick surround with a sack to cover the gap. It was more permanent than the 'leader's', but then it would have to be; its function was different.

The 'leader' who had helped to dig my cave, and the others', seemed very proud. 'This is just for you', they said.

Then it was time to go. My feet inside my wellies were blue with cold and so were my short-trousered legs. The 'leader' said, 'Let's go', so we called the dog and walked in line back across the dew wet grass towards the light.

Chapter 4

Play types and the playwork menu

In the early days, playworkers used to describe what they saw children doing under one umbrella heading, 'play'. Certainly, we knew that within the overall term children talked, ran, swung, climbed, created and acted out, but these were all parts of the same thing, play.

More recently, developments in the literature and greater awareness in the field of playwork itself, have made it possible to break 'play' down into some of its component parts, parts which have meaning in their own right. These component parts, which I believe to be discrete and which can be differentiated from one another, are becoming known more generally as 'play types' (Hughes, 1996a).

For playworkers this is a useful development. The playworker's main function is the creation of good play environments. But the play needs of children vary, depending on their developmental progress, and particularly on their experience. For example, a child from a big family may not need as much social interaction as say, a child with no sisters or brothers. A child from a cramped home will need more space than a child from a home with plenty of room. A child from a high-rise block may not need elevated perspectives as much as a child from a bungalow, and a child who has had the opportunity to build and create will not have the same urgency to engage in building and creativity as will a child who has not had such opportunities.

If play can be broken down into various types of engagement, i.e., if play can be explained in terms that show that different ways of playing perform different developmental functions, then as playworkers, we can begin to describe how it is possible to address deficits in certain kinds of specific play behaviours in ways that are focused on those behaviours in particular.

Breaking play down into its component play types gives the playworker a tool for focusing expertise, resources and time onto particular areas of need. If, for example, most of the children who come to the playground, or playcentre or After School Club, are not able to run freely in their home environment, there will be a deficit in what is known as locomotor play. This deficit will not be addressed by providing opportunities to paint, but will be addressed by being given the opportunity to run about. Thus by analysing the child's home context from the perspective of the child's own experiences of playing in it, the playworker can more accurately facilitate a type of play that child is being deprived of.

Facilitation means making the props for all play types available; it may mean allocating specific spaces for particular play types, or making sure that children are aware that, in the play space, certain behaviour that might be frowned on elsewhere is enabled. I am using the term 'enabled' rather than 'positively encouraged', because that would imply an intervention on the part of the play-worker(s) to encourage a child to do something and that is not what I am describing. Being enabled always leaves the choice to engage or not with the child. It is not a function of playwork – except perhaps in therapeutic playwork environments – to encourage children to do anything. Playwork's job is to make all types of play possible, so that if a child is driven to engage in play, it can happen.

Without a clear and unambiguous description of the various behavioural groupings that make up the overall term 'play', playworkers are in much the same diagnostic situation as were doctors before the categorisation of illnesses and diseases, when all symptoms were seen as a part of the same malaise and treated as such. The real medical breakthrough arrived when different sets of symptoms were ascribed to different medical conditions. Similarly, an analysis of need in playwork terms can only be undertaken when specific play deficits can be linked to playwork prescriptions, which are specific to particular play types.

The development of an analysis of play using play types carries with it all manner of implications. For example, if play as a total phenomenon is essential to human development and evolution, which I believe it is, then it follows, in the absence of any evidence to the contrary, that every type of play is also essential. However, playworkers and providers often discriminate between those play types they allow to be facilitated and those they do not.

Some types of play are not viewed as problematic. Imaginative play, creative and fantasy play, for example, are normally viewed as totally acceptable to most adults engaged in working with or providing for children's play. However, loco-motor play needs a lot of space, and many play spaces are far too small to engage in quality locomotor activity. Rough and tumble play, although seen by researchers as 'precisely the cause of social bonding' and having a positive effect for children (Baldwin, 1982) is often banned by adults, often for reasons of political correctness rather than as a result of a playwork analysis of need.

Deep play is also banned in many settings, even though it can be viewed as a mechanism for children to access an understanding of their mortality. Deep play may enable children to devise risk-assessment strategies as a way of dealing with what Stanislav Grof (1975) called, the 'agonising existential crisis', which results from an increased awareness of the nature of death and dying.

Play types and the play environment

It is relatively easy to provide for most play types and on the whole what they describe is self-explanatory. Disposable and scrounged materials, loose parts, dressing up clothes and props will cater very adequately for many of them. However, thought also needs to be given to their location and the playworker may need more than one, or even several of some things. A variety of materials will certainly facilitate *symbolic, creative, fantasy, role, dramatic* and *imaginative* play, although dramatic play may benefit from a specified area too, like a stage.

Rough and tumble can take place on any surface but, if there is concern that children will hurt themselves, the playworker should provide a soft play area and take care that any rough and tumble that does happen does not develop into a real fight. *Socio-dramatic* play is often more the realm of a therapeutic environment, although children will always dramatise and play-out what is happening to them in 'real-life'. As with dramatic play I would be tempted to provide a specific area where both dramatic and socio-dramatic play can be engaged in by children. Because of the potentially explosive nature of the socio-dramatic narrative, I would expect that area to be a particular focus of a playworker's peripheral vision.

Like *locomotor play, social play* often takes up lots of space. Playworkers should never be satisfied with the tiny excuses for play spaces I have visited over the years. Many were far smaller than Playground B, as I described earlier. Adequate levels of social and locomoter interaction are crucial to health and well-being, but without social play children cannot understand what and how they feel in social situations, or decide on their own rules of engagement with other human beings. As well as enabling children to socially calibrate themselves, i.e., How close do I stand? How hard do I touch? How loud do I speak? etc., they are also faced with learning to solve the puzzle of what other children's faces and bodies are saying, when they are playing. This particular form of what is known as meta-communication (Bateson, 1955; van Hoof, 1972; Else and Sturrock, 1998) is an incredibly sophisticated device we humans have evolved, which has the effect of topping up what we say with words – using emphasis, pitch and volume – with body movements or stances, and complex facial expressions, involving our eyes, our eyebrows and our mouths.

This is a very interesting area for the playworker. Children are invariably socialised to trust and believe adults and they rarely question whether what adults say is true or false. However, in the child conducive atmosphere of the good play setting, children will immediately challenge adults when they detect a conflict between what the words are intended to convey, and what that adult's face and body tell them. It is both a developmental and a survival skill to be able to do this quickly and accurately. A skilful command of meta-communication will help children to decode and encode the complex interactions that go on between adults, and between adults and children, and help them to decide on appropriate courses of action in some circumstances. This has obvious advantages if children are approached by strangers who might also cause harm, but it can also be useful in understanding how to deal with manipulative, exploitative, bullying or oppressive older children or adults.

Games like tag and hide and seek, which also have a locomotor ingredient, and adolescent games like spin the bottle and knocking down Ginger, all contribute to a better understanding of how children network and relate to one another. So much of human relationships involve what Wilber (1996) calls the 'subtle' realm, and require acute observation, memory, mimicking, rehearsal and hearing co-ordination on the part of the child.

There are arguments for and against a specific space for *creative play*. If one can only provide for painting and model making, this can probably happen anywhere and should be happening wherever the children are. But some play projects enable children to engage in more sophisticated creative activity, making jewellery and candles and so on, which requires special areas and has health and safety considerations. I have often wondered whether this kind of highly specialised activity, which invariably has to be supervised and taught to children, belongs in a play space, or whether it would be better kept in the school environment, which is more suited for it. However, if it is there and children do engage with it, a special area specifically designed to cater for the use of hot, sharp, delicate, expensive materials and tools is an essential. One final word on this. The playworker should ask, who is this for? Is it for me, or for a more artistically inclined worker? Or is it really for the children, because I have assessed a deficit in the level and type of creative play they engage in?

Resources are always under pressure and they may be needed elsewhere. If they are used to fund access to a particular play type, be clear that it is the children's needs that are being met. I remember visiting a play project some years ago, and was bemused to see twelve table tennis tables in their indoor accommodation. When I asked, 'Why so many ping-pong tables?,' I was told the senior worker plays table tennis!

A great deal of *communication* play will happen without any facilitation, although prompts like nursery rhyme murals, music and books may stimulate it. Perhaps the most important point to make is that the playworkers should try not to censor how children communicate.

In Hughes (1996a) I described communication play as the way we access vocabulary, nuances, fun and rude words and duel meanings. Sometimes we forget that language itself is not just words, it is the meaning of those words in different contexts and with certain emphases. And as I described above, communication is not only about language, but includes body posture and meta-communication too. In my experience, children are not conscious of the meaning of words until they are made conscious either by the reaction words get when they are used by others, or by the reaction they get from others when they use them. Children are rarely intentionally offensive, but if the use of words creates a reaction, they will use them again and again to get that effect.

The following two extracts were overheard from two small children at an open air festival:

* Willy-bum, willy-bum, poo, poo, fart pants.
* What's the message? Fart, fart, that's the message.

These words were probably picked up either individually or in groups, in other contexts and then strung together to make sounds that make the children (and the rest of us) laugh.

Sometimes, children learn words or phrases that other adults regard as offensive. Dealing with these words or phrases needs great sensitivity on the part of playworkers. In the context of my analysis the play space is where these children come to experience adult-free play. The playworker's main function is to facilitate that. Some professionals would argue that one of the characteristics of good play provision is the protection it offers the children using it. However, in this specific context this may mean protecting one group of children from another group of children's language by stopping those children using certain words or terms. I am not sure how appropriate or even ethical that is, even if the words do cause we adults offence. It may be an intervention too far.

Children have to sort out language and other forms of communication as they go along. If one child calls another child 'four eyes', for example, should we step in and stop the child doing that? When do we intervene? If a child uses racist language, which it has clearly learnt form a parent or relative, do we step in, and if we do, how? Many adults say that racist language, for example, should be confronted. But as far as playwork is concerned, I do not think we are in the business of confronting four- or five-year-old children, who are behaving perfectly normally having absorbed their local language. If that child had been playing out in the street or in the wild, a playworker would not have been there to intervene, so why do it in a child's play space?

To address these problems, I restrict my intervention to when it all begins to be less about communication and more about persecution. When the perpetrator is apparently enjoying the discomfort of his target, when the target is obviously feeling uncomfortable and showing it, when an innocent remark escalates into a linguistic feeding frenzy.

Language and communication can all be very complicated. At Playground C, I heard a child shout, 'Fucking Paki', only to turn around to see two brothers, both from a Kashmiri background, squaring up to each other, with one of them shouting this racist insult at the other.

At another play space, local middle-childhood boys, six to ten years of age, were very homophobic in their language. Whilst I did not feel it was my function to be overtly or systematically educative in the play space, I did judge that it was part of a playworker's function to insert question marks into what children perceived as correct or obvious. To do this with these children, I went and bought an old bicycle, a woman's model, with no cross bar. In that location, where status was very important and where to have the latest mountain bike, trainers, stereo, mini-disc player or whatever was an absolute esteem essential, to arrive on an old bike was bad enough, but to arrive on a woman's bike was total heresy. My point was, 'Do you understand what any of this homophobic stuff is about?' Their reaction to this was amazement, then laughter, then a real decrease in the homophobic language.

All too often, what with peer pressure, TV fashion pressure, music biz pressure, this pressure, that pressure, children often do not have a clue about the meaning, or more importantly the impact, of what they are saying. So they need to be given a chance to learn meaning, before we pile in team handed to 'teach' them, often leaving them feeling inadequate and humiliated because we perceived ourselves as better censors of their language and behaviour than their own humanity.

Exploratory play requires loose parts, puzzles and space. A playworker in Northern Ireland said that she kept a big box containing clocks, locks and things like old radios, so that her children could pull them to bits, see how they worked and then try to put them together again. Another interpretation of the term, exploratory play might be playfully exploring the play environment and that has other playwork implications. It is a good idea from time to time to look at the environment one provides for children and ask, 'Would I have wanted or been stimulated to play here?' Or, 'Would my children want to play here?' The answer would probably be a resounding 'yes' to both questions if the play space is an interesting place to be. Visual effects from pictures, projections, structures, planting and building all change a bland space into one to explore. Sounds, like recorded or live music, running water, or no sound, new languages and the radio all stimulate exploration. Mazes are great. Being able to go from an area of high activity to one of isolation is stimulating. Moving from a flat area to a high area, shielding off part of the environment with cloth or paper, anything that means the only way the child will find out about where s/he is, is to explore it. That was one of the great things about the inflatable maze I mentioned earlier – it had to be explored.

Except in adventure playgrounds, and in children's free play in the wild or at the seaside where access to it is guaranteed, providing for *mastery play*, is very important, but it does seem to be losing ground. I know people have problems with the term 'mastery', but as a play type, access to it is vital. In many of its manifestations it could just as easily be called elemental play, because it is often about mastering the elements.

It is quite difficult to provide for mastery play indoors, unless the playworker has a spectacularly large environment to work with, because in mastery play the child is learning about trying to master different features of the natural environment. I use the term 'learning about trying to' because it is about doing, it is about the process, about interacting with the forces of nature and learning about what can be controlled, what might be controllable with more knowledge, practice or information. In this sense it is not exclusively about damming or bridging streams, or digging caves.

From a play perspective the term describes a very effective and enjoyable, although not altogether risk-free engagement, that children undertake with a whole range of geological, botanical, elemental and atmospheric aspects of their habitat, in ways which often have a basis in engineering, science and construction.

Mastery play is a vitally important way of engaging with the world in a 'child-scale' format and learning important lessons by doing, observing and reflecting. It is a great deal about asking questions about the natural world and exploring what can be controlled, what should be controlled, how things can be controlled, and so on. The fun is often in losing control or in never having control in the first place, rather than in any form of environmental domination. Like trying to hold back the tide and by so doing playing with the notion of futility. It is also about working with nature in an interdependent way. For example, building a camp out of natural materials not only tells children it can be done, it is also a recognition of the security that the natural environment can give them, and this too is an important play lesson. One which many children are never able to learn because they do not have the opportunity to engage in mastery play.

Mastery play not only provides information and questions about the context that is being played with, it helps children to question in the first place – other play types do much the same thing in their own particular area of experience. Children should not need to be taught to question, their play should contain such unexpected and unimagined experiences, i.e., experiences that contain what Koestler (1967) called the 'aha reaction', that questioning should be a natural corollary to play.

Object play, or problem solving play as it is otherwise known, needs loose parts, and an interesting environment that throws up problems for children to solve.

Deep play, although vitally important, is another of the play types that is losing ground, partly I think, because of our increasingly litigious culture, but also because playwork has become so obsessed with safety in recent years. Apparently children do not get hurt when they play. They do not graze their knees when they play, or get a bang on the head when they play.

I believe that deep play exists to bring children in contact with mortality. I do not mean it exists so that they can kill themselves or nearly kill themselves. Rather, that it is a playful acknowledgement that death, dying and the personal inevitability of them is real, that they happen to us all. This play type helps children to come to terms with what is difficult knowledge, both to comprehend and accept. To stop or inhibit children from engaging in deep play is, in my view, a very serious issue, and like censoring any play types from children's behavioural repertoire, is deliberately disabling and ethically unacceptable.

Like all play types, deep play brings children into contact with a particular aspect of being. In the case of deep play, this aspect is risk and risk-assessment. Because of how the play process works – it happens when the child chooses, it is under the control of the child, it involves repetition, gradual escalation, immersion, evaluation, insight and does not acknowledge the notion of failure – play is an incredibly effective way for children to gain understanding of where they are and of what they are doing.

Most children are neither stupid nor suicidal. They are not going to deliberately go beyond the limits of their known skills. But to evolve at all they must take much of what they do to that limit and test it. When we see a child engaged in something 'dangerous', we are making that judgement from our standpoint, not from theirs. For them what they are doing may be exhilarating or fun, but they are not going out to deliberately maim themselves. It might, however, be a part of their computation that injury, whilst not a probability, may be a possibility.

All human beings have to learn to risk-assess, and where better than a play space – a space devoid of hazards, a space which is supervised/operated by someone who understands what is going on and who will almost certainly have a first aid qualification and be in touch with the emergency services – to do this experimentation? It is not often I would sing the praises of artificial play environments over the natural environment but I would in the case of deep play. To understand caution, to compute risk, to respect the built and natural environments from the perspective of the dangers they contain but not to be afraid of them, is essential to personal survival, it is need-to-know material and most of it can be accessed in a high quality playwork space.

But a huge change needs to take place in modern parenting before this can happen. Parents currently seem to have made the same discoveries that all other parents have made and have had to live with, but they appear to have reacted differently. Many modern parents seem so petrified of their child getting hurt or injured that they are doing exactly what is needed to virtually guarantee that it will happen. Play is nature's way of training children to navigate the environment they find themselves in. If we stop them playing then they cannot learn that navigation, and a simple operation like crossing the road becomes a huge ordeal.

Like parents everywhere, I never wanted my children to get hurt or injured or hit by a car or assaulted. But whilst I recognised that feeling this was normal, what was also normal was the acceptance that these things might happen, as awful as they are. There is a point in a child's life when the child has to be allowed get on with it, as there is in the lives of the young of every other species. Children cannot be carbon copies of their parents. They will have their own friends, their own relationships and, importantly in this context, their own ups and downs, including illnesses and accidents. The more equipped they are to deal with life's problems, the better they will be at dealing with what life throws at them. Wrapping them in cotton wool does them no favours at all, it just makes the inevitable more painful when it happens.

We live on a planet. It is a dangerous place, and in the end, it is we as individuals who have to deal with the experiences we encounter. I had a serious car accident a few years ago. The injuries were bad enough, but what was really awful was the realisation of how simple it was, that this could happen at any time. I had to get my own head around that. Nobody, not my mother or anyone else could do that for me, and it is the same for our children. There is a point when we have to say a kind of metaphysical goodbye to our babies. That does not mean we do not love them and will not support them, but it is a recognition of reality.

So where better than a happy, exciting, vibrant, colourful space full of other children and all sorts of wonderful experiences to play with and challenge themselves with, to come to terms with that? Where better to begin to develop the realisation that there is a lot more to life than death and fear of dying? Playing opens up infinite doors of experience children are previously unaware of and will continue to be unaware of unless they play. But it has to be joyful, exuberant play, that is not ridden with anxiety and worry.

There is a phrase currently in vogue, 'Go for it'. Whilst all too often that can be interpreted as do what you want and do not worry on whom you tread to get there, it can also mean: 'This is not a rehearsal, if you do not do it now, it may not come around again, go for it.'

There is a wonderful optimism in such a sentiment. Play makes it possible for us to make the most of our lives. I do not mean vocationally or in terms of status, although it might indirectly do that too. Rather, I mean in terms of increasing our awareness, of developing our consciousness, in terms of our well-being and appreciation of what it is we are involved in and a part of. Play brings us into contact with everything else, both inside and outside of ourselves. It demonstrates that we are an intrinsic part of a greater and beautiful whole.

So, like all other types of play, deep play is a must for children. However, the playworker should ensure that the deep play experience s/he facilitates are what they purport to be, that they do not contain any hazardous 'surprises' that are the result of negligent playwork. I am not highlighting this just to protect playworkers. Playwork is nothing if it does not honour and respect the children it serves, even if it does appear a hard-nosed friend at times. But if children do come to a play space operated by a playworker, not only is it essential that risk is accessible, it is also essential that danger/hazard is not. Then there can only be two sources of injury to the child.

1   A genuine freak accident and these can happen anywhere at anytime.
2   If the child is not taking personal responsibility for his or her safety and tries to perform outside of his or her known ability.

Note: There will be children who, because of play deficits or disabilities, may not be aware of their limitations. At a swimming pool, for example, there is always the possibility that a non-swimming child will jump into the deep end. We should be aware of similar possibilities in play spaces and must always be vigilant. But for those children who use the play space regularly, they will know the limitations both of the environment and of themselves, and if they get hurt, hopefully they will have learnt a valuable lesson from the experience.

Knowledge of play types is useful for two reasons. The first and more practical reason, as I suggested earlier, is that by dividing play up into its components, we can more effectively facilitate it in total and we can also address the issue of particular play type deficits.

The second is that sub-dividing play into a first level of component parts gives us a better understanding of the mechanisms of the play drive. Earlier I compared the play drive to a genetic river and that is a useful analogy, but perhaps a better one in this context is that it could be seen as a high energy cable with fifteen cores, each of which energises a particular play type. At one end of each core is the child playing, whilst at the other end is a monitoring mechanism that is computing which play type, or combination of play types, are most appropriate for the child to engage in to ensure the development of essential skills and characteristics, including balance and flexibility, language and problem-solving.

Play types do occur singularly, but they also appear as composites, like mastery, locomotion and imagination. Perhaps the very young only manifest play types singularly, but as experience grows and perception becomes more complex, so the way we interact with the world through play types becomes more amalgamated.

This does not necessarily change the notion of play as a drive, or as an energy source, but what it does suggest is that either the drive can exist in fifteen different forms, which can manifest themselves simultaneously and which may be relatives in a particular neurochemical family, or that the delivery mechanism for each play type is different in some way.

The playwork menu

An equally useful way of organising practice is by using the playwork menu. This subject has been looked at briefly before (see Hughes, 1996b) under the title, the 'Playwork Curriculum'.

The playwork menu enables playworkers who view their practice as a series of unrelated activities, to use its simple organisational method to more clearly rank what they offer children, under four basic headings. It is designed to make it easier for practitioners to analyse and prepare the play environment by using these headings in advance of the children's arrival. Thus, when the play space is in use, the playworker is then free to generally oversee what is happening, rather than engaging in programming activity and by doing so risking dominating the children's choice of activity and methodology for engagement.

The menu categorised playwork practice into four areas:

1   Senses
2   Identity
3   Concepts
4   Elements.

The rationale for the menu was this. Play is a fundamental learning mechanism, that begins with absolute basics like touch, where the interface between the child's skin and the world exists. Play is primarily a process that has no external motivation. Therefore what is gained during play is for the benefit of the child as an organism. That is, play has no interest in future career, or a particular relationship, in travel or in any conscious objectives. In that sense it is raw biology. The menu tries to reflect that.

Diversity, balance and depth

Because play exists to enable flexibility, adaptation and evolution, it is not fuelled by end-products. Instead it looks to diversity, balance and depth of engagement or understanding for its motivational base. What I mean by understanding, in this context, is that one of the benefits we gain from playing is not understanding as comprehension, so much as it is understanding gained from immersion in an experience, through a fusion with that experience. For example to playfully understand mud or water, it is necessary to have more than an appreciation of its chemical composition or its physiological benefit. There is a level to playful interaction, which is about a coming together, a combination or symbiosis between the play object and the player, that puts a value into the object so that it becomes a 'whole' which transcends the sum of its parts. Actually playing with mud or water, for example, enables children to gain a whole other understanding of texture, viscosity, temperature, impact and so on. Playful immersion in toys develops this deeper special quality, so does immersion with places, people and other species.

For example, anyone who has ever owned a cat will know that they can study all sorts of things about cats; their habits, history, psychology, their illnesses and so on. However, no amount of knowledge will tell them about that cat as a living and breathing entity. Ask cat lovers about their cats and they talk about tactile sensations (stroking etc.), auditory sensations (the purring and mewing noises they make), their movements and the affection they give – this is more than understanding through knowledge, it is a transcendence of perception brought about by a level of immersion, in the cat as a live reality. Like the cat lover, the playing child is also engaged in immersion. But where the cat lover is only engaged in immersion on a mono-dimensional level – the human and the cat – the child engages in immersion on a multi-dimensional level – the child and the Universe. So the playing child is not just making factual sense of the world as it plays, it is also making sense of it on emotional, psychic and sensory levels too.

The four areas of the menu are intended to give playworkers guidance about the fundamental areas with which children will be interacting.

The first area is *senses* – hearing, sight, touch, taste and smell. Each of these sensory interfaces certainly tells the child about different aspects of its play experience, but it is more complicated than that. To simply say, for example, that the *sight* sense enables a child to see what it is playing with is to totally understate the experience. What the child sees is shape, colour, context, applications, form, depth, perspective, size, and so on. I am not asserting that the child would be conscious of each characteristic in its early years, and I am not saying a child would describe things in this way. What I am saying, however, is that in an increasing form of completeness – over time – these are the building blocks which are being formed at an atomic or sub-atomic level, and they are what the child is seeing.

Similarly, *sound* can be equally understated. Many play environments will have music in the background or in the foreground. Thought should be given to the musical experience children are engaging in, so that they are not only able to access what is currently fashionable – although they will want to do that too – but also enabled to experience music and other sound spectra as a total portfolio of what sound is and can be, including a developing consciousness of its overall complexity and the effort taken to create it. As well as having the opportunity to listen to music, children should have the opportunity to be able to make it. More importantly they should know that they can and that the props for doing it are continually available.

As I have suggested earlier, social play is an important source of fundamental sound building blocks. During social play children learn, by simultaneously watching another child's meta-communication and body posture, to understand intonation, emphasis and pitch and to discriminate between the match and mis-match of the spoken word and the other communication protocols.

Tactile diversity is also a crucial experience, and its effect on the child can also be understated. Where do we gain the building blocks to express emotions by gesticulation, by drawing, stroking and massaging, hanging on to structures and holding tools if not through play? Where do we gain the fine motor co-ordination required to differentiate between the pages of books and newspapers? Textures, pressures, palms, fingertips, manipulative movements, holding, acute motor movements, are all important characteristics of the tactile experience that a play environment should give the child the opportunity to engage in. Good play spaces offer a wide range of opportunities for tactile interfacing, so that children can begin to develop a tactile relationship with metals, woods, fabrics, ceramics, plastics, papers, etc.

Diversity, balance and depth in what they see, hear and feel when they are playing gives children an overview of their existence, which is awesome rather than ordinary. For each experience is not only valuable in itself, it also makes comparison and analysis possible. Why do I like that? Why do I not like that? Why does that tune do that to me and that one does that to me? Why does some music make me want to dance and some music make me want to sob? Why do some experiences make me feel better or worse, what do those terms mean anyway? Each play experience should provide interesting and useful additions to the child's experiential portfolio and the play environment should be assembled in ways that make that possible.

Children should always be able to play with the senses of smell and taste too. Whether that is by cooking on open fires, making scent from wild-flowers, trying new foods, enjoying BarBQs, or evoking house or school or even cinema smells or the smell of animals, straw or cut grass.

Knowledge, awareness and, above all, appreciation of smells and tastes is an important prop for imaginative play, a subject for discussion in social play, and introduction to cookery and chemistry, and might be a life-saver too. But more importantly for the playworker, playful access to each of these sensory universes helps children to appreciate the minutia of experience. It enables them to listen, look, feel, taste and smell with delicacy and wonder, to transcend the 'take it for granted' way in which many adults live their lives, and be conscious of the reality of the sensory interface, that it is 'the world telling us what it is'.

The second area is *identity*. Identity is about at least two questions. Who am I? Who do I want to be? A good play environment can give children objective feedback on the first and facilitate decisions about the second.

I am particularly interested in the idea of identity. I have worked for some years in Northern Ireland, a location where for many if not most children who live there, a specified and allocated identity is all but unavoidable. As a child I always thought that people were whoever they wanted to be. I do not recall ever being put under pressure to change who I was. I was called 'skinny' and 'four eyes', but I do not think anyone expected me to binge eat, or take my glasses off as a result. But in Northern Ireland, being of a particular identity is viewed by some both as a badge of exclusivity and of exclusion.

Whilst I appreciate that to many adults, giving their children a tribal, class, national or a school identity means a great deal to them in terms of their tradition and heritage, there seems to be little accompanying awareness of what a human catastrophe this categorisation brings about in play terms, creating as it does both a conceptual barrier between children, and a false view of self in the children it affects.

For playworkers, children can only be children, the young of our species. They cannot be perceived of as coming from a particular religious, ethnic, national or economic group. As Cairns (1987b) writes of Northern Ireland, if they are allocated a particular social role, then, 'children come under enormous pressure to take sides'. At Playground C, the children came from several economic, social, religious and ethnic backgrounds. Should we have treated them differently? Were their play needs different because of their parents' religion? Certainly, we were respectful of perceived differences. But professionally every child's needs were assessed using the same criteria, in much the same way a doctor would assess illness.

I interpret Article 31 of the UN Convention of the Rights of the Child to mean that the Right to Play is the right to play freely, in diversity with other children. Insisting on this right being enforced will not make problems vaporise, but where divisions do exist, it would make life more difficult for those who would try to segregate and separate children from one another. The impact of segregation is frightening. A mini-survey, carried out in Northern Ireland in 1998–9, for example, showed that eighteen out of twenty-one people interviewed there (from a wide band of ages, both genders and from both main traditions) had not had any friends from the other main tradition, until they were at least fifteen years old (Hughes, 2000).

As with our senses, the development of the building blocks of being conscious of having an identity and comprehending what it is, starts very early. But if a child starts with only part of the information – like a jigsaw puzzle with only half the pieces – s/he will only get half the picture, and may never be able to overcome the problems caused by that deficit later in life.

Much of the racism and sectarianism that exists is not simply the result of the institutionalisation of these phenomena. Certainly they exist in many institutions, but when children will not even cross the road to play with other children – a matter of some 20–30 metres – as was the case in a part of Belfast, something more powerful than propaganda is at work, something deep within the psyche of the individuals involved.

Children are not born racist, sexist, sectarian, homophobic, criminal or whatever. These are things they learn from other people, but what is it they actually learn? The previous section on senses gives us a clue. Just look at touch. A parent only has to give a child a tiny anxious squeeze of the hand, a tiny tactile cue, whenever a particular word is said or a particular context mentioned, for that child to begin to associate feelings of anxiety with that word or that context.

It only needs a consistent raising of the eyebrow or a disapproving twist of the mouth for a child inadvertently to link that look to a particular person or group of people. It does not need a patronising manner or downright rudeness or violence to create the links; they are just the heavy guns that may come later. The real building blocks, as with everything in childhood, are much more subtle. Children, particularly young children, are totally sensitised to small changes, they have to be, because small changes are what are happening around them. The child may be oblivious to the bigger picture, because s/he is operating at the atomic and molecular level.

The props children use to play with the idea of identity and with their own version of it are only that, props. An ostentatious hat, for example, does not really tell us whether a child has an ostentatious identity or whether the child is insecure, and from a playwork perspective it does not really matter. What matters is that children have the time, props and opportunity to explore who they are and what that means, so that they can be both secure and happy with what they discover or look to ways of changing themselves, if they are not.

Playwork is not about making judgements about children's identities and this is where I have problems with some of my playwork colleagues who feel that certain child identities are, by definition, bad or wrong. I cannot agree with that for the reasons I have stated. Their concerns normally lie with children who take on racist, sexist and similar identities. But what if a child takes on an identity which is viewed as disruptive, or negative, or irritating? Are these regarded as inappropriate identities too, and if not why not? Their impact may be equally hurtful. Why are some playful manifestations of identity regarded as worse than others?

That does not mean that some behaviour will not be viewed as intolerable, and perpetrators asked to stop it or invited to leave the play space, civilisation has to be maintained. But this should always be a last resort, based on safety rather than political or social correctness. Alienating children because they come from a particular background is only inverted discrimination and play spaces exist for all children, irrespective of their origin. The play space is a raw environment, it has to be, to facilitate much of the raw behaviour which is at the cutting edge of the play drive.

If a child has only just discovered a piece of information which, after time, could fundamentally alter his or her view of the world, playworkers have to acknowledge what is happening. Forget for a moment that some playworkers might actively display dislike for children from, say, racist context. Imagine that a child from a racist context does begin to question its racist certainties because s/he has discovered that all children with pink hair do not stink, in direct contravention to everything about children with pink hair that the child's family has taught. Whilst the inappropriate playworker might be saying to the child, 'See, see, you were wrong', the child is having to weigh up the pros and cons of the reality of this revelation.

How does one reconcile the discovery that one's parents are wrong, that one's aunts and uncles, brothers and sisters, friends and their families views are inappropriate? What does one do with this knowledge now that one has it? I have met many people in Northern Ireland who find this kind of discovery about the 'other side' almost impossible to compute, because the meaning and value of everything, *everything*, every preconception, everything that makes life worth living, membership, belonging, history, tradition, powerful symbolism, music, family, is thrown into question. 'If I am not that, then what am I?' That is a big enough question when you are four or five years, but imagine asking it when you are 60 or 70 years of age!

Many people go into denial over identity, afraid to be who they are because of the preconceptions of others. Others retreat into their own ghetto, not wanting the complication or reality to ruin what they now know to be a fantasy, and a pretty nasty one at that.

The playworker's job is not to alienate any children but to help them to feel secure enough, both in the play environment and in themselves, to explore who they are, either on their own or in the company of other children. This is particularly important for children who find themselves growing up in a context where identity is a foregone conclusion, but where the impact of adult imprinting has not yet 'hard-wired' that child's identity.

Playworkers also need to hold in their mind, particularly when they are working with young children, that much of what they see as expressions of identity is work in progress that they can facilitate – although they shouldn't concern themselves with the outcome of the processing – if they provide children with opportunities to engage with identity as a general idea and with their own identity in particular.

Identity can be explored in any number of ways. Mirrors, dressing up clothes, other props – hats, gloves, jewellery, bags, even guns, musical instruments and clip boards could be made available. Photographs, personal stories, flags, hair dressing and historical viewpoints are all useful. We need to be clear that we are facilitating an exploratory process, that there should be no subjective limitation on what is explored.

The third area is *concepts*. My *Penguin English Dictionary* definition of a concept is: 'an abstract or general idea'.

I have just been discussing identity (which is a concept) in the context of racism (which is also a concept). We've mentioned death (which is a concept) and we've alluded to fairness and justice (which are also concepts).

This section is not so much about what concepts are, as it is about acknowledging that they exist and making it possible for human beings to describe ideas that come to them, which might be shared and even valued by many other people.

The notion of democracy, for example, is recognised by many human beings as representing a preferred way of being governed, of conducting debate and of decision making. Most of us are not totally clear what democracy is, any more than we are totally clear what the notion of justice is, or love for that matter. These are more the terrain of philosophers. But irrespective of our personal comprehension of abstract ideas, they are important to us and perhaps as important to us now as are sensory interactions, because they are at the very root of how we live our lives, our beliefs and how we perceive everything from time to numeracy.

The playworker's role in facilitating play with concepts is relatively simple. Our function is to ensure that children are given access to concepts on a sensory level and on an intellectual level. That is, they are assured that exploring, discussing and having opinions about ideas is expected.

As with the previous section, it is essential that the playworker sees him/herself in a facilitative role. We exist to help children to access, not to predetermine outcome. The play space is exploratory ground, and so at the playground, democracy is not 'right' any more than is fascism. Islam is not 'right', any more than is Buddhism. Vegetarianism is not 'right' any more than is omnivorism. What is 'right' and 'wrong' is more the philosophical province of the world outside the play space, the play space is where children gather insights by playing with ideas.

But access to ideas should not only be diverse and deep, it should also be balanced. If the play space has access to the Internet, for example, that may cause problems of bias, which only the space's ambience and general approach to playful enquiry and balanced conclusion can hope to influence. Any more intervention than that and the project becomes an arm of school with all of school's cultural and moral absolutes.

If play is essentially an adult-free experience, and if there is even a suspected relationship between that adult-free experience and the development of vital characteristics that aid our understanding and evolving consciousness, it is essential that playworkers do not corrupt that relationship. I say essential when it is probably unavoidable – the question really is, 'How much can or should adults legitimately intervene in children's play?' My judgement would suggest a sliding scale from 'not at all' to 'as little as possible'. Others say, 'as much as is necessary to get the result adults want'. Irrespective of how child-centred, etc., they say they are in coming to that conclusion. I feel that that is an infringement of the child's biological and psychic integrity on the playground.

I have said before that, outside the boundary of the play space, whatever that is, I recognise that adults rule and children are not normally perceived in the way they are being described here. But, in the past, children have been able to get away from adults to form their own, often contradictory view of the world, which is an essential developmental process if we are not all to become identical clones of some preconceived normality.

Currently it is increasingly difficult for children to do that. Often it is impossible. To counter that disastrous deficit, for first-hand unregulated learning, we ourselves have to learn how to accept and provide for non-conformity, and play provision based on evolutionary playwork principles is a good start.

If we cannot recognise that the engine for our evolution as a species – this includes social evolution too – is play, if we cannot recognise that the more we try to control and constrain the play drive, the more we will damage the very essence of our young, the more likely it will be that their development, and that of our whole species, will be thrown into reverse mode.

Increasingly, children are manifesting dysfunctional behaviour. They are not at ease in the narrow confines of what adults feel is appropriate for them – contexts that are rarely what adults experienced themselves as children. Parental obsession with safety has turned many children's lives into little better than that enjoyed by battery hens (Huttenmoser and Degan-Zimmermann, 1995). Play can help these children, but parents have to accept that there are inevitable risks. Risks which will increase the longer the situation drags on. A psychic shift in the current perception that parents have of their children is long overdue. Children need adult-free play experience more than they need safety. It is the parents who say children have to be safe, and who transfer that onto their children, not the children themselves.

Something has happened relatively recently to cause this imbalance. On Playgrounds A and B, it did not exist. But at Playground C, it was full blown, with safety experts everywhere. Many of these people are now performing intricate U-turns, aware of the potential damage they may have caused to the development of the children. Some of the 'safety' scares are inevitably caused by media excitement and the need to sell a story; some of them have come from quite close to playwork itself, where organisations have been trying to sell the idea of childcare by frightening parents; some of them have come from safety experts, as I mentioned above; some of them have indeed come from a bandwagon within playwork, where individuals apparently terrified of not appearing politically correct have also overemphasised the importance of safety. Hypersensitivity towards safety issues has also permeated the home, as parents have become increasingly paranoid about traffic, and the potential for their children to be abducted, or worse, by predatory adults.

As a parent and grandparent, I too have all these fears. But I also recognise that they are malignant fears that can eat away at the rational thought of any human being who does not want to experience loss, or see their children injured or frightened.

Providing children with access to concepts may seem a long way from this debate, but it might be that parental distancing from thinking about conceptual and abstract things in the round is what is making them see the world in the way they do. A kind of hide-under-the-bedclothes-and-hopefully-it-will-all-go-away, view.

I did not know there were such disciplines as philosophy or economics until I was in my mid-teens. But if a child knows that things exist, even if that child does not know what they are or what they mean, the child's own curiosity, a neophilic attraction to the unknown may drive him or her to investigate (Morris, 1964). One cannot investigate if one cannot imagine. And one cannot imagine if one does not know. Imagination is limited by experience, and that includes experience of the conceptual, the abstract.

The fourth area is *elements*. The elements, in this context are earth, fire, air and water.

Although these have been discussed in detail elsewhere (Hughes, 1996b), I would like to spend a little more time exploring one aspect of playful elemental interaction further.

Elemental interaction is another crucial experience for the playing child. For as well as bringing children into contact with life-giving materials, like air and water, and through this contact reinforcing the importance to human beings of free and unpolluted access to these essentials, it may also have a deeper significance.

There are at least a dozen theories about why human beings play. One of them, Hall's Recapitulation Theory will be explored throughout the text. G.S. Hall (1904) was significantly involved in the genesis of what is now known as developmental psychology, and his ideas about recapitulation are very interesting in the playwork context.

What Hall, and Reaney (1916) who later expanded on Hall's work, suggest is that a child's play is a recapitulation, or re-play of what its ancestors did; not in their play, but in their adult life. I will be exploring possible reasons for this later.

Hall's and Reaney's thinking is explained further in an interesting examination of their work in Helen Schwartzman's book *Transformations* (1978). In it, Schwartzman says the following:

> What she [Reaney] proposed was that 'the various stages of childhood could be divided into 'play periods', that corresponded with the various stages of human evolution. For example, she suggested that the animal stage

or period (birth to age 7) was reflected in swinging and climbing games; the savage stage (7–9) exhibited hunting and throwing games; the nomad stage (9–12) was reflected in skill and adventure games and 'interest in keeping pets', and the pastoral and tribal stages (12–17) were characterised by doll play, gardening and finally team games.

(p. 47)

What Hall's and Reaney's ideas imply is that when children are playing, some of what we are seeing is a re-run of their ancestral evolution, a recapitulation of their ancestral past, in the form of Reaney's model of children's evolutionary play stages.

My interest in this theory is that some of what we see as playworkers may actually be that process of recapitulation at work. Why this is pertinent to playing with the elements is that elemental play, which can involve anything from digging, sowing seeds, cooking over open fires and children's rituals and ceremonies, has always struck me as very primeval and instinctive, not of this time at all. Yet children engage in it quite naturally and spontaneously without prompt or encouragement if the context is conducive.

In my own play, elemental interaction was a big part of what I did. We often had fires and built shelters, in the form of tree dens, straw bale dens and caves. But what impresses me most about it now is the way we exposed ourselves to the elements by playing outside a lot of the time. I can remember on windy spring days, playing with my shirt open to the wind and I can still evoke the feeling of exhilaration, virtual flight, and importantly what I can only describe as the feeling of 'looking through the eyes of ancients', that came with it.

It is true to say that we carry our past with us in our genes. For example, Jones (1993) writes of Freud's belief that behaviour was controlled by biological history (p. 227). It may be that play is a manifestation of all our genetic echoes, a reconnection with our own ancestors. We are, after all, the most advanced form of the amalgamated genes of many generations of human beings, whose life experience was encoded into their genes and passed on through the ages. As the Hall/Reaney models suggest, each of us is standing on a pyramid of our own past, going all the way back to the beginnings of time.

Whilst I do not think that play is only about recapitulation, I do believe that some of play is playing back in time. Unconsciously reconnecting children with what are now only faint imprints of times long gone. In fact, recapitulation may carry a highly symbolic role for the human child. That it is not alone on the frontier of time, but is connected to a personal and unique history, which it may feel driven to play out, to actualise, in order to derive stability and comfort from, in its present circumstances.

Whatever the realities of recapitulation, it is too important an idea for us not to give it attention, and in the play space it is easily accommodated, if the props are there. In this case they should include a fire area and water buckets; elevated areas that enable children to view panoramas and experience wind; there should be puddles, stand pipes and paddling pools, even small streams to enable children to engage in water-play; and timber, cloth and digging tools for children to build dens and shelters. If recapitulative play is a significant feature of the play space, children may well begin to play out rituals using body paints, fires and music, too.

A fuller exploration of recapitulation can be found from page 233.

Chapter 5

Evolutionary playwork values and play-deprivation

Current playwork practice has not evolved out of any theory and, although attempts are being made to develop a theoretical playwork base now, to compensate for the theoretical deficit over the years, playworkers have generally relied on various philosophical or political rationales for their playwork practice.

Currently, there are three written versions of these rationales. Two appear in Hughes (1996b) and the other in Playwork NVQ material (NCPET, 1995). Each version will be examined below.

1. Playwork values and the National Vocational Qualification in playwork

The NVQ values were radical for their time, although closer inspection reveals a philosophical base tailored to fit a formal service, provided perhaps by a local government department or a voluntary agency. A form of service that is beholden to voters or funders rather than one designed to authentically underpin the facilitation of a biological process or a discipline independent of politics.

Terms like 'child-centred', 'empower', 'respect', 'equality', 'care', 'consideration' and 'co-operation' abound in a context that also states that children have the right to play safely, in a stimulating and challenging environment, which is not controlled by adults (NCPET, 1995: 6).

In terms of personal preference, there is little to disagree with here. I would also like life to be less difficult but it isn't like that, any more than play is, can or should be co-operative, caring or equal. And describing play in this way reflects perhaps more the desires of adults in terms of what they would like play to be, rather than what they know it to be in reality.

However, deriving playwork practice from a list of values that have the effect of redefining play as a social, rather than as a biological phenomenon is as unfortunate as it is also contradictory. Certainly playwork is a social phenomenon. It only exists because the march of the built environment has so reduced the child's opportunity for adult-free experience, that we feel driven to make special provision so that it can happen. But play provision and the playwork that takes place there will only be special if it ensures that children are able to play, and that means that it has to facilitate an adult-free, often socially unacceptable, fundamentally biological process.

Obviously, this becomes less possible if there are rules in place governing the space and children's behaviour in it, which so limit play that it is changed beyond recognition.

The NVQ values state that 'adults should always be sensitive to children's needs and never try to control children's play'. But even this statement ends with the phrase, 'so long as it remains within safe and acceptable boundaries'. This seems to negate the previous part of the statement. Whose safe and acceptable boundaries? The adult's or the child's? The implication is that the boundaries are set by the adult, but what is implied by the terms 'safe' and 'acceptable' is not clear, and no clarification about the criteria against which these terms are judged is given either.

It is regrettable, but the NVQ values appear to remove the child from the realities of adult-free experience, so that they risk becoming a statement of desired outcomes of some, as yet unstated, social policy programme.

The whole point about adult-free experience is that children gain a perspective on life that is their own. An individual view that they can then use, as they grow up, to evaluate the rules and standards of the adult world from their own perspective, what King (1988) described as making 'informed choices'. The closer the supervision, the more imposed the standards, the more the behaviour has to conform to some prescribed 'norm', the less truly independent 'informed choices' will be made.

Adult-free play experience guarantees children's integrity. It alone gives them control to make their own mistakes, to engage in trial and error and to develop their own opinions and their own rationales. If that is taken away or diminished by over-controlling adults – adults who not only control behaviour, but thought too – all children end up with is a viewpoint predetermined by those adults and that is a kind of totalitarianism, although I do not believe at all that this is what the NVQ intends. But playtime is the only chance that children get to address their own emotional and perceptual agendas. Every other waking minute is already taken up with adult expectations.

My own view is that the freedom to explore and experiment, without adult intervention, is precisely what was implied when the UN Convention of the Right of the Child gave play the status of a human right. They did not intend that the right to play meant that children's play behaviour should be controlled and programmed by adults, however well meaning those adult intentions. My interpretation is that Article 31 is a way of acknowledging that children have the right not to be dictated to by adults when at play, however benignly that might be done.

If the corollary to this is that we do not know how yet to provide non-directive spaces for children's play, or that we do not want to provide it, that is a different issue. If adult society genuinely finds it too difficult to sanction the kind of play spaces that put children more prominently in the play driving seat, then that should be urgently and professionally addressed, given what is at stake. It should be seen by playwork as a problem that it is imperative for society to solve, rather than one we pretend does not exist, or one that can be solved by re-writing play to suit what adults want it to be, rather than what the facts tell us it is.

The problem is fundamental. And it is certainly not my intention to demonise either the NVQ or its supporters by exploring it here. But what could be interpreted as expediency by the development of values like those underpinning the NVQ, could have the effect of contributing to what Lloyd George described as 'deep and enduring harm' to children, rather than the reverse, which is what I assume was intended. What this particular articulation of 'playwork's values' underlines more than anything else is how complex are the problems that result, when the child's play habitat is supervised or operated by adults.

However, as I mentioned earlier, there are other sets of values too, and one might feel that they suffer from similar flaws. If the NVQ's values seem over-controlling, perhaps those that I wrote in Hughes (1996b) (see p. 71), are too naïve and esoteric, and, as a result, equally unhelpful?

I believe that the authors of the NVQ values were genuinely trying to solve a difficult problem. I do not think they were successful, because in attempting to create rules for funded and acceptable provision, they left play, or at least the play I recognise, out of the equation.

2. Playwork values and *Play Environments:* A Question of Quality

- Trust the child
- Children's interactions with one another are essentially non-competitive
- The content and intent of its play is determined by the child
- Children are whole environment citizens
- Children are independent beings with human rights
- Children are lone organisms
- Children are individuals deserving of respect
- Playwork is child-empowering
- Playwork and equal opportunities are inseparable.

Perhaps what I did here was leave political realities out of the frame. Instead, what I wanted to do was devise a set of standards for playworkers that were rooted in a non-social view of children and play. I wanted to do this because, for a great part of my own 'playhood', adults hardly featured at all and when they did, it was normally in the form of a hostile interface.

I accepted the teachers' rule at school, I respected my parents' rule at home and for much of the rest of the time, I expected and accepted moderation by the police, shop-keepers, other children's parents and so on.

However, this does beg one serious and important question. What territory do children hold? Which bit is theirs? If adults dominate all of your time and all your space, where do you exist?

I existed when I was with my friends, when we went out to play. We ranged the fields and hedgerows, the railway line and woodland stream and later on the building site. But we were only able to play in these places if we avoided adults.

Although I articulate a view of the development of playwork as being a response to recent inroads being made into the child's habitat, that is only part of the story. For space, territory, has never really belonged to children for play, except perhaps the ubiquitous fixed play space and even that is plagued by adults.

Perhaps I am suggesting two things.

- That the march of socialisation into the child's psyche is going too far. That children must be able to differentiate between themselves as unique individuals with their own integrity, and themselves as members of a forward looking and advanced society. I am concerned that, even in playwork, not enough attention is being given to this, to the need for children to develop their own unique sense of self by playing, rather than simply becoming conditioned as consumers of fashion and lifestyle items.
- That perhaps adult society should begin to consider formally legitimising space for children. We try to do it now but it is fraught with difficulties simply because many of the adults involved cannot perceive of children as anything other than recipients of services. Seeing them as imperfect adults, in need of care, rather than as entities with brains and rights of their own. However, there is a debate there, waiting to happen. Perhaps adults should consider dedicating some larger tracts of land for children's use as well as smaller play spaces? Adults have National Parks, why not children?

The non-social view of play, to which I allude, is at the root of the values I expounded in *A Question of Quality*. They are more than personal observations of the playing child made from the perspective of a playworker. They are an attempt to capture an essence of childhood in spite of the prism of socialisation through which we view it all.

In John Steinbeck's book, *To a God Unknown* (1935), one of the characters has a very primitive, animist types of experience in a glade containing a large rock with a stream of water flowing from it. It impressed me deeply when I read it, long before I ever became a playworker.

What it said to me was that human beings come together to form social groups for reasons of safety and security, but that they are much more than a purely social or gregarious species.

The incident in Steinbeck's book gave me an insight into a deeply spiritual side of myself that I had not even recognised before. But although human beings are multi-faceted, our social nature, the emphasis we put upon our sociological identity, may be creating layers of its own – money, holidays, qualifications, position, prestige – which are stifling other equally important characteristics, what we are as human beings, from also informing our identity.

We are social, but we are also spiritual, and we are a species among other species – a facet of our humanness that is being totally buried beneath our apparent desire to commercially exploit natural space, even if that is at the cost of every other species. We seem to be out of touch with who we are and where we are, and this is particularly apparent in the priorities we apply to our children.

I want to be able to write here that playwork has the answers to these problems, but it does not. However, intuitively I am convinced that good playwork – where children have the time, space, props and opportunity to discover who they are in a context in which everything that exists is not viewed necessarily as for our exploitation or gratification – can make a significant contribution to finding solutions. It enables our children to reflect on where they are going in terms of their evolutionary direction and address it, if they feel it is appropriate.

Needless to say, this is not a majority viewpoint. Some would say that it is not even a fringe viewpoint, and yet it is a view that is expressed by playworkers. It may be rooted in the intense immersion in childhood we experience as playworkers. Perhaps, because of that, we are more sensitised, more aware than others, of the intense primeval forces in which children's play is rooted and from whence it springs. There is something deeply significant about seeing children as the guardians of our species' evolution.

I am convinced that, in the longer term, the ideas underpinning playwork will become part of some form of mainstream social policy perception, somewhere. However – and I share this analysis with other playwork colleagues – contemporary society is just not in the right mode to seriously consider some of what playwork is offering at the present time. It is a problem of the interface between a 'magician' and a 'non-magician' system (Palmer, 1994). And governments seem happiest listening to pragmatic individuals who hold views that fit into their prepared policy jigsaws, and one can hardly blame them for that.

The implications of playwork on society are huge and similar to those which accompanied the alleviation of the impact of urban violence on children in the United States, where Perry (1995) concluded that 'nothing less than a transformation of culture, including radical changes in child-rearing practices is required' (p. 140).

3. The Ten Newcastle Points

The final set of values is called the Ten Newcastle Points and was born out of a training session I ran with a group of playworkers from Newcastle upon Tyne in 1985 (see Appendix 2 for a full list).

Its main conclusions were that quality play experiences will help children to:

- think for themselves
- make their own decisions

- have confidence in their abilities
- develop empathy
- develop values
- test out strategies without the stigma of failure
- resolve contradictions and inconsistencies
- communicate their needs, beliefs and desires more clearly
- have an understanding of the life process
- to develop an understanding of the interrelationship of everything
- to question everything.

This list could be construed as having a social emphasis too, although it was derived from practical observation and is not a wish-list. It also reads like a curriculum for the 'citizens of the millennium', although that was not how it evolved. Rather, the playworkers in the group saw the play spaces they operated as separated from adult society by metaphorical 'air-locks', which because of that had the effect of enabling children to engage in new experiences, and test and explore them, until what they learnt became a part of the child's view of the world. In other words, they saw the play space as a laboratory where children explored experiences, and where some kind of resolution to the problems that exploration exposed could be reached.

It is a statement of belief, born out of observation, rather than the statement of a position or a list of desires, and it makes some very important playwork points. For example, coming to terms with mortality (No. 8), how everything is interrelated (No.9), being able to test strategies without the stigma of failure (No. 5), and being responsible for yourself and your actions (No. 1).

Values are a useful tool for articulating the beliefs which underpin playwork, although even articulation is fraught with problems as I have attempted to demonstrate. For reality we must rely on research and hard evidence, which in playwork are still rarities, although the situation is improving.

However, there is a very serious side to these values statements that is less about individual or group descriptions of what they believe playwork to be and more about the impact of play-deprivation, and this brings me back to the playwork NVQ. The other two values statements I have included here, are there to be read, discussed or ignored as playworkers see fit. They do not underpin a formal process of qualification, but the NVQ values statement does.

There are two implications within the NVQ values statement that cannot be ignored. The first is that, in my opinion at least, its implied expectations may change the nature of the play experience for children so radically that I am unsure whether children would be experiencing play at all, either as I know it, or as the literature describes it.

The second is that these conditions also seem to lay several traps for children who may have come to the play space from abusive or racist households and for whom respect, care, consideration, equality and co-operation may be alien concepts. It is feasible, and perhaps likely, that playworkers, in their desire to provide a model of good practice, using NVQ criteria, will feel obliged to exclude such children from their projects. This might result in children who are already damaged by their living environment being damaged further by a play environment which the NVQ itself states, 'must be accessible to children'. I appreciate that this particular value is probably talking about wheelchair access, but play spaces should also be accessible in other ways. Just because their face or language does not fit, is no reason to exclude a child from a play space, particularly when by so doing that child may be deprived of what might be its only opportunity to engage with a quality play experience.

play-deprivation

Although I will explore this concept in more depth later, (see Chapter 8, Stimulation theory) it is worth spending some time on it now.

The existence of play-deprivation is more a question than a statement of fact at the present time. No one is sure if it is a damaging reality or a theoretical possibility, although evidence of the impact of being deprived of certain sensory and other experiences is increasing all the time.

What is not clear is what happens to children who do not, or cannot, or for reasons I have expressed earlier, are not allowed to play. What happens to children who are potentially play-deprived?

Although only currently under evaluation, the effects of the lack of interaction with the world, which play-deprivation implies, may be catastrophic. Studies on other species record aggression and social incompetence (Harlow and Suomi 1971), whilst children, especially from 'economically disadvantaged backgrounds show less frequent and complex fantasy and socio-dramatic play' (Smith *et al.* 1998).

However, it is recent studies in Romania and Switzerland that provide the clearest insights into the potential impact of this phenomenon.

Huttenmoser and Degan-Zimmermann (1995), for example, referring to what they describe as 'battery children', attribute play-deprivation to the effects of traffic and parental fears of predatory adults.

Battery children, they say, are 'often aggressive and whine a lot. By the age of five they are emotionally and socially repressed, find it difficult to mix, fall behind with school work and are at much greater risk of obesity.'

Studies on children who have been without play and who have become stimulus deprived report 'mental problems, physical de-sensitisation, and restrictions in brain-growth' (Chugani, 1998), and severe learning difficulties, erratic behaviour, difficulty in forming bonds, depression and withdrawal resembling autistic children or hyperactivity and loss of control, like children with ADD. 'The neurological cost [being] that regions of children's brains are utterly devoid of electrical activity' (Tobin, 1997).

Because play is cited as a major influence in the development of skills from communication to creativity, and from social interaction to problem solving, it is reasonable to postulate that any effect of play-deprivation would be to diminish the ability of the children affected to communicate, be creative, to problem solve and to socialise. In other words, if we create a play-deprivation matrix, for example Figure 5.1:

Play type	Intensity of deprivation									
	1	2	3	4	5	6	7	8	9	10
Symbolic play										✓
Rough and tumble play										✓
Socio-dramatic play										✓
Social play										✓
Creative play										✓
Communication play										✓
Exploratory play										✓
Fantasy play										✓
Imaginative play										✓
Locomotor play										✓
Mastery play										✓
Object play										✓
Role play										✓
Deep play										✓
Dramatic play										✓

Figure 5.1 A play-deprivation matrix.

we can see that because their environment was apparently totally devoid of stimulation, *and* because they were unable to search for stimulation elsewhere, the children to whom Tobin and Chugani refer may have been suffering chronic, i.e., long-term, play-deprivation and the reported condition may have been the result.

Because the deprivation suffered by Huttenmoser's battery children is less severe – the environment is less stimulus deprived, and they are able to go elsewhere, even if they have to be transported by parents – it may have resulted in acute, rather than in chronic symptoms. Perhaps their matrix would look something like Figure 5.2.

By definition, most children will suffer some level of play-deprivation of most play types at some time during their childhood. I have no idea, and I doubt whether anyone else has, what the effect of being mildly deprived of, say creative play, might be. Although I would hazard a guess that children so deprived would initially feel frustrated at not having a creative outlet. In fact, frustration might be the Level 1 warning signal for every form of play-deprivation. (I choose the term frustrated, because the child would be unaware of what it was his or her warning systems were communicating, or even that they were communicating, and might just feel mild annoyance, frustration or unease because of the embryo of a deeper feeling of being unfulfilled.)

Some say the play drive will manifest itself under all conditions, and they cite, for example, that children were known to have played in the concentration camps of World War II.

Play type	Intensity of deprivation									
	1	2	3	4	5	6	7	8	9	10
Symbolic play					✓					
Rough and tumble play					✓					
Socio-dramatic play					✓					
Social play					✓					
Creative play					✓					
Communication play					✓					
Exploratory play					✓					
Fantasy play					✓					
Imaginative play					✓					
Locomotor play					✓					
Mastery play					✓					
Object play					✓					
Role play					✓					
Deep play					✓					
Dramatic play					✓					

Figure 5.2 A 'battery child' play-deprivation matrix.

I agree that as a basic human urge, the play drive in children, like the sex drive in adults, will be potentially active the whole time, but equally, like the sex drive, without the appropriate conditions – in the case of play, time, security, permission and something to interact with – it would probably remain potential rather than actual.

Certainly children will consider playing in any environment in which they find themselves, and frustration and boredom will result if that environment is sterile or restrictive.

But if the gradient of deprivation increases, if movement is restricted, for example, or if the period of deprivation moves into hours or days, we can imagine that any latent desire to engage in some play types, e.g. locomotor, social, rough and tumble, symbolic, mastery and deep play, may just evaporate. Other play types might linger much longer as children so deprived played to entertain and stimulate themselves. Gradually though, these – socio-dramatic, creative, exploratory, object, role and dramatic – would also decay. With silence, and without sensory stimulation, the child would be left to talk to itself for comfort and engage in flights of fantasy and imagination.

I write later (Chapter 8) of my concern that children chronically deprived of company and sensory stimulation, but who still have some props in the form of toys, may begin to dwell in a world in which fantasy/imagination and reality become indistinguishable.

There are probably many hypotheses about the factors surrounding the murder of children by children. Mine begins in this realm, the realm in which some children, for all sorts of reasons – some obvious, like sexual abuse, some less obvious, like loneliness, or low self-esteem – find themselves in a space inside their heads where they can freely manufacture fantasies, and having found this space, find it difficult to leave, perhaps even preferring it to their reality.

I imagine that if the phenomenon of a fantasy-driven reality does exist, that children in such a state, unable to know the difference between projections generated by external experience and those generated internally, would be capable of committing acts of great cruelty and violence.

The human mind, even in childhood, is quite capable of concocting fantasies of nightmare content, which, if transported into the external realm, may not only be responsible for murders by children, but for certain types of violent crimes committed in later life. This is only conjecture, but childhood is a delicate time and enormous damage can be done then which may emerge later in life, not necessarily as conscious vengeful acts, although this may happen too, but as violent games that confuse fantasy and reality.

I once interviewed a man in Belfast about his childhood. He was from a Catholic background, but in his early years, he had lived in a predominantly Protestant area. I asked him to draw me a life-line. (A life-line is a device many trainers used to help those they are training to organise their memories and their recall.)

His life-line from 0–14 years was divided into three pictures. The first 0–5 years contained a large flaming bonfire, a house, three adults and a small child sitting on a trike, a toddler's tricycle. The second picture, 6–9 years, contained a miniature Gaelic football pitch, a bike, a church and a school. The final picture, 10–14 years, contained a drawing of a soldier, an army barricade, a gun and a corpse.

0–5 years. The interviewee told me that on his third birthday his parents had given him a red trike. Two months later, on the twelfth of July, a number of adults – he said they were Protestants – had lit a large bonfire so close to his house that the glass in the windows cracked. At some time they took his trike and threw it onto the fire, where it was destroyed.

6–9 years. Shortly after the Troubles started he and his family moved house and he found himself in a Nationalist enclave where he was free to play and to express his culture.

10–14 years. In the early 1970s, he joined a paramilitary organisation. During the 'Troubles' he was imprisoned for long periods for his paramilitary activities. He told me it was 'Get even time, them bastards burnt my trike.'

While I do not know for certain if this man was telling me the truth about anything I have described, I do know that it is possible. I have known many children who have images imprinted on their brains of the great cruelty, neglect, abuse and humiliation they have suffered at the hands of adults. They then want to get even, and some, as this example demonstrates, do.

Whether this man would have done so without the onset of the 'Troubles' is anyone's guess, but I believe that his story was true and I also believe that deep down, the burning of his birthday trike created a time-bomb that the 'Troubles' themselves only exploded.

Depending upon the severity of the conditions of deprivation, eventually even the child's capacity for communication, fantasy and imaginative play would also disintegrate. For Chugani's (1998) children this would probably happen in their early infancy, as neglect and an almost total lack of contact with anything outside of their imagination, took its toll.

However, for Huttenmoser and Degan-Zimmermann's (1995) battery children, it would take many years and would probably never happen. These children would just continue to whine and suffer the discomfort of an unsatisfactory relationship with the world, becoming socially and environmentally disabled as a result. But it is doubtful that the play drive would begin to dry up, although they would probably experience increasing difficulty in initiating play and could end up needing help to start the play process off.

Reflections 2

Play is often about learning how to survive, except you do not know that while you are actually doing it. Children build dens, cook, hunt, track, hide and develop all of the other skills which make survival possible. Sometimes they go to incredibly sophisticated lengths to create homes for themselves. This reflection is concerned with three play types – mastery, deep and social. It also demonstrates the power of recapitulation, when children are driven by their ancestral past to engage in complex behaviour that has little current purpose save that of developing motor skills.

However, this complicated narrative would not have happened if the characters had been interrupted by an adult, and the playworker must be sensitive to this dynamic. Children can only engage in this kind of deep immersion if they feel the security and lack of pressure that makes it possible.

Reflection: tree dens

'Come on Rob,' he said, straining. He was pulling and I was pushing a railway sleeper up to his tree den which was on an intersection between the trunk of the tree and a big branch.

This was only one of lots of tree dens we had, and would have. It was 30 feet from the ground, but overlooked the river which added at least another 25 feet to its height. I suffered from vertigo and he didn't. But to simply say he didn't would be a total understatement. He was the Navajo Indian of trees and tree dens. As completely at home as I was out of my depth.

To build this den, he had scaled the tree by driving six-inch nails into it, and using them as a form of ladder. Then he had wrestled huge pieces of timber from the ground to the branch, quite alone.

Although I didn't like heights very much, I loved trees. Especially the feeling you got when the wind was passing through the leaves and rocking the branches. It was incredible in strong winds.

The problem was that I found it really hard to climb trees. I'd give it a go. No self-respecting kid wouldn't, but I was useless. It wasn't any big deal, 'Rob just wasn't any good at climbing.'

So when he wanted help with the sleeper after school, the thought of sitting swaying invisible, under the canopy, made me overcome my fear, and we did it.

Although different, in this respect, we were also very similar. I know he loved the solitude he got from being in dens. Sometimes he would disappear all day, and only later would you find out where he'd been. The countryside was a part of us both, and it became whatever we needed it to be.

Our games would make it a war zone, or we would explore. Sometimes we would sit for hours, and just look and listen to the water in the Valley as it trickled over the stones making musical sounds, while we talked about whatever was happening.

Both of us carried catapults and we were good with them, and sometimes he would carry a serious sheath knife, although it was only for cutting switches and carving. Cutting real people was something which happened on crazy Saturday afternoon matinees, not in real life.

With a final shove and a final pull, the weight of the sleeper was transferred to the branch. As he undid the rope, and manoeuvred the sleeper to its position, I trembled the last few feet to the den. It was a long drop, and he was no help at all, not being able to comprehend my problem. He had a hammer and nails up there and used them to fix the sleeper. He also had a bottle of Corona. After a couple of swigs of that, and a belching competition which had us both in hysterics, we lit the one fag we had. He was lost in his own thoughts. I was already worrying about how I was going to get down.

Reflection: rape

When this event occurred, I had no idea about what to do. Had there been a rape, or was it just a cruel joke? The problem is, that these clichés about sex do have some basis in truth, at least in as much as the child sees it. How do you know if someone fancies you? How far is far enough and how far is too far? How are you supposed to know what the opposite sex likes? These are difficult issues for children, even older children. They are complex in the extreme for children who have had little or no chance at developing the range of social skills to necessary facilitate the beginnings of sexual exploration. This Reflection alludes to a complex collision between sexuality, social cruelty and naïveté. Not a particularly rare combination of ingredients in playwork, youthwork or teaching. But in the early days of playwork, this was profoundly difficult to deal with as a lone playworker, without training or support.

He stammered and stammered and stammered, and I thought I would die. He was scared, terrified. He just didn't understand.

He shook and looked about him, as if waiting to be floored, and I thought, 'Oh shit, I hate this.' I just wanted to say, 'Don't worry, there's nothing to worry about', but that wasn't the way it was – he'd been accused of attempting to rape one of the girls.

My initial thought was that you could have accused him of many things, but not rape, for God's sake, but is that not always the way men's minds work?

He was a kid with problems. He was a difficult kid, too. He always hung around the fairgrounds, mainly pulling jobs on the dodgems, collecting money and being macho by riding on the back of them when they were going around, but he wasn't really that type of cowboy, believe me.

I suppose his label could have been 'retarded' or 'with learning difficulties' or 'hyperactive' or any of those explanations which take away your identity and turn you into a 'problem' instead. He certainly had behavioural differences and they often resulted in problems for him. He used to stare into people's faces and it would irritate other kids. He stammered unmercifully but what he said normally made sense, certainly as much as most of the other people I ever came across.

But inevitably he was already deeply into the 'System' by the time he arrived at the playground. I don't remember him arriving, I just remember him being there. He had a temper, but then who didn't? He wasn't exactly normal, but then who was? Certainly not me!

He liked to think of himself as a rocker, a greaser, grebo, biker, although the nearest he ever got to a bike was a leather jacket with tassels and studs. And now the word was out that he had attempted, or even done, something dire and the world was after him, particularly that breed of male who, in the absence of any ethical limitations themselves, suddenly become the guardians of public morality at times like this.

'Sod them,' whatever my lack of knowledge, training and understanding of the subject, or even how I felt about it, 'I'm going to get to the bottom of this.' You can't have people going around abusing and violating other people. Neither can you have people being accused of things they haven't done.

I sat down behind what passed for a desk in the office, all strewn with paint and petty cash and all the other flotsam of a playground.

'Andrew, what happened?' For brevity I'll paraphrase the conversation. Suffice it to say that his first sentence started, 'I, I, I, I, I, I, I,' as his stammer got the better of him.

Apparently he'd been up at the local park and a couple of girls who also used the playground happened to be there too.

I suppose he might have fancied his chances and went to sit with them. They thought that he was a bit of a prat and a bit vulnerable and had a joke with him about his experience with girls, and he misunderstood and made a grab for one of them. No rape, no assault, no intention.

But comparatively, he was a big sod, and he frightened the girls, and the more they told him to 'Piss-off' the more frightened and confused he became. He tried to calm the situation, tried to tell one of them that he didn't mean anything, but she was noisy and screaming for him to just 'Fuck-off' and he grabbed her by the arm and tried to shake her, to shut her up, to get her to realise that it was all a mistake. But it was going too far.

Nothing happened. No blow. No strangulation. No finding half-clothed bodies in ditches. Not this time. Just raised voices. Panicking children. Inquisitive adults. A young guy running to erase the noisy incident from his ears. Just a mistake.

And now the cops were after him. The vigilantes were massing. The girls said he tried to rape them. And he was alone, with his stammering, his inarticulacy and his fear.

'Is that it?' I said. 'Is that what happened?' It was.

'Listen Andrew, if you're having me on, you won't need to wait for the cops.' He wasn't having me on.

'I'm warning you, this is serious. There are people out there who would string you up for this before the cops even got near.' And I believed it. He knew it was serious, but he hadn't done anything.

I walked up to him and stared him in the face. He turned away. 'Look at me. Have you been messing around with those girls? Have you?' I shouted it. I was scared too. He was going to be seriously damaged five minutes after he left me if we didn't get somewhere. He hadn't. It just all got out of hand.

'Andrew, between here and your house are a load of kids who are determined to fill you in. The only thing at the moment between them and you is me, and I'm not going to be a lot of use anyway. What happened up there?'

He was crying by now and so was I inside my head. This has got to stop soon; I'm beginning to hear myself as the Gestapo. What to do?

I quietened down. 'Andrew, look, if there's been a mistake, we'll sort it out. But if you've – done something – let's have it out in the open. At least we'll know what it is we've got to deal with.'

No, that was it. He'd said what had happened. He didn't know why the girls were telling all those lies about him.

'OK,' I said, 'then that's where we'll have to start.' What was I supposed to do? Administer electric shock? Beat him senseless? Throw him to the wolves? No way. He was one of the kids and whatever had happened no one was getting at him.

I put the word about to leave him alone. That wouldn't guarantee a great deal, but it might put the punch-up artists off for a while.

I talked to the cops shortly after they'd interviewed the girls. After a while they gave more or less the same version of events as he had. It was all a joke that had got out of hand and he had frightened them.

No charges were brought, but it didn't stop the same girls from taking the piss and shouting at him for weeks after. His response was to arm himself against attack with a bike chain and a knife. But most of the time they were only defences against being alone, because all he was, was isolated within his own permanent isolation.

I always thought he was a sweet kid, although he annoyed the hell out of me with his staring.

In the end, the event was overtaken by others and forgotten. He came back to the fringe of the crowd again and life perhaps wasn't so bad. But doesn't it get out of order sometimes?

Reflection: the cut throat wedding dress

Because it is both spontaneous and goalless, engaging in play can be very cathartic and the playworker must be vigilant that some children will need to engage in play for that reason and make that possible by sensitive observation rather than intervention. Whether this Reflection describes a cathartic episode or whether the child is simply engaging in a synthesis of creative and deep play is unclear. I just found this incident very shocking.

Siobhan was the eldest child, with three brothers and a sister. Her parents were kind and loving as far as I could ascertain from the amount of contact I'd had. But all of them, the children and their Mum and Dad, always looked tired and worn out, living in an almost derelict two-up two-down. Certainly there were times, when like any other children, they got excited and sparkled, like the time the youngest sister came to the Venture still dressed in her angel clothes, direct from the school Nativity play. But the wear and tear of an untypically hard life often left them on a behavioural spectrum which only ranged from depressed to explosive.

On this occasion Siobhan had come over straight from school, and after hanging-out for a while, she went into the space we reserved for arts and crafts and began to paint. I was busy doing other stuff, as she fixed a sheet of paper onto an easel and began to draw a female figure in pencil. Later, I noticed that the figure now wore a dress.

When children are engaged in any play activity or narrative it is essential that they are not distracted, so I tried to watch the progress of Siobhan's picture as inadvertently as possible – I have always felt that one of playwork's most important skills is good peripheral vision.

The dress turned out to be the kind of traditional Western wedding dress. Long, white, and very full, but no veil. Siobhan spent a long time, outlining the figure and the dress in pencil before adding skin colours and white for the dress.

I suppose I assumed that that was it. She had painted a woman in a wedding dress, perhaps it was a dream of hers to get married in such a dress, or perhaps she had seen someone getting married, or whatever. I had no deeper psychological armoury to draw from, and it didn't seem such an extraordinary picture for an adolescent to be drawing, male or female.

But what happened next was different. You have to visualise this picture on white paper, a long white dress, and very pale skin tones. It had a very pre-Raphaelite quality. Then I saw that she also had some very deep red paint, and before I realised what she was doing, she had dipped her narrow brush into the red paint and drawn it across the throat of the female figure. For a second there was just a thin red line, but then the paint began to run. First of all it ran down the throat of the female figure, but soon it was trickling down the front of the dress too. Siobhan had cut the throat of the female figure in the wedding dress.

She stepped back and looked at her creation. Apparently satisfied, she took her brushes and washed them at the sink, turned and walked away from the painting and out into the sunshine.

Of course one could read anything into what had just happened. Was it deeply symbolic; was she out to shock us, or perhaps herself? Was this a proxy execution, or a proxy denial? I never asked. It was my practice to let the kids come to me if they wanted to talk or if they had problems, either that or to go to one of the other workers. We were on hand, and the kids knew that.

But it wasn't our normal practice to intervene without an invitation. Siobhan wasn't crying, or behaving in any way differently to the way she behaved on hundreds of other occasions, so we assumed that it was a statement that would reveal itself over time.

We never saw Siobhan again. The family moved that evening, to another part of town, and although the others came to see us, Siobhan never came with them. Was the picture a representation of the end of her relationship with the playground, or was it something else? Like so many playwork episodes, it has to hang in the air.

Reflection: the sand-play children

This Reflection is a study in immersion and recapitulation. It demonstrates that when a play space operates effectively even the most unlikely individuals get drawn into complex and absorbing play narratives. Their use of sand and water as their main materials is also interesting for two reasons. The first, is that both Haeckel and Hall allude to the child's drive to pass through evolutionary stages when s/he plays, and the use of sand and water are a clear demonstration of the child's affinity with two elements that underline our past as sea dwellers as well as land dwellers. The second is that Nicholson (1972) maintained that the best play environment was the sea-shore, which although it contains many different play ingredients – disorder, mobile components, a large variation of both living and non-living objects, blue light, illumination and the noise of the sea – is dominated by what he calls 'slush' – the area where the sea meets the land, and which also contains strong resonances with our evolutionary past.

It was a hot, sunny day in the middle of the school summer holidays. The morning had been busy with children wanting to play in the paddling pool, splashing each other and throwing water about. The afternoon promised an extended water fight, with hoses, and buckets, perhaps even water bombs made from water-filled balloons. Water fights were always great fun, but the skill was to make sure that the big kids didn't frighten or soak the little ones, and to try to ensure that the water stayed outside, that the fight didn't move indoors, where there was equipment and electricity.

The morning session finished around 12.45, and by 1.45 the temperature was really climbing. Ideal for the expected watery activities.

As we opened up, the children signed in, filed through and dispersed to the shady areas, to get out of the heat.

Strangely the expected water fight never materialised. Instead, a group of about a dozen local 12–15-year-old boys came in. They weren't regulars, and I was a bit anxious about what would happen next. I needn't have worried.

As one, they gravitated towards our sand-play area, a large box about 10 metres square, with sides about 40 cm high. It was filled with fresh sand. What was to follow was as extraordinary as perhaps it should have been predictable.

The boys jumped over the sides of the sand-play area, and each one got down on his knees and began to dig away at the sand. Realising that it needed to be damp, one of them came to us and asked for something to carry water in. We gave him one of our fire buckets and pointed him to the nearest stand-pipe. He filled the bucket with water and took it over to where he had been digging in the sand. Some of the other boys in the group watched as he poured water into the shallow hole he had dug, and seeing that this made the sand firmer and less likely to cave in, asked us to let them have some water too.

Soon our entire collection of fire buckets was in use, and water was being continually transported to the sand-play area, where a dozen adolescent boys were totally engrossed in the business of tunnels, bridges, pools, dams, streams, underground caverns and subterranean worlds, for about four hours, without taking breath. Each of them had taken off their shoes and socks and, on their hands and knees, were immersed in the sandy, watery world of the beach.

Tiny flags were erected over sand-castles. Dinky toy cars and small plastic people from *Camberwick Green* and *Trumpton* passed over deep gorges on rickety bridges, whilst monsters lurked in the depths of the sand, like extras from *Dune* or *The Empire Strikes Back*.

The magic of that combination which is sand and water, which continually regresses young and old alike to their primeval human roots, had triumphed once again, over the prevailing ageist and sexist assumption that boys, and in particular older boys do not play (except cricket and pool, of course), and certainly not with basics like sand and water, and especially not in front of girls.

Chapter 6

Evolutionary playwork methods

Modification and intervention

For years, many playworkers' rationales for modifying the play environments they operated and their rationales for intervening in children's play have, from a playwork perspective at least, been somewhere on a scale between arbitrary and intuitive.

They have normally done what they thought best in what are often very difficult circumstances, either coming to an individual decision based on their knowledge of the local children, their own childhood preferences, or what they judged would have been appropriate for their own children. They would probably have discussed things as a team and decided what to do on the basis of a democratic vote, standard practices and legal guidelines.

The NVQ values state that play opportunities should always be provided within the current legislative framework relevant to children's rights, health, safety and well-being.

The legal context

Whilst I appreciate the legal requirement to operate within the law, playworkers themselves should also be giving the lawmakers guidance about whether the law, as it relates to playwork practice, is always appropriate. Recent academic concern about over-intervention and too much safety in children's lives are cases in point (Ball and King, 1991; Furedi, 1999).

My view is that the criteria on which decisions are made, relating either to environmental modification or intervention in children's play, should in the first case be based not on what is legal, or on what is good practice in another profession, i.e. social work, but on the outcomes of professional discourse about the impact of playwork practice on children and their play, within playwork itself.

This would mean that playwork practice, i.e., playwork's professional rules of engagement would – in the first instance – be more likely to be derived from the biological/developmental principles that underpin it, rather than from a political or social analysis as it seems to be currently.

One of the more negative effects of the implementation of the Children Act (1989) was to bring social workers into play spaces as inspectors of good practice. This proved to be a broadly unpopular and divisive development. It also caused widespread problems except in those cases where projects being inspected had a professional and mutually respectful relationship with the department or individuals concerned. What eventually transpired in many places was that the Social Services Departments gave playworkers or play development workers themselves the responsibility for inspection, and criteria derived from objectives that were closer to playwork's were used.

As a consequence, some projects that had been under threat of closure because they did not meet Social Services standards were reprieved, whilst projects which did not meet new 'playwork' standards were closed if they did not improve.

The positive side of this was that the debate about what constituted good playwork practice became more focused, and moved considerably from the arbitrary/intuitive position I describe above to one of greater clarity.

Another example of the potential difficulties arising from legislative imposition on playwork reality can be illustrated by 'fall height' regulations.

Like other playworkers at the time, I had been building structures for many years, and some of them had been upwards of 30 feet high with a fall height of 30 feet as well.

I had seen children engaged in acrobatic feats on these structures, day after day. It was not shocking or even remarkable to see children engaged in activity that 'off-site' would have been prohibited. But that is one of the points about having specially designated spaces for play. Children need an outlet for their play drive. And if they have it in the form of a good quality play space, then the attraction of engaging in risky play where there are adult hazards and dangers seems to decline.

However, new recommendations from the field (NPFA, 1984) recommended that anything with a 'fall height' of 2 metres or a maximum height of 6 metres should be discouraged:

> that the maximum overall height of ... structures should be 6 metres [and that] any part of a structure where a vertical fall of more than 2 metres is possible must be protected by [measures] which reduce the possible fall-height to less than 2 metres.
>
> (p. 53)

Suddenly children whose play had included negotiating considerable heights had to be told that adults no longer regarded that as appropriate.

The situation has softened over the years. Although the general approach is not to be prescriptive but to risk-assess, (Melville, 2000), Section 5.6.1 of *Risk and Safety in Play* states, 'Generally it is recommended that the maximum height for any platform or walkway should be 5 metres [and] guard-rails will normally be indicated on any part of a structure where a vertical fall height of more than 2 metres is possible (PLAYLINK, 1997).

I agree with the spirit of the concerns covered within this guidance. No one wants children to injure themselves. Playwork practice should always be of the highest quality, and publications like, *Risk and Safety in Play* should always be consulted and their advice seriously considered. But in my opinion these fall height developments had the effect of adulterating practice.

As I have argued, my concern from the biological perspective is that risk is an essential feature of playing – that the play experience is impoverished without it. When *Towards a Safer Adventure Playground*, the precursor to *Risk and Safety in Play*, was written, the field was moving into a tense period where that sentiment would have been considered heresy. Not because it was contrary to the literature or to playworkers' experience, but because employers and professional and lead organisations were becoming increasingly nervous about playwork in general, and about the possibility of litigation in particular – together with the resultant bad publicity for both provision and 'the field', that would result if an accident occurred.

This is the problem about integrating legislation into playwork without proper professional debate – practice guidelines become decidedly arbitrarily. And although it may make sense from an adult perspective, inappropriate implementation of legislation can have the effect of inhibiting the quality and benefits of playing – often the very opposite of what is intended.

Obviously playworkers have to obey legislation, unless, that is, they consider it unethical to do so. But this should not be one-way traffic. Playwork needs a mechanism for analysing the legislation that impacts on its practice and feeding its views back into the legislative process, so that legislation in the future can be more in tune with what playwork is trying to do.

Modification

What modification means is taking a space that has been designated for play and changing it so that the features which it then contains more accurately address the assessed play needs of the children who will play there.

Environmental modification is a continuous process. It attempts to address the needs of the children as they change, as they grow up and as new children arrive. It is also a dynamic that the children themselves will engage in with the playworker or in their own right.

Part of the rationale behind modification is that, if children are an intrinsic part of a constantly changing space, then change will become a part of their own internal dynamic and this will positively impact on their ability to adapt. Their involvement not only makes an important contribution to some of the essential physical environmental change that keeps the play space interesting, it also oils the wheels of the child's own adaptation, a core essential of the play process.

Sylva (1977) described play as a dialectic relationship with the environment, which 'natural selection would favour'. Although this 'dialectic' could take a sensory form, it could also take the form of one or more play types, assuming of course that the modified play space facilitated them.

This dialectic could be described as a continuously flowing exchange between the 'soul' of the child – in a whole variety of forms, depending on the play type in which the child was engaged – and the 'essence' of the environmental feature the child was having a dialectic with, whether that was a tree, a fire, the act of painting or a conversation.

What might happen during Sylva's dialectic, is that as the child playfully interacts with its environment – and here I must re-emphasise that play is a very particular mode of interaction that requires the child to freely immerse him or herself in the experience in which s/he is engaged – information about the nature and the changing nature of that environment is absorbed by the child through its senses at an atomic or sub-atomic level.

In other words – and Jones (1993) deals extensively with this nature/nurture dynamic – one of play's functions could be that it acts as a kind of intelligence-gathering mechanism for adaptation. This means that sensory, or immersion information collected at play is not only used to enable the child to have an immediate forecast of its environmental conditions on many different levels, but that it is also used to provide the child with longer term forecasts, stored genetically and utilised for adaptive purposes. Perhaps the child as a biological entity draws on the information it has gathered to make changes or adaptations to its physiology and/or its behaviour, in order better to survive as environmental conditions change. This is perhaps why natural selection 'would favour the most playful individuals' (Sylva, 1977).

In the last paragraph I used the term 'on many different levels'. This theoretical capacity to access information in numerous forms simultaneously is, for me, one of the absolute beauties of human play. Many scientific instruments can sense, identify and measure all manner of things, from colour, to wavelength, from mass, to pressure. But the human child at play probably does each of these and many, many more at the same time – that is one of the reasons why working with children in playwork situations is as awesome as it is.

For example, let us say that a child is engaged in creative play. What is creative play if we begin to unpick it? Let us say that the child is painting, with a brush and with a variety of colours. What can painting tell the child?

- there are different ways of holding the brush
- the different holds create different strokes
- strokes can be deliberate and controlled
- strokes can be tentative and fragile
- strokes can express sensitivity
- strokes can express anger
- strokes can create images
- some images symbolise figures, like parents or pets
- some images symbolise places or spaces
- co-ordinated movement can form representations of reality and fantasy
- there are different colours

- colours can differ fractionally
- colours can differ dramatically
- colours can be mixed
- mixed colours produce an infinite variety of other colours
- like strokes, colours can express anger
- colours can express beauty
- the sky can be painted using many different forms of blue
- the sky can be other colours, too, and grass can be red
- houses can fly
- the sun can be touched
- painting can be representative, impressionistic and abstract
- to paint something 'good' requires a unity of physical discipline and psychological clarity
- the act of painting is very satisfying
- the act of painting is very exciting
- the act of painting is very frustrating.

The list goes on. Painting tells the child a great deal about the nature of existence:

- there are many ways of doing things
- there are no right ways
- the child is in control
- painting has affective, i.e., emotional, content
- painting has representational content
- painting has symbolic content
- the child can move from reality to fantasy and back again
- there are many different viewpoints, there is no right one
- huge and tiny changes can have similar impacts
- affect can be expressed physically and creatively
- no perception is correct
- reality can be rearranged
- practice and application opens doors into rooms of greater complexity
- painting has cathartic qualities.

Even this rather clumsy exercise serves to illustrate that simply painting a picture can tell a child many things. Less mature children will perceive these things on one level, more mature children on another.

There are many creative forms all of which have a different tale to tell, and there are fifteen play types, all of which enable children to access different sorts of information at different stages of development. Play may also be an amalgamation of several play types where information is being accessed in different forms and at different levels, all at the same time.

On one project on which I worked, children were able to access craft and creative materials at all times. One of our older girls painted the cut throat wedding dress picture I mentioned earlier. Although this picture may have been a comment on marriage, or on the girl's own life, more than anything it seemed to be about personal control. That she was stating that when she played, she should be able to access any form of information and put it into any new combination, however shocking or unusual, because by doing that, by moving through what she perceived as her technical or creative limitations, she was genuinely able to engage in original exploration and experimentation. Not necessarily to shock, but to move into a space that was absolutely new. I think for this child, creating this picture and knowing that it was OK to do it, even though it was so obviously shocking, may have helped her to transcend her current situation and move on.

I would contend that modification helps children to interact with the different facets of a play environment on many different levels. But the modifier, in this case the playworker, must be aware of the need for continuous evolution of that environment, if it is going to retain its neophilic attraction to children. An interesting but static environment may not retain a child's interest for long. Normally, children would range when they play, rather like many wild animals, moving on to a new space when interest – rather than food stocks – becomes depleted.

Desmond Morris (1967) then Curator of London Zoo, coined the term 'neophilia' in relation to play, suggesting that it is their instinctive attraction to novel things and situations that keeps children interested in playing.

If this is the case then retaining that feeling of the 'novel' requires alteration and change on the part of the play space. At one project, we deliberately moved and hid equipment and props so that children would approach the space in a more exploratory and cautious mode, after we had noticed that their behaviour was becoming increasingly stereotyped. That is, every day they would come out of school, run to the play building and all head for the same piece of equipment, fighting each other off as they went.

I felt that the play space should not be contributing further to any of the children's anxieties and that this uni-directed flow has the effect of channelling all the children towards just one experience. I deduced that if they were given the opportunity to think, by removing some of the predictability from the site, they might be just as happy to go and do something new.

Moving things around broke the flow, by slowing it down, and it did appear that children took more notice of the environment as a whole. The result was that the majority of children broke out of their previous 'tunnel thinking' and engaged in other aspects of the play space.

The lesson here, for playworkers, play space developers and designers, is that it is not really enough to plant and landscape and build, if that process is just a 'one-off'. Planting, for example, should be continually changing the nature of the environment, perhaps on the basis of sensory characteristics. For example, the first tranch of planting might emphasise plants with smells or perfumes, the second, plants with interesting colours, the third, tactile characteristics and so on.

Landscaping could focus on hills, then gullies and then water, or a mixture of the three. All too many play spaces I visit are the same years later. However, that is not to say that the play space should be the subject of continuous and frenetic changes. Not because it would not attract children – it would – but rather because other facets of play, like socio-dramatic play and some mastery play, like building, might be discouraged.

As I have said, for children to engage in what I would consider 'real' play they need to be able to immerse themselves, and immersion is not conducive to the kind of environmental change which feels as if it is outside the children's control.

So change is essential, but it must be 'context sensitive' and should never be at the expense of the process being facilitated. Social play, for example, which often takes place as conversations interspersed with locomotor activity like tag, is actually helped by the stability of the setting for many children. It is the very sameness and reliability that enables them to relax and communicate on anything other than a dysfunctional level. Insensitive change would interrupt the delicacy of such interactions.

Change as constant and gentle evolution seems most suited to the play space. Where change happens at a pace which is sympathetic to the child's need to adapt, it gradually integrates into their playscape. I would imagine a five-year evolving strategy, where the play space was completely transformed over each five-year period, with some less disruptive changes or essential maintenance taking place more frequently.

Needless to say, implementing this kind of 'strategic rejuvenation' has resource implications that will require the play space to be moved out of the 'begrudged grant' bracket, and into the 'perceived as essential' bracket.

Modification, as I mentioned earlier, is also all about compensation for, and assessment of, children's general living environments.

Modification and tools for environmental assessment

Some years ago, I developed some rudimentary tools for assessing children's play and living environments for features that would enable or disable children's opportunity for quality play experiences. They are primitive, and their measurements comparative, but they give playworkers a fix, what Sturrock (1997) called a 'North or South', from which to begin to develop more accurate techniques. I have always been a believer in the philosophy that it is better to create a square football that can be kicked about and made round, than not to develop a football at all!

The first of these tools is a Sensory Audit. This requires the comparative allocation of marks out of ten for the level of different types of sensory stimulation in or around a particular play environment. In time, various criteria will be developed for each of these tools which will help in their accuracy. Figure 6.1 gives us a simple example of a comparative basic sensory audit.

Sense	Play space A	Play space B	Play space C
Sight	7	5	4
Sound	7	4	6
Taste	5	2	7
Smell	3	2	5
Touch	7	6	4
TOTAL (out of 50)	29	19	26

Figure 6.1 A Sensory Audit.

Where an environment scores less than a predicted norm, say 30, then particular sensory deficits should be addressed.

The second tool is called a 'Spiral', an early prototype of which was developed by the Merseyside Playwork Training Project from a primary school model, nearly 20 years ago. It can be used in several forms. Figure 6.2 shows an example of a Spiral, which can be used to make a comparative measure of the availability of different play types, either in children's immediate home locality, i.e. the estate, or road where they live, or on a particular play space.

Similarly this Spiral can be used to monitor change in three different ways:

- in the availability of play types in the living environment
- in the availability of play types in the play space
- in addressing whether or not the play space is actually compensating for the non-availability of some play types in the child's living environment.

Other Spirals, Figure 6.3a–c, can be used to measure other factors that might facilitate or inhibit children's access to quality play experiences. Again they can be used to make measurements of the spaces the children are actually coming from, i.e. the home/play environment, and the play space they are coming to.

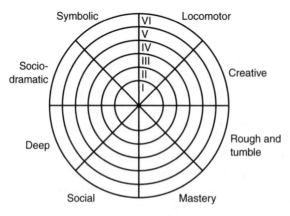

Figure 6.2 An example of the Play Types Spiral.

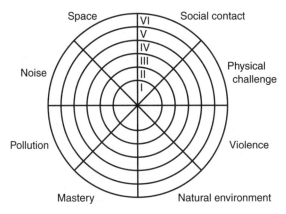

Figure 6.3a An Environmental Deficits Spiral.

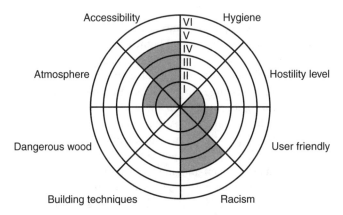

Figure 6.3b A spiral for other types of deficits.

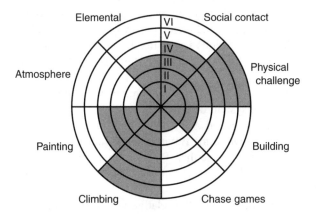

Figure 6.3c A spiral for different types of play experiences.

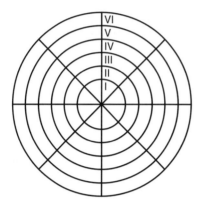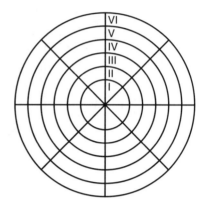

Figure 6.4 The Dual Spiral.

They can also be used to make comparative measurements to ensure that the play space is compensating for deficits in the general home environment.

Figure 6.4, the Dual Spiral, makes comparisons easier between the quality of more than one play space or more than one local environment. For example, when trying to make a case for changes to provision on a particular estate, the Dual Spiral could be used to demonstrate that the deficit level of certain play-enabling characteristics was higher on estate A than on estate B.

Each segment on each Spiral provides a measurement (0 = absent, 5 = high). With frequent use, a playworker will soon get used to judging what levels to award each feature, particularly when making comparative judgements. The playworker will find it useful to note why a score of four has been awarded to one play space and a score of three or five to another. As these comparisons are analysed, so a clearer idea will emerge of what each of the categories means and the criteria being used to make these fine judgements.

Similarly, it will help if each playworker in the team measures living and playing environments independently, and then compares results, discussing why their measurements differ. These Spirals have already been in practical use on several occasions, most recently by the Design and Build Team at Hackney Play Association in 1999.

The final tool is less visual but is preferred by some playworkers as it comes in list form and uses a scoring system of low/medium/high, rather than 0–5, or 1–10. There are two lists. One is called A Play-Enabling Environmental Indices Checklist, and the other, A Play-Disabling Environmental Indices Checklist.

As with the Spirals, scores from either Play-Enabling or Play-Disabling Checklists, can be totted up, and total scores or individual component's scores, can be used comparatively.

With both methods, local factors, like the relative involvement of particular child populations, the relative pollution caused by a factory chimney, or the

INDICATOR		LEVELS	
	Low	Medium	High
1 Elements – water, etc.			
2 Natural space – trees/vegetation.			
3 Variation – landscaping, etc.			
4 Open space.			
5 Opportunities for height/movement – for co-ordination and games.			
6 Opportunities for indoor/outdoor.			
7 Opportunities for modification – tunnels/ dens/gardens.			
8 Opportunities for creativity – crafts/arts.			
9 Range of play types – rough and tumble, fantasy, mastery, social, socio-dramatic, creative, etc.			
10 Social opportunities – peers/adults/seniors.			
11 Care/welfare.			
12 Opportunities for other species.			
13 Intellectual opportunities/problems.			
14 Peace/quiet/privacy.			
15 Security and safety – playwork, surfacing, lighting, design			
16 Visual stimulation – colour, etc.			

Sub-total to be carried forward.

Figure 6.5 A Play-Enabling Environmental Indices Checklist.

INDICATOR		LEVELS	
	Low	Medium	High
1 Incidence of dietary/malnutrition/health problems.			
2 Dogs.			
3 Traffic.			
4 Poverty, i.e. general socio-economic status.			
5 Local fear of predators.			
6 Unemployment levels.			
7 Noise.			
8 Pollution.			
9 Desolation, i.e. lack of visual/tactile stimulation.			
10 Psychological referrals.			
11 Poor housing stock. Interior overcrowding. High density. High rise.			
12 Isolation, i.e. auditory/social.			
13 Tranquilliser prescription.			
14 Compound abuse.			
15 Lack of alternative experiences and attitudes.			
16 Depressing or oppressive environment.			
17 Concrete.			
18 Sexual/physical assaults on children.			

Sub-total to be carried forward.

Figure 6.6 A Play-Disabling Environmental Indices Checklist.

relative level at which local children engage in deep play activities away from the play space (e.g. playing chicken) can be included for monitoring. Sharing and comparing results will enable these methods to be used with greater consistency and accuracy.

Analysing the results

These tools have been created to enable playworkers to improve the quality of the environments they operate, by increasing their skill at making judgements regarding the process of environmental modification. The purpose of modification is to enable the play space, the play environment, whatever label it has, to be a more appropriate, stimulating and secure place for children's play, after modification, than it was before.

The Audit, Spirals and Indices Checklists can all help this process, but a playworker's eyes and feelings about a particular space, although less methodological, will also be invaluable. A playworker should ask: 'As a child would I have been attracted to play here?' and be rigorous with their response. They should ask: 'What *specifically* do I like/dislike about the space?' Unless it is obvious, like it smells, it is next to a main road, or it has electricity pylons going over it, they should ask: 'What is it about *this* space that I do not like?' Sometimes places just have an intangible 'bad feel' and children will pick that up too. Playworkers should also ask: 'Would I want my children to play here?' If it is not good enough for their children, it is not good enough for other people's children either.

Designated play spaces are statements that say everything about how we view our children's play needs and what priority we give them in relation to everything else. Many serious problems in the adult population were triggered during childhood. Problems which access to a good play space or to a good playworker might well have reduced or alleviated.

It is every child's right to have access to good play experiences, but it also makes good economic and social sense. Proper investment in play and playwork could make all sorts of expenditure unnecessary in later life.

Intervention

Sophisticated models for intervention are developing; for example, Else and Sturrock (1998) offer this four-part intervention hierarchy:

- play maintenance
- simple involvement
- medial intervention
- complex intervention.

I would also offer the following guidelines regarding intervention. Intervention in children's play is appropriate under a number of different conditions. The *first* being if the child asks for it. That is s/he indicates that s/he would like help from or interaction with a playworker, either by saying so, or by using some form of meta-communication, or by issuing what is becoming known as a 'play-cue'.

The playworker's skill, in this context, is to be sensitive to the fact that children may both expect and need some playworker intervention from time to time. For, although I have stressed that the playworker's primary function is preparatory (prior to the children's arrival), and supervisory (when the children are there), children may need a game or a piece of equipment from the playworker, they may be lonely, or an expected friend might not have arrived, or they may just be bored or uncreative that day.

However, there is another perspective on this level of intervention. Smith (1994) states:

> For example, Vygotsky (1978) postulated the importance of the 'zone of proximal development' (ZPD) in understanding how children enter into a social and cultural world. The ZPD is the difference between what the child can achieve unaided and what he or she can do with the aid of a more experienced, probably older person to help.
>
> (p. 189)

He continues:

> This argument has been developed by Wood, Bruner and Ross (1976). Using the metaphor of 'scaffolding' – (also used by Bateson and Martin (1999)) – they have described just how a more experienced person can help: for example, by pointing out salient features of a task, breaking up a large task into smaller components, helping with sequences and so on. If operating within the ZPD, or scaffolding slightly more difficult play, the adult can help the child learn more and play at a more complex level.
>
> (ibid.)

Whilst I accept this as a perfectly legitimate offer to practitioners, I feel that it could put the playworker into a contaminating frame. The play space is not school, and whilst learning may be an important playwork priority, what is even more important is how the child learns and whether s/he retains control over prioritising what is learnt. Play is a process of trial and error in which the error is as valuable to learning as is the success.

Within playwork we generally define play as behaviour which is 'freely chosen', 'personally directed' and 'intrinsically motivated' (Hughes, 1984). The definition is seen as having authenticity by playworkers because it recognises not only the child-centredness of play, but its experimental nature (Eibl-Eibesfeldt, 1967, 1970).

The Smith, Vygotsky and Wood, Bruner and Ross approach could have the effect of depriving the playing child of the valuable lessons which come from learning by playing freely – lessons that seem to make play so unique as a neurological developmental medium (Sutton-Smith, 1997) – by proposing that 'someone older' points out salient features, breaks up large tasks and helps with sequences.

Certainly playwork experience suggests that this would, in general, be an unnecessary intervention. It is not what play seems to be for. It implies that children playing in adult-free spaces will, in some way, be disadvantaged without adult help. Certainly if the child initiates an intervention then limited help should be given, but the onus for learning in the play space should normally be on the child.

However, the biggest problem with the 'zone of proximal development' approach is that adult help will introduce 'short-cuts' to learning that will leave the child with gaps in its understanding or in the neuronal pathways that are formed as a consequence of new learning, that may make it difficult or impossible for the child to undertake similar tasks unaided.

The great strength of play is that, because the child chooses what to do, does it in his or her own way and for his or her own reasons, a task or object is learnt on every sensory level until the child has exhausted the thing's learning potential. This process may teach the child many, many different pieces of information about that task or object, simply because the child is not aware of any pre-determined way to conduct its play.

If this awesome process is steamlined, if a solution is alluded to or its discovery simplified, what the child gains from that experience is also streamlined and simplified. This may not be a problem if all vital pieces of information from that experience are still learnt by the child, but who can know what 'scaffolding' an experience might omit or how important that omission might be in, for example, adaptational terms?

Certainly when a child asks for help we should respond, but we should be aware that the more help we give the more the experience is adulterated and the more the child may become dependent upon help that would not – in adult-free circumstances – have normally been available.

The *second* condition arises when the child has not asked for a playworker to intervene, but is clearly unhappy, distressed or isolated. An intervention here requires great sensitivity. Children, even when feeling bad, do not always want a cuddle or to be asked what is wrong with them, or 'Is there anything I can do?' An insensitive intervention in this context is often more about what the playworker needs than it is about what the child needs. It is quite common for children to come to the play space to be miserable in peace, when something has happened elsewhere. At home, for example.

One way for the playworker to check if s/he is welcome may be to move into another kind of zone, a 'support zone' – near enough for the child to be reasonably aware that the playworker is there, say 3 metres – and watch to see if the child is receptive to meta-signals or play-cues. If they are not picked up on the second or third attempt, and the playworker has cause to be concerned, i.e., s/he knows things are going badly for the child at the time, then s/he should move away, and observe.

Judgements in this context have to be very subtle. This child may have lost a friend, s/he may be distraught, s/he may be embarrassed and the playworker may be the last, rather than the first person s/he wants to talk about it with. So the playworker should be respectfully, not intrusively, concerned. Having said that, movement into the 'support zone' will often be enough of a cue for the child – if s/he does want someone or some support – to make it clear that s/he would like to talk.

In artificial environments, in particular, privacy can be a rare commodity, simply because of the lack of space and the number of children using it. So if a child does give the appearance of needing peace and quiet, playworkers should not draw attention to him or her unnecessarily, but observe from a distance (Hughes, 1996b).

The *third* condition arises in more exceptional cases, when, for example, a child might be suffering from a condition that makes it difficult for other children to recognise the play-cues they themselves are issuing. Using the example of children with Attention Deficit Disorder (ADD), Else and Sturrock (1998) state:

> They issue play-cues to the containing environment as indicators of their commencing internalised gestalts. These are not picked up in the time the child allows. The return cannot be framed and either dissipates or prematurely returns and is annihilated. The child re-issues the cue, now laden with increasing anxiety. These then repel the possibility of shared gestalt (because other children or the worker sense that something is 'wrong' and do not play), and return to annihilation before the internalised gestalt can be fully, or meaningfully explored. The complete play cycle is truncated and the whole activity becomes speeded up.
>
> (p. 23)

In this example the playworker is advised:

> intervention by a sensitive worker, where the . . . child, assured that the cues were being picked up [and] as an almost immediate result, the firing off of cues, the hyperactivity slowed down and adjusted to normal periodicity.
>
> (p. 24)

The *fourth* condition arises when there are disputes between children. These can be very complex and require great sensitivity on the part of playworkers, as the situation – which might involve cultural, self-esteem, status, racial, historical, or any number of other issues – could be made worse by heavy-handed intervention.

At Playground C, for example, we had children from both genders and a whole range of cultural, economic and religious backgrounds and ages playing in the same space.

In conditions of such obvious complexity, any intervention needs to be moderated by previous continuous observation/scanning, hyper-sensitive hearing and good intelligence. If the playworker is not up to speed with what is happening in the play space, an initial and speedy move into the 'support zone' will do three things:

- the playworker will be that much closer to the action, and will therefore be made more quickly aware of the current temperature of any dispute
- the playworker's very presence might have the effect of restoring some perspective to the situation for the children involved
- the playworker will have a better idea of the cause and therefore the likely method of resolution, i.e., is it a shouting match or is it likely to escalate and turn to violence?

Situations involving several children, and which should easily be resolvable by them, can become goaded into escalation and end violently. Once in the 'support zone', if my presence is registered, i.e. the noise level drops, or heads turn, I might lean over and say politely, 'Anything I can do?', which is often enough to take the sting out of a situation.

The playworker should try to remember that the dispute in question might be the result of a parental feud or a political event. Children, particularly from minority communities, may feel deeply emotionally driven to defend their (or their parents') country of origin against political ridicule, aggression and media attention. As I write, India and Pakistan are in a confrontational mode that may well be transferred to children where there is a play environment interface between the children of these two Asian communities. This certainly happens between children from communities adjacent to 'peace lines' in Northern Ireland.

Another complication arises if a dispute is being progressed heatedly in a language other than those understood by the playworker. What is being said? What are they shouting at each other about? Is either of them being deeply insulting to the other, saying 'Your Mum . . .' or something similar? In this situation monitoring and analysis of body language is essential and the playworker should be alert for weapons or a change of posture, which telegraphs an escalation in any dispute.

Abusive language can be another complex problem. Take for example the two Kashmiri brothers I mentioned earlier, who called each other 'Fucking Pakis', or the situation in which a child from a Traveller background was surrounded by children from Asian and Afro-Caribbean backgrounds calling her 'a tramp'. These are not the stereotypical faces of racism we know, but in communities of children from many backgrounds, things are rarely straightforward.

Playworkers are taught to confront or challenge racism, but as I discussed earlier, my preferred route is to assume that most, if not all, young children are only following adult leads and have no idea of the possible meaning of what they are saying or what is being said back – it is a consequence of where they live, much the same as are traffic and pollution. I tended not to make a big deal of it until children were older and then I would take them to one side. The little ones would normally get a ''Scuse me', a play-cue, and a game of chase, to take the heat out of the situation.

Now and again playworkers have to take the brunt of racist language. It has to be seen as coming with the territory and not something to take personally.

The *fifth* situation arises when a dispute manifests itself as a fight or if it ends in violence. Children do engage in physical battles, particularly, although by no means exclusively, when adults are not around. The playworker needs to be able to acknowledge this and see it as a normal, although perhaps regrettable, manifestation of human behaviour. As with adults, children renege on agreements, their negotiations fail or are bypassed and violence is viewed as a legitimate means of settling disputes.

The frequency and intensity of violent episodes is often a function of the culture and the levels of affect being experienced locally.

In each of the projects I described as case studies earlier, violence was a significant and relatively frequent feature. It normally took place between individuals or groups of children, but sometimes it took the form of a confrontation between a playworker and a group of children, an older brother or sister, or one or more carers.

Whatever form it took, it was unpleasant. In some situations playworkers and children can feel very vulnerable to attack.

Conflict resolution: a playwork perspective

Any intervention in a violent situation should be moderated by what I can only call 'graduated caution'. Implicit within that should be the recognition that the playworker's intervention is based on a predetermined strategy, which does not contradict the principles of playwork as facilitating play in an adult-free space. In other words, persistent fighting should be viewed as negative dysfunction manifested in anger, and intervention should be diagnostic and curative. Where possible it should be kindly, supportive, and never taken as an opportunity to be seen as the bigger bully.

Small children

Minimal caution should be exercised if small children (under five years) are involved in violent interaction. However, it should be brought to a halt immediately, with a one-to-one team intervention, i.e., a team member is allocated to each fighter and the children literally picked up and separated by, say, 10 metres. Do not take little children to other spaces unless they have sustained injuries, in which case, first aid and perhaps an ambulance may be necessary – the playworker's employers will have a procedure. Taking them further than a separation zone may frighten them and make them feel totally, rather than just momentarily, out of control of the situation.

Older children

Exercise moderate caution. For children aged between 5–12 years, my strategy would be that I either pretended not to see them immediately, or I reacted quite slowly. This may sound cruel, but those children who create friction, knowing playworkers will intervene, may become addicted to their protection. Intervention that is too early – and which has not allowed enough time to pass to let nature take its course – or which is perceived as unnecessary, will destroy the play space's credibility with those children who, although 'hard', are not generally bullies. In other words it is vital that playworkers are not seen to 'collude' (Sturrock, 1999) with certain kinds of behaviour.

All sorts of children come to supervised play spaces and some of those who come will provoke others and then hide behind the playworker for protection. In adult-free space this could not happen and it is important that the playworker does not destroy the inevitable natural authority of some children in the play space and unwittingly replace it with a 'please Miss' attitude.

If a fight continues for any longer than, say, 2–3 minutes, then it should be brought to an end, with something like, 'Excuse me, I think someone wants you over there', pointing in different directions for each protagonist and breaking the cycle the children are in. Only if it continues should the playworker resort to reason, or eventually to her or his own authority.

I once separated two boys who were fighting by walking over to where they were with two fire buckets full of water, placing one bucket beside each fighter and just tipping the buckets over so the water went over each individual's feet – it was enough to completely defuse the situation.

Adolescents

Adolescent fighting, whether it is girls or boys, can be very different to the other two examples. It can be very bitter and quite dangerous, and weapons may be involved or at least available, so maximum caution should be exercised. Playworkers may need to draw on their local intelligence to ascertain what is going on, but they must not try to stop it on their own, whatever their analysis. Adolescents fighting may be a matter of face or pride, and bringing a fight to a humiliating conclusion, just because the playworker has the power, simply amplifies in the children's minds that this is not their space.

If a fight is terribly uneven, if one child is on the floor, or crying or pleading for it to stop, it should be slowed down or stopped by direct intervention, appealing to the victor, 'She's had enough', or if that fails, by stopping them by restraint.

But if it was fair and needed to be passed through, i.e., it would have happened even if it had not happened in the play space, it is vital that the playworker recognises that any intervention says at least as much about the playworker as it does about the children's behaviour – that we may need to intervene, that intervening may be important to us, for our own reasons.

The playworker should also be aware that because a supervised play space is an artificial environment, with an adult presence, it will attract some children into the vicinity of other children, when normally that just would not have happened. Sometimes these children may unwittingly be exposed to a level of violence which has not been a part of their normal play experience in the past, and which may terrorise them.

The playworker should also be aware that such children may never have had to develop the survival skills that would enable them to defend themselves. This is a powerful argument for provision to be local.

Where appropriate, move fighting adolescents out of the play space, in order to protect other children, particularly younger children. If weapons are involved the police should be called, for reasons of everyone's safety, not least that of the fighters themselves.

Siblings or relatives

Like other violence, sometimes this just has to happen and very often the only space where claustrophobic disagreements can be exorcised is the play space. These events should be treated in much the same way as violence between older children. With sympathy for both protagonists, and an analysis that this was probably the unavoidable result of dysfunctional affect between them.

Bullying

I was bullied a lot as a child. It is a thoroughly unpleasant experience, but personal experience of bullying is probably the best reason to resist intervening. I stress the word 'resist'. In the end, if bullying persists, if it is cruel, and a flagrant breach of the other child's right to play, then intervention is unavoidable.

However, like so many intervention judgements it is essential for the playworker to ask, 'What are the valid playwork reasons for this intervention?' My response to that question is that like many of the forms of violence covered by the various headings above, bullying is a form of dysfunctional behaviour, i.e. something has happened to that child, that has made bullying an acceptable strategy for him or her to adopt. I knew a child once who bullied other children unmercifully. I found out that the reason she felt safe to bully was that she had access to uncles who, if challenged by the playworker, she could call on for reinforcements. What I also found out though, was that these 'saviours' bullied her, they were just violent people.

So some respite for the victims of bullying is essential, but some respite for the perpetrator of bullying is also a playwork necessity. Showing the bully the impact of their bullying, but caring about them too, can have the effect of inhibiting bullying behaviour in my experience.

Perhaps except for the very young, it is an essential playwork requisite that children should be left to sort out their own problems and develop their own conflict resolution strategies. It is essential to their own skilling through play. When this strategy is not so successful is when behaviour is dysfunctional, i.e., when it is driven by affect, and children are less aware of the reasons why they are doing what they are doing, and importantly, when they will have done enough. Then tempered intervention is unavoidable.

What playworkers should always avoid is the personal desire to stop fights and disagreements, often because there is a high level of transference happening, i.e., the playworker because of his or her own childhood experiences, is feeling the pain of the children. They should resist this identification by de-centering their approach in the same way as medical professionals do. That does not mean that they cannot have feelings – acknowledging feelings is also an essential ingredient of good playwork – but in addressing the child's needs, the feelings of the playworker, although important, must come third or fourth to those of the child.

Violence against workers

Whilst this final piece is not really relevant to the notion of playwork intervention, its subject is a possibility and does happen, so I will look at it briefly.

First of all, if children are fighting, particularly big children, then the playworker should take care not to become embroiled in the violence.

Second, whereas with the children, the playworker should be flexibly interpreting the situation as it evolves, workers should always have contingencies for the possibility of violence directed against them, or more commonly against their vehicles.

I am always reluctant to call the police. In some of the areas in which play spaces are situated, the police may not be respected for all manner of reasons, and calling them is tantamount to announcing the demise of the play space. Calling the police also provides a vivid demonstration to the children of the playworker's loss of control and credibility.

The most sensible strategy is for playworkers never to put themselves in that situation in the first place. They should not be prepared to work where they are vulnerable, especially after dark. If they are working in an area where violence is possible, they should leave when the children leave, at least until they have a better idea of what might happen.

Difficulties often happen at the most unlikely times. Saturday afternoons used to bring drunken older brothers to projects I have operated. One successful strategy I adopted was just to stay out of their way until they got bored and went away. Another potentially difficult time is just before the play space closes. If problems arise then, the team should present a united front and remind possible aggressors that they are known and that the best thing is for everyone to go home. The reality is that playworkers can read all the books they want on 'dealing with violent behaviour', but behaviour is so diverse, and circumstances so unpredictable, that the situations they are confronted with will almost certainly not have been included.

The best insurance policy, is to have playworkers on the team who are from the local area. That reduces the possibility of violence dramatically, simply because they are local, they know the culture and the language and therefore cannot be reduced to 'fucking students', or whatever other label might be used as a dehumanising justification for violence.

More importantly, perhaps, is that a powerful link between the local community and the play project should be established, and that can mean that not only are playworkers less vulnerable to attack, but that there is a more comprehensive understanding of why the play project is there and why it needs to be there in the first place.

Conclusion

So, authentic playwork intervention should only take place on one of three occasions. i.e. when the playworker or playwork team judges that:

- the actual physical environment of the play space needs further modification to provide additional novel experiences for the children who use the space for play – landscaping, building, planting, etc.
- a child, who is using the space for play, needs an interaction with a playworker for short-term support or longer term therapeutic reasons. This would take place in the 'support zone'.
- mediation to alleviate 'normal local', or dysfunctional behaviour manifested in disputes will enable the play space to continue to operate as a useful resource for the children who use it for play.

Intervention in any of these areas requires fine judgements that have a great deal to do with the overview the playworker has of the play space and the children using it. Things like:

- is the play space looking tired and worn out or is it well used and familiar?
- is the dynamic between the children and the play environment energetic, exploratory and enthusiastic, or is it lethargic or on remote control, i.e. in entertainment mode?
- is the play space really interesting and different or is it predictable and created to a formula?
- do the children using the space reflect the total, local constituency, or are they a reflection of the playworker's personal, behavioural preferences?
- is the playworker still excited by and interested in the play environment s/he operates and in the way the children are using it? Can the playworker still stand back and analyse it and the children's interaction with it, with a view to improving it for the developmental benefit of those children?

IMEE, the reflective practice tool I used in the case studies, not only requires that as playworkers, we think and reflect, have direct experience and are well versed in the appropriate literature. It also requires that the resultant process should not only stimulate the children, it should also stimulate the playworker. If it does not, then something is wrong.

Successful playwork, in other words, has to be an authentic dynamic amalgamation of the following:

- the space and its special characteristics and what it can offer to the play process
- the play needs and skills of the child users in a local and wider context
- the playworker's feelings, experience and knowledge.

Where a commitment is made by the playworker to invest a high level of personal reflection into this dynamic, asking, for example, 'What would I feel like? Why are we doing this? Who is this for?', then the playworker is engaged in a continual interrogation of his or her adult/human motivation for doing what is being done.

Although only in its early stages of development, playwork has already shown a capacity and a potential for playing a major guardianship role in the lives of the children it engages with and who, in return, engage with it.

In a period in time when physical and psychological space and childhood are all under attack, playwork is providing a conduit, a map, a route for the child's soul/spirit/psyche, allowing them further to evolve, to transcend their current view of the world by engaging in a playful interaction with it.

However, the playworker must always be on his or her guard against any external or internal pressures to adulterate the space, the children's play, or their own motivations. In the end, the play space and the playworker should only exist for one reason. That is, in combination to genuinely attempt to add something fundamental to the lives of the children who engage with them.

Playwork cannot be Care, containment or entertainment, simply because they are manifestations of an agenda of adult needs to have children looked after or diverted. From a developmental or transcendent perspective they have nothing to offer the free spirit that is the child.

At its most minimalist, play is a word that describes the freely-chosen or non-adulterated journey of a child through its own childhood. It cannot do that if it is unable to range, is addicted to TV, or if its mind is made up by an adult, who is playing out his or her own repressed childhood.

It is a cliché, but this is not a rehearsal. If the child does not experience that 'ecstasy of variety' during childhood, I believe s/he will spend the rest of his or her life feeling unfulfilled and searching for fulfilment. Good quality play gives children the stability and balance to approach the life they have in front of them – which in itself can be a daunting prospect – with the joy of the voyager, the experimenter and the explorer.

Summary of Part I

In recognising the enormity of the subject, both in terms of scope and importance, to those new to playwork, Part I tries to gradually immerse the reader into the main areas of knowledge and controversy. It begins by providing the reader with a general overview of the basic principles, ideas and methods employed by evolutionary playworkers. It introduces the notions of adult-free space and adulteration, it begins an exploration of environmental modification and playwork intervention, and highlights the importance of risk and elemental play.

It provides a description of the criteria that determine what is play, describing it in terms of its 'defining characteristics', and its sub-divisions of 'play types', likening them to the notions of flexibility, calibration and non-specialisation – features intrinsic to individual development and species adaptation and evolution – explored in detail in Part II.

Part I, explores the nature of the play environment and playwork operational practice, analysing three case studies to demonstrate how different factors are considered. It shows how applied knowledge of play types and the playwork menu can facilitate the development of comprehensive play spaces and how 'distance' playwork can enable children to have more control over what they do and how they do it.

Chapter Five provides the reader with an analysis of NVQ values in relation to those postulated in this volume, and also explores the idea of play-deprivation.

The final chapter provides an in-depth look at the relationship between the child and its play environment and suggests some tools to enable the comparative measurement of play-enabling and play disabling features.

Part I finishes with guidance for intervention in a variety of circumstances including when children engage in violent interactions with one another or with playworkers.

Part II

Some advanced evolutionary playwork concepts

Chapter 7

The evolutionary playwork construct of the child

Children are increasingly seen as gene carriers, or as cultural entities, and more 'cosmic' views of children that describe children in terms of their planetary, astronomical or psychic/spiritual context tend to be unfashionable. And yet, children are members of one of many evolving species; they live on a living planet and look out to a galactic backdrop which is as overpowering as it is beautiful. To provide an analysis of anything children do without putting their actions into that context not only insults them but also avoids a great deal of what makes children what they are. Therefore, whilst some forms of out of school provision may use education, containment and entertainment rationales, evolutionary playwork attempts to draw from this 'cosmic view' – as its starting point, as a way of determining what support children need, if any, and how that support should be delivered.

The term 'child' does not mean the same to everyone. To the United Nations, it means anyone under nineteen years of age, but to many others, 'child' would probably mean someone who was under the age of twelve or thirteen. From that age on, the term 'adolescent' would be seen to be more appropriate.

For the playworker, the meaning of the term 'child' has a particular resonance, because how we describe children in a general sense dictates what our job is and informs how we do it.

Reading the literature and reflecting on what it offers gives us a particular insight into the child's dilemma and into a description of 'child' that is of most help to those whose function is to facilitate play. It is this dilemma that I intend to explore in this chapter.

In Hughes (1996b) I suggested that the most useful 'construct' of the child for playworkers, was that children are:

lone organisms, on a hostile planet, in the middle of nowhere

This does not mean that this is the only construct of the child that would be accurate and sympathetic to the notions of play or playwork. Rather what it attempts to do is break down the idea of a child into a very basic format to provide playworkers with some insights into:

- what a child might need to address in order to survive and develop
- what play's role is in addressing those needs
- what playwork's function is in facilitating play.

The lone organism

Birth is the beginning of a lone journey for us all. For, although we may spend much of that journey surrounded by family and friends, colleagues and acquaintances, what these terms mean, the value we put upon them, the help they are to us, the nature of the bonds we forge and the quality of relationships we share, depend on what we do as individuals to communicate and to establish those relationships. Only then, assuming that there are family or friends or whoever to make friends with, can we establish relationships.

So the first part of this playworker's construct is that playwork is fixed upon the premise that, as human beings, we are alone and a number of things need to happen if we are not to be alone. We must do things to establish links with other humans, or with other species and systems, and we also need some luck.

For many of us the notion of luck in this context is a nonsense. But if we had been born into the stereotype of a Romanian orphanage, or into a civil war somewhere, or into any number of circumstances that could exist in any part of the globe, the guarantee that we would have access to a loving, caring, supportive family structure would itself be the nonsense. Playworkers cannot assume that the life of any child with whom they work has any of these ingredients, particularly in the context of practical playwork. However, what playworkers can assume, if they see the child as a lone organism, is that it will be driven to develop the means of communication if it is to stop itself being alone.

And what are these means? They are the spoken word, body language, metacommunication and mobility. Without one of these, unfettered communication is not possible.

The spoken word is what children are developing and rehearsing when they are engaged in communication play. It can take the form of simple noises, which form the beginning of deliberate sounds; it can be the formation of words themselves; it can be the repetition of fun noises and words, or songs, stories, poems and rhymes. But more than each of these, communication via the spoken word relies on expression, on intonation, emphasis, pitch, affective content, clarity and accent. Exploring, testing and absorbing these are the subtle content of much of children's communication and social play. For, in this context, language is not something we hear, rather it is something we interpret, in conjunction with other forms of communication.

Body language, for example, gives us an indication of the feelings and intent of the communicator. How we sit, where we put our hands and arms, where we place our legs, whether our head is back, forward or to the side will all go into the equation when a child or adult is trying to understand what another person is trying to communicate. What we try to communicate is vastly complicated.

Trying to communicate love, or hate, or gratitude for example, requires us to express feelings that may be impossible to express by the spoken word alone. The child needs to learn how to express itself in these incredibly complex areas and, similarly, it needs to learn how to read others' expressions when they are being communicated. Body language is one method we have developed to add something to our language to express more than we are able to say.

Meta-communication enables us to add yet another layer to what we are trying to express, through changing facial expressions. Smiles, grins, grimaces, scowls, all communicate different messages which, when combined with the spoken word and body language, more accurately convey what children are actually trying to communicate to another person. It is necessary for each human child both to be able to read what is being communicated to it, via this triple prism, and to be able to communicate to others using it.

Perhaps what is even more critical to the young child is the development of the skills that enable us to discriminate between, for example, what is being said and the truth, or otherwise, of what is being said. The words say one thing, but the body language or meta-communication may say another. 'Of course I love you', may be the words, but do the eyes, the body or the face convey what the words imply?

I remember in one training session, a young male playworker described feeling that he had been sensorily deprived as a child by his parents, because of their persistent lying. He knew they were lying because he could read their meta-communication!

Play is the art of the experimental – because it is non-detrimental, because it is the mode of the explorer, because it allows for endless repetition, and variation, and because it can be fun, and is certainly interesting – so it is the tool human beings use to embark upon a journey of breaking out of their own hermetic bodily package and establishing links with others.

However, another ingredient in the communication equation is mobility. For communication is all very well if everyone the child wants to communicate with comes to him or her. But what if s/he has to go to them? To reach another space from the one s/he currently occupies requires mobility, balance, co-ordination, spatial awareness, even mental mapping skills. Each of which evolves from a playful interaction with the world.

(I should say here that playworkers should not only be very sensitive to the need for children to have each of these communication skills, but should be even more sensitive to the catastrophe of not having them. Developing communication is hard enough with sight or hearing, for example, whilst developing communication skills with a sensory disability is many times more difficult.)

Communication requires effort, and the effort expended needs to be acknowledged in some way to justify its continuation. The good play environment will enable and stimulate children to travel and traverse many interesting routes successfully to develop communication and mobility skills. It will be a space in which it is acknowledged that children are exploring language and experimenting with it. It should be a space in which the complexity of mobility is acknowledged and facilitated in as many ways as possible.

What it must not become is an expression of our adult behavioural agenda. Children need to be able to make mistakes, to hurt each other and themselves, to see the look on the other's face and experience how that feels for themselves. Humanity is more about shared errors than it is about shared perfection, and the play space is the error ground in which that learning takes place.

There will be many times when children will actually prefer to play the lone organism. Tiredness, frustration, a need for solitude, a time to think things through, the peace of tranquillity, all require separation from the crowd. However, for most of us these are moments of choice, times when we choose to separate ourselves from those with whom we have relationships. For that choice to exist, however, the lone organism needs the opportunity to play, to develop the skills that enable it to make connections with others. Only then is it able to control to some extent how lone it chooses to be.

From a playwork perspective the use of the term 'organism' is also very important. For, all too often, we forget that human children are also biological as well as social or cultural entities. Using the term 'organism' helps to sensitise the playworker to the biological nature of children. It reminds us that as well as needing the social and cultural trappings of family, friendship, art and education, children also need energy and nutrition, they need warmth and shelter, they need clean air and they need to play. The term 'organism' also serves to remind us that much of what they need to engage with, and discover and explore through playing, has less to do with other human beings than it has to do with sharing a planet with many other creatures, other living things and other systems. And finding a comfortable sense of place within that diversity is crucial to mental health.

For, unless children are able to perceive themselves as organisms too, unless they recognise in their development processes that they are one among many, and act with respect to non-human flora and fauna, they may unwittingly engage in the destruction of many of these things. And, as a consequence, they may be faced with an increasingly impoverished play space and a negatively spiralling play prognosis.

The hostile planet

Although it is obvious that the human child at birth is vulnerable to violence, disease, starvation etc., what we tend to forget is that hostility is ever present and human organisms need to develop physical and psychological defences against it very early on in their lives if they are to survive and develop.

Something that is less obvious is that play is a general human tool, irrespective of where we are born or what culture we are born into. It is a mechanism that makes it possible for us to adapt to wherever it is we find ourselves, by enabling us to interact with our local environment, so that we learn the in-depth nature of where we are. So, whilst gaining knowledge of tigers, snakes, spiders, earthquakes, tidal waves and changing meteorological conditions, will be factors for some human children, for others the major hostility factors may be traffic, economics, pollution, guns, lack of space and potential human predation and abuse.

In order to be able to overcome the problems associated with environmental hostility and develop the skills to enable adaptation – both where they are, and where they might subsequently go – children need to be able to play in spaces which reflect the various hostile characteristics in some way. Exposure to them will mean that children can explore them, gain an understanding of how they function and develop strategies for avoiding, confronting or, in some other way, solving the problem they present.

I do not mean that a play space should contain hazardous ingredients, but I do mean that children need to quickly become aware that 'hostility' exists in many forms and that they need to be prepared for them in a general sense. I am reminded of a quote in Sylva (1977), which says, 'What is acquired through play is not specific information, but a general [mind] set towards solving problems that includes both abstraction and combinatorial flexibility.'

Through playing the child is engaged in the following proposed equation:

Play + Environment = Experience + Evaluation = Molecular/Atomic
Building Blocks
(applicable to most
similar situations)

In short, playing in appropriate circumstances enables the child to do two things. One is that it enables the creation of the neuronal networks that make high speed computations about new situations possible. The other is that it enables the application of the resultant potential for higher skills that make the analysis of problems possible in the first place. So play builds, as well as uses, the brain (Sutton-Smith, 1997).

Another useful characteristic of a 'good' play space, in this context, is its unpredictability. If the space the playworker creates is forecastable by children, it will be a comfortable and secure space, which may be an asset, but it may not present any hostile challenges or adaptational problems, and may not be very useful as far as adaptational skills are concerned as a result. Unpredictability injects just that into the child's evaluation mechanisms – a kind of 'What if?', ingredient, that means children will learn not to put all their eggs in the one basket, will learn to hedge their bets and base their judgements upon possibilities, rather than perceived certainties.

What part of the human adaptational mechanism seems to be about is that, by playing within a changing and unpredictable environment, the child is able to build up a vast reservoir of different responses to different conditions and situations, some of which are only slightly different to one another and some that are markedly different. Then, if adaptation is required because of a change of circumstances, the child is able to use the facility of combinatorial flexibility (see page 136) to mix and match potential solutions to its adaptational dilemma, until it finds a solution that fits most, if not all, of the requirements of his or her adaptational problem.

Children have to be able to develop the building blocks that enable them to address whatever problems and adaptational contexts that confront them. These can include wars, natural disasters, domestic violence and abuse, as well as more mundane issues about growing up, moving house and learning to cope in a new class at school. One important feature of children having access to good play environments is that, if the adaptational problem they experience are simply person or place specific (i.e. they need to learn how to deal with a particular individual, say, a bully, or a particular place, say a housing development where there are lots of dogs, or cars) then they will develop a strategy for dealing with those particular situations. However, how they do that will not necessarily be applicable in other, even similar, circumstances. But if they are given a comprehensive, challenging and unpredictable play experience, it will not only equip them for their specific location but will provide them with a foundation for solving similar problems anywhere.

Additionally, if a child is only adapting to a narrow range of consistent problems, s/he will get a very biased view of the world, which could be disabling in a broader context. For example, part of the play experience is about ranging, i.e., journeying to places outside of one's immediate area of experience. If ranging does not happen, then little of the variety and diversity of the world outside of the child's experience is discovered and the child may, understandably, think that the world he or she knows, and his or her learned responses to it, are appropriate everywhere. Then s/he may discover that much of what is appropriate behaviour locally, given the problems that need to be addressed there, is totally inappropriate somewhere else, where nothing like those problems exist. A good play environment dispels this myth early on. At the same time, whilst it may not be able to correct the experiential imbalance the child is currently accessing, what it can do is let the child know that the narrow world of, say, bullies, dogs and cars, is not remotely representative of what is in the world, even a few miles away. People may speak with a different dialect, the geography might be different, customs and local culture may vary, even the micro-climate may be significantly different.

Obviously, this puts an onerous responsibility on the play space to continually address the child's need to range, to expand its depth and diversity of experience, and to see its own problems in a context of growth and optimism, rather than in a context of predetermination, narrowness and pessimism. This means that playworkers need to be consistently active in attempting to evaluate the play space's effectiveness and developing and re-developing it to ensure its continued relevance.

The middle of nowhere

Even if the child is successful in making friends and communicating success-fully, and even if it does develop survival strategies appropriate to its needs, it still has one more very difficult problem to contend with. I refer again to Grof's (1975) 'agonising existential crisis', and how it relates to the child's realisation that s/he is a 'frail and impermanent biological creature'. How can playworkers help children to deal with this psychic nightmare?

Play and playwork can help children to address this problem on several levels almost simultaneously. For example, playworkers can ensure that both the resources and the atmosphere exist for children to engage in deep play so that they can come to a realisation and analysis about what mortality is – not just the realisation of their own mortality but that of friends and loved ones. I am reminded of the horror on the faces of many playworkers I have trained when we have discussed the need for children to engage in deep play. Where children are able to engage in different forms of risk taking behaviour, as a natural tool for coming alongside the notion of death or near death. Yet without experience of factors that contribute to death – height, speed, strength, aggression – how will children learn to avoid it and perhaps even more importantly, how will they learn to know the value of life?

Adults forget perhaps, that unlike old age, two point four children, mortgages and jobs, which all come later, children need the metaphysical wherewithal to deal with death, their own death, from the moment they become conscious of it as a possibility. From a relatively early age, nature provides them with a medium through which to explore this inevitable consequence of life. Deep play – as well as being thrilling and exciting – provides children with the closest pos-sible access to real risk whilst minimising unforeseen danger. The child is in control of how far the experience should develop – s/he is in control of his or her own level of fear.

Thinking about it now, perhaps deep play is less about experiencing near death than it is about experiencing real fear, the cancer which eats away at lives, long before they become consumed by disease. But because it is play, the child is allowed to make stage by stage decisions about the development of a deep play experience, throughout.

1 There is the tree, shall I try to climb it or not?
2 Shall I try to climb it today or another day?
3 After each foot of ascent, at each branch junction, as each new vista is revealed, the child is free to ask, 'Do I want to proceed?' And free to decide, 'No! This is as far as I want to go.'

However, the notion of the middle of nowhere is not about death alone. Death is not the only ingredient of the 'existential crisis'. For as well as having to contend with the reality of its own and everyone else's mortality, so the child also has to contend with being marooned on a planet, circling the sun, in the middle of the solar system. Where the planet on which it is marooned is subject to enormous turbulence, both from without and within, and which, it is predicted, will eventually be consumed by its own sun. We only need to watch any of the many 'space' documentaries to know that the crisis is also about insignificance, and about 'the point of anything'.

I am trying to outline throughout these pages my contention that play has evolved as a biological mechanism to enable human beings to come to terms with what and where they are and have some control over and understanding of what is happening to them. That, through their playful interactions with their physical and psychological environments, they develop an individual and collective relationship with these environments which enables them to make some sense of human existence.

However, if children are play-deprived or if play is adulterated, then these perceptions will not be universally held. Wilber (1996) provides us with a scholarly analysis from which I infer that if one of play's effects *is* to enable humanity to feel 'at ease' with its situation, it has only met with partial success. In fact, he assigns a great deal of our history of conflict to our collective and individual inability to cope with these huge and devastating realisations.

Grof's (1975) solution is 'transcendence'. I certainly believe that access to diverse and authentic play experiences throughout childhood can help children to look further than their mortality. I believe there is a spiritual or psychic dimension to play that enables an appreciation of life which is more than rational.

Some years ago, on a working holiday in the Western Isles of Scotland, I stepped out of the caravan I was staying in, into the blackest night I had ever experienced. Then I discovered, as my eyes became accustomed to the darkness, that the sky was ablaze with stars, something I had never encountered to such an extent before. The feeling I experienced in the face of that void was one of great joy of being a part of a magnificent interstellar hologram, rather than a member of an isolated species on one planet.

This incredible and vast context in which we journey through life gives us a perspective of what is valuable and important, as much spiritual as it is material. This marks an evolution in playwork itself. For, even as recently as a decade ago, to have mentioned the terms 'playwork' and 'spiritual' in the same breath would have been viewed by many as unacceptable. Yet now, primarily through the work of Sturrock and others, who have brought the depth of psychologies into our frame of what playwork is struggling to facilitate, the spiritual dimension of existence is also a playwork consideration.

Chapter 8

Stimulation theory

Selfishness, aggression, confusion and withdrawal are normal human states which are usually subsumed into each child's total personality, only showing themselves on rare occasions. Most children, most of the time, are playful, stable, optimistic and friendly individuals who, because of this predictable norm, enable playworkers to develop particular operational criteria.

However, not all children playworkers meet are like this. Some are very angry and highly aggressive. Others seem lost, existing only on the fringes of groups. Some appear spoilt and arrogant, communicating their apparent contempt at every opportunity, whilst others are nervy, frightened and constantly lacking in confidence.

When these children come to play spaces, playworkers may need to adapt their operational criteria accordingly, but what might this mean? How do children become extreme in their behaviour and what can playworkers do to contribute positively to these children's play experiences?

By exploring the theoretical impact of different types and levels of environmental stimulation on how children might view the world, this chapter offers an analysis that provides tentative insights both into the development of extreme behaviour and the prognosis for the children affected. It also provides some guidance on practical playwork remedies.

Human beings rely on environmental stimulation for their playful interaction with the world to have any sensory content. With every contact we have, be that visual, auditory, olfactory or tactile, we rely on the world sending us messages about its nature via the stimuli we receive.

When a child is interacting with the world, it is because it senses the world of stimuli, that it is able to develop a sensory picture of the world around itself. Hard things are hard, soft things soft, things that are warm, others that are cool or cold, things which smell or taste good or bad, pleasant and unpleasant sounds. The child learns to discriminate between different temperatures, between different tastes and smells, and begins to build up the ability to understand that the world can be a medium of illusion. A world where, in order to understand anything about what is happening around it, or to be able to predict and forecast, the child must learn to analyse and evaluate the information arriving as stimuli and try to develop an increasingly informed view of what things mean. For example, what is the weather going to be like? How long will it take me to go from A to B? Is that smile covering up other feelings? Is that person really my friend? And so on.

Although these stimuli can be described in sensory terms, smells, tastes, tactile feelings, sights and sounds, they can also be described as two different forms; POSITIVE stimulation (which I will sometimes abbreviate to '+ve' in the text) and NEGATIVE stimulation (which I will sometimes abbreviate to '−ve' in the text).

Positive stimuli are the ones humans would normally describe as pleasant, negative ones as unpleasant, and because to some extent, which is which, is dependent upon individual perception and mood − for example, I like that colour, I do not like that taste − they are open to subjective interpretation. However, many stimuli are sensed by us in more or less the same way. We all either like them, or dislike them. If someone hits us, in general we humans tend to find that a disagreeable experience, whoever does the hitting. Whereas, if we get a smile or a hug, we generally like it.

What stimulation theory offers us is a rudimentary theoretical analysis of the effect of different types and levels of stimulation children are experiencing at home, with their peers and in the built and natural environments. Its purpose is to encourage playworkers to have both a better idea of the 'stimulus state' of the children they are working with and therefore a better idea of what to offer them, as *additions*, *alternatives*, or *compensations to or for that state*, to ensure that they have access to a balance of experience. A balanced experience will perhaps equip them better to survive and evolve in a whole variety of contexts, whilst acting positively to affect their health and well-being.

I made my first attempt to articulate a stimulation theory for playwork with Hank Williams (Hughes and Williams, 1982).

One of the next attempts appeared as an article for the *Leisure Manager* (1988). Since then it has gradually evolved, although it still has a lot of scope for development.

What was suggested was more or less what I have written above − that children live in a world of stimuli, some wonderful, some horrible and it is the child's job when it plays to encounter, explore and learn about their different effects, develop responses to them and gain an understanding that different stimuli have different uses. Although, later models predicted that in the extreme, particularly if exposure was chronic, both positive and negative stimuli could actually be very harmful (Hughes, 1996b).

Positive and negative stimuli are opposites, like tickles and nips. And in general, for each nice, beautiful, interesting stimulus experience, there are equivalent, nasty, ugly and boring ones. When children play, the potential for one often compensates for the potential for the other, thus encouraging children to keep playing.

For example, if a child wants a bird's eye view, s/he might choose to climb a tree, but needs to be aware that the higher s/he goes, the more s/he will hurt him or herself if s/he falls. Of course, like everything, the child needs to experience the reality of the situation before that calculation has any real meaning. Some experience of physical and psychological pain and pleasure is essential to making informed and balanced judgements, and it is when the child is at play that the spectrum of pleasure and pain can be most effectively evaluated, thus enabling the child to make the vitally important calculation:

What pleasure is worth what pain?

This is a vitally important 'curiosity versus realisation' computation for the child at play to make. It provides the child with a basic, push/pull, attraction/repulsion mechanism, which is at the heart of intrinsically motivated play. For even without any external goal or reward, the playing child still engages in what Sylva (1977) calls a 'dialectic', weighing up the pros and the cons, before undertaking action.

The playworker should be aware of the importance of his or her role in facilitating this dialectic. For example, how the play environment is presented to children will have a significant impact on their curiosity (Morris, 1964). The range of both positive and negative experiences on offer will act as a limitation on it, or as an attraction to it. The narrower the range, the more impoverished the play space, the greater the limitation imposed on the child's neophilia; the higher the level of novel experiences, the more enriched the play spaces, the greater will be the child's neophilic drive.

For the child, play should be both a discovery and a balancing experience. It should be a discovery experience, so that the child is able to constantly update its perception of where it is. By which I mean, when the child is playing, s/he is constantly engaged in a process of 'deepening' his or her understanding of the planetary and universal context in which s/he finds him or herself – whether that experience is visual, like looking at sunlight as it passes through the leaves of a tree, or tactile, like the feel of air on skin as the child is in motion on a swing.

Children require a balancing experience because, to be able to authentically evaluate the nature of their everyday play and other experiences in their home context, they need access to experiential contrasts that enable comparisons to take place. If the play space offers access to a balance of both positive and negative stimulation, that will enable the child to experience a form of 'stimulus normality'. Although not affecting the child's general circumstances, this will enable him or her to be conscious of alternatives to feeling picked-on or feeling privileged.

My playwork experience has led me to conclude that a majority of the children I worked with already inhabited this 'stimulus middle-ground' of play. Their everyday experience of the world, although diverse and deep, fell within the comparative parameters of, say, plus or minus 5 on the Stimulus Spectrum in

Extreme   **Extreme**

++ve   +ve   Balance   −ve   =ve

10–9–8–7–6–5–4–3–2–1–0–1–2–3–4–5–6–7–8–9–10

Figure 8.1 The Environmental Stimulation Spectrum.

Figure 8.1. As play environments, their homes and the areas around their home were moderately stimulating and varied, and offered much of what they needed both in terms of experience and novelty. Therefore my playwork contribution to these children was to offer alternatives and supplement some deficits – like access to new friends, interfacing with additional risk, and accessing water and fire play. For many of them the play space's greatest value was that it provided somewhere where they could do what they normally did, but away from adults. This is probably the case with many children who live in 'playable environs', where they have access to dirt, trees and water, but still choose to use supervised play spaces, like adventure playgrounds. The attraction is not just neophilic, it is also about a reality born out of perceived independence.

However, there was a significant, and in my view growing minority of children who attended each of the play spaces I have operated who did not experience this 'stimulus middle-ground' of play. Their everyday experience was either more extreme (they experienced high levels of negativity or positivity, on a daily basis) or the levels of stimulation they were subjected to fluctuated wildly (making it impossible for them to predict or forecast) or the levels of stimulation were unhealthily low (causing them to experience a degree of sensory deprivation).

The four doors

Imagine a room where there are many doors and behind each one is revealed a new, vibrant, interesting, although perhaps difficult, and even risky, play experience. This is the world many children inhabit. A world of diversity of experience, of unpredictability, a world which requires children to be endlessly flexible and adaptable, learning from each experience and evaluating its value and meaning in the light of what s/he already knows from the experiences s/he has already had.

Now imagine a room where there are only four doors. Each door representing either a stimulus extreme or anomaly.

The over-positive or indulged door

This door gains entrance to a world that is always positive, where the sun always shines, and where children are indulged, protected and get every plaything they want. When a child knocks on this door s/he is always welcomed and feels special.

The over-negative or de-sensitised door

This door gains entrance to a world that is always negative, where it's always cold and raining, and where children are disliked, shunned, even threatened, and have to struggle to get anything they need. When children knock on this door they are rejected and feel unwelcome and inferior.

The Z1[1] or erratic door

This door gains entrance to a world of contradictions, that can be anything from frustrating, to very frightening. Children in this world can be indulged or rejected for doing the same thing. They can experience love and hate only moments apart, promises are made, broken and made again. Playthings are provided and withdrawn without explanation. When a child knocks on this door, sometimes it opens, sometimes it does not, and the child feels insecure, unable to trust his or her own judgement or that of others.

The Z2 or de-humanising door

The final door gains entrance to a world in which very little happens, where at best it is boring and at worst, numbing. Where children are ignored, left for hours and have to invent what they need from within their own imagination. When a child knocks on this door, nothing happens and s/he feels lost and alone.

Many children experience each of these metaphorical doors and the worlds they give access to at sometime in their lives, and from the perspective of healthy development in an environmental context that is probably all to the good. Experience of each of them is probably useful to the development of skills that make it possible for us to survive and thrive in a whole variety of situations.

However, it is also likely that many of the children with whom the playworker works will come from home and living environments all too often biased towards one or other of these doors/worlds. These will be children whose experience of experiential balance or other experiential alternatives is so limited that most of their judgements and strategies come from one sort of experience and one sort only.

Stimulus extremes

The over-positive or indulged door = Extreme +ve bias

Play Behaviour(1) + (+ve) stimulation(1) = Reinforced Play Behaviour(1)

Reinforced Play Behaviour(n) + (+ve) stimulation(n) = ++ve biased play world view

---

1 In *A Question of Quality*, categories Z1 and Z2 were referred to as 'Zero A' and 'Zero B' respectively.

What these equations suggest is that for play behaviour to do its job, we must evaluate the experiences we have as we are playing. The idea being that as the world presents different experiences to us, and as we explore them with our senses – propelled by our evolving movement, co-ordination and dexterity skills – we take those experiences and consider them in the light of what we know already.

If a child hurts itself, for example, if s/he receives a bang on the head, initially s/he may ignore it if it did not hurt much. S/he may have done it before. If it did hurt, or if s/he keeps on doing the same thing, s/he will eventually look to the source of the pain and begin to make the connection between it and him or herself. S/he will begin to calibrate him or herself in that particular space (see Chapter 9). It may take a large number of knocks – for example, some young children spend an inordinate amount of time banging their heads by standing erect when they are under tables, with all of the accompanying noise and tears – before the calibration lesson sinks in. But it is a vitally important and essential lesson on many levels and, if not experienced, will deprive that child of necessary life knowledge.

Children need to know about pain. Pain tells them about their nature and their mortality and, like it or not, it is a huge feature of what makes us all human. Pain is an important part of our day-to-day survival mechanism. Little cuts and bruises when we are children, particularly if we get them from vigorous and enthusiastic play, from a vital interaction with the world, are essential indicators of the nature of that interaction. Too many cuts and bruises and we moderate the impact of the interaction; we are more careful. If we are not, then we get bigger cuts and bruises, until we do moderate our behaviour or we really hurt ourselves; in which case, we have to evaluate our behaviour in the light of that experience, or we have a survival problem.

The child's need to learn about pain is not helped by over-eager or inappropriately-timed adult intervention, or by only playing in an environment that is over-ridingly positive. Understandably, most parents/carers do not want their children to hurt themselves, and most or us do not like the sound of children crying, but it is essential that we understand that, without a lot of knocks, our children will not survive either physically or psychologically, in a dangerous world. Some parents/carers cannot or will not accept this and instead of giving their children access to balancing experience, do everything they can to protect their children from everyday scrapes which disable them as a consequence.

The over-positive or indulgent adult may see the child as their life's greatest accomplishment, or as a kind of ornament. The child might be the focus of huge amounts of 'transference', if, for example adults either have been badly hurt themselves, or have a vivid imagination when it comes to injury or distress. In wanting to forgo the experience themselves they project this onto the child's world and intervene continuously to stop the child experiencing either what s/he, the adult, has experienced in reality, or what s/he is imagining is possible. Alternatively the adult may see the child as a piece of property, where the child's free interaction with the world undermines the feelings of power the adult gets from controlling the child's behaviour.

Whatever the reason for the intervention by the adult, if the child is over-protected, it will become an unwitting accomplice in a process of biasing its own world view. On the other hand, indulgence might not just be about protection, it might also be about the constant reinforcement of the 'specialness' of the child by the parent. Specialness, as I suggested in the context of identity, tells the child that it can do no wrong; that it is always the other children. The child may be constantly smothered with positive stimulation, whether in the form of food, or hugs, or words, whilst pathways in the child's brain are being formed that set this feedback as the expected norm for that child. In other words, because the stimulation the child gets is excessively positive ($+ +$ve), and because there is no balancing negative stimulation to moderate the child's expectations, it will expect over-positivity as the norm.

An over-positive play world view would describe a scale from a naïve view of what that child might expect from playful interaction, to an egocentric protective view.

The naïve view

Because it has always been protected by its over-anxious carer and may never have experienced a fall, or banged its head, the naïve child will not have developed the survival building blocks which link personal safety to the calibration processes that are reinforced by the negative stimulation of pain. This child may be spatially clumsy or even reckless, when it comes to height or speed. Risking personal injury, because s/he is unaware, or not aware enough, of the risky nature of the environment.

The egocentric protective view

Alternatively, the child's anti-social behaviour may have been positively reinforced by an over-indulgent carer. Or the child's abhorrent behaviour may be explained away as 'cute'. Consequently, s/he will not have developed the building blocks that link successful social interactions, to behaviour which is perceived by others, as reasonable. Because of this deficit, the child may become selfish, perhaps bullying, unable to understand why other children do not give in to his or her every demand. And, depending on its physique and guile, the child may begin to use physical force to get his or her own way, thus, reinforcing the child's own perception of his or her 'specialness' or superiority, or retreating instead, confused and bewildered at not getting his or her own way.

The child who is always protected at home may find the play experience daunting, in which case s/he may get a negative reaction from children who have experienced less protection, which s/he will not like. Alternatively s/he may find play exhilarating, taking silly risks, perhaps hurting him or herself or other children. Either way, whether s/he finds play daunting or exhilarating, because the initial building blocks for calibration and social interaction are missing, or not fully formed, like a computer with a half-formed operating system, s/he will not be as able to function as s/he should, and may move onto a path of resentment or one of perpetual criticism as a result.

Children who are over-indulged by their parents/carers will find the play space a difficult place to navigate socially. Although most groups of children have some kind of in-built hierarchy, much of what is decided is through negotiation. Children know that each of their peers has a parental, school and behavioural context, and consideration is given to each of these when decisions are being made about where to go, what to do, for how long, etc. However, this system breaks down or is undermined by the entry of an over-indulged child into the group, who, because s/he knows no better, will expect every decision to go his or her way. That is, if the child's early stimulus experience has been primarily positive, if s/he has not experienced contrary views, which act to persuade him or her that his or her judgement can be wrong as well as right, then s/he will not be familiar with negotiation, and may continually attempt to force his or her view on the rest of the group. The result being that s/he will either begin to dominate it by force or be jettisoned. Either way, this child's view of the other children will be diminished. Force, in this context, is not the won power of having to fight to survive from an early age, it is the force of relative size, or ability to intimidate, or use tactics like crying to achieve the desired ends.

Children whose play environment is over-ridingly positive, where they always get what they want, and whose play experience is not governed by a 'real' world curriculum of danger, disappointment, frustration, poverty and potential injury, are also at risk of a positively biased view of the play world. They will find it difficult to operate with children whose expectations have been lessened by experience, who have learnt to do without, to compromise or to share. The child from an over-positive environment may well find it easier to function in the over-positive, predictable world s/he experiences at home, to one in which s/he has to 'give ground' to other children. This child's discomfort might be such that s/he begins to dislike the children who do not get everything they want, perceiving his or her world as somewhere that is special and which needs to be protected from them, growing up into an adolescent whose world view is at least disparaging of those who have materially less.

Taken to the extreme, these over-positive children (+ +ve children) have a considerable potential to become embittered with the real world outside of their cosseted space. The reaction of the world to them will be to either reinforce that view, in which case they may become more reckless or violent, or it will reject them or attack them back, in which case they will feel vulnerable and become increasingly overtly or covertly violent, as a result.

Theoretically it should be possible with concentrated opportunity for good, balanced play experiences, for these children's play deficits to be addressed. They should be able to recover the building blocks without the experiential gaps

– rather like retaping over a badly recorded song with a better recording – particularly if they are enabled to re-engage in early/middle play again but this time with a programme designed to address the deficits and their symptoms. However, Huttenlocher's (1992) imaging findings on brain plasticity (1992) imply that this would need to be done at a relatively early age to be totally effective. The additional synaptic potential to which he alludes (p. 64), and which the child would need to utilise, would only be available for a few years, and by ten years of age much of this potential will have been lost.

Less recent material from the literature, including Harlow and Suomi (1971), Novak and Harlow (1975) and Einon *et al.* (1978) support this strategy, implying that short periods of quality play can have the effect of overcoming serious deficits in social skills, for example. Although whether this is as true for human children as it is for other species is not known.

Good supervised play environments have a lot to offer + +ve children. They are happy, fun and welcoming places to be. Children have freedom to do what they want, in a context of some compromise and negotiation, where appropriate. They are reasonably well resourced. They are staffed by experienced and knowledgeable playworkers who, by ensuring that the space is interesting, novel and addresses many different play types, facilitate a whole range of experiences. Like other 'normal' children, over-indulged children may find the supervised play space attractive and interesting and find it relatively easy to adapt to their new situation. Giving ground or playing less recklessly may be perceived by them as a small price to pay for friends and happiness. In other words, fundamental human needs might over-ride dysfunction and have the effect, at a neurological level, of replacing incomplete circuitry with a more complete version drawn from the missing experience.

What can the playworker do when over-positive children come to play?

Some proposed indicators of an over-positive play bias:

- inability to navigate the play space
- difficulties with other children
- reckless or clumsy behaviour
- high expectation of immediate access to materials
- always has sweets, the latest toys, the latest fashions
- smokes at home
- engages in destructive behaviour
- has bodily adornments including tattoos, studs and particular hair cuts from an early age
- expects favours
- talks loudly, intrudes into others' space
- obesity

- looks through other children
- adopts a particular tone when s/he wants something, but ignores or dismisses children the instant s/he gets it
- egocentric – expects to be the centre of attention
- sulks, has tantrums
- walks through other children, never around them
- rarely says 'Thank you'
- exhibits bullying behaviour.

It is important that playwork practice is not focused on treating specific indicators of indulgence, but on recognising the root causes of the child's situation. The child should be enabled to play through his or her difficulties, rather than be criticised for his or her behaviour. S/he will be more socially competent and less of a danger to him or herself and others as a result. More importantly what might have been serious experiential deficits that could have led to de-sensitised, and perhaps, eventually to de-humanised behaviour, may have been repaired by the child's own engagement in the 're-play' process.

This means that our expectation of the indulged child should be exactly the same as those of any other child. Except that, because we are aware that s/he may have some serious experiential deficits, our supervisory mode should be at medium-close proximity to enable us to intervene if there is a dispute between this child and others, or if this child's behaviour represents a danger to him or herself or to other children.

The level and nature of any necessary intervention will also differ. As indicated in Part I, the playworker's presence may be enough to make some children re-evaluate what they are doing, whereas others may need more direct intervention where materials, tools or other children are removed with the minimum of disturbance to that child so that the frame of the child's behaviour is changed (Else and Sturrock, 1998).

However, playworkers should always remember:

- that change may be slow, and that dysfunction may return several times before it is overlaid with new behaviour
- the playworker's most important function, for that child, is to engage with him or her in such a way that s/he continues to come to the play space. If s/he is confronted directly or embarrassed, s/he may never return.

The over-negative or de-sensitised door = Extreme =ve bias

Play Behaviour(1) + (−ve) stimulation(1) = Undermined Play Behaviour(1)

Undermined Play Behaviour(n) + (−ve) stimulation(n) = =ve biased play world view

The problem for the over-positive child is that whatever strategic choices s/he makes when s/he plays are either:

- confirmed as appropriate or correct by her over-indulgent carer, or
- made to appear correct by an over-protective carer.

However, the problem for the over-negative child is the reverse. This child's self-image and perception of self, is continually being undermined by events that are occurring in the home/living/playing environment.

When a child playfully interacts with the play environment, s/he is receptive both to positive and negative experiences, sensing them as either pleasurable or unpleasant. The child has evolved to expect a range of experience, and if those experiences are invariably of only one type, i.e. only positive *or* negative, the child will begin to adjust his or her expectations of playing. These expectations will become manipulated by his or her experiences. The child who experiences only positive effects will have expectations that are manipulated towards the positive, i.e. the more positive effect s/he derives from playing, the more s/he will learn to expect. Similarly, a child playing in an environment that only contains negative experiences will have his or her expectations manipulated towards the negative, i.e., the more negative effect s/he derives from playing, the more negativity s/he will learn to expect.

Just as with the over-positive child, where a child's expectations are manipulated by a bias of negative experience, serious consequences ensue, both for the child affected and for other children.

A positively-biased child will expect things to be positive, to go his or her way, s/he will make all sorts of assumptions about the world. The impact of his or her experience upon his or her neurological structures and brain chemistry leave the child with no other choice. When s/he plays, if his or her view of the world is not confirmed, and the child realises that – for example s/he may discover that many children do not have what s/he has and do not share his or her preconceptions – the reaction will be confusion, which may eventually result in fear of loss and eventual *defensive* anger.

Alternatively, a negatively-biased child will expect things to be negative. This child's neurological structure and brain chemistry is also determined by experience. His or her world view is that bad things always happen and s/he adapts to that perception, adopting either 'a shoot first and ask questions later' view, or a 'keep your head down' view. When s/he plays, the child will expect the experience to be verbally or physically violent and anticipate that. However if, when s/he plays, the child's view of the world is not confirmed, if, for example, s/he sees that everyone has not been treated as s/he has, then his or her initial reaction may be shock, perhaps even shame, but this will eventually turn into *offensive* anger.

Thus, for children suffering an extreme negative play bias the prognosis is more or less the same as for the over-positive child – violence, although for offensive rather than defensive reasons. The older these children become the less effective will be any attempts to enable them to balance themselves by playing with experiential alternatives.

What can the playworker do when over-negative children come to play?

Some proposed indicators of an over-negative play bias:

- taking over equipment or materials from other children
- ignoring the playworkers
- flinching or ducking when playworkers or other adults are in close proximity
- looking physically or materially neglected
- punching or pushing with little or no provocation
- bullying behaviour
- being 'old before their time'
- exhibiting high levels of attention seeking
- stealing
- violent interactions between siblings
- very defensive
- trying to make playworkers fearful – manifesting threatening behaviour
- destructive behaviour.

It is very tempting to create a self-fulfilling prophesy with over-negative children. Having said, 'You do that again, and you're out!', one should not be surprised that they do indeed do it again and that they do have to be excluded. These children know they are going to fail and they know that the consequence of failure may be being shouted at or hit. So if the playworker gets angry, that instantly reinforces their preconception. It is better to recognise that the negativity they bring to the play space can be a force for good – these children often like to help adults. However, because of their violent potential, our intervention mode should be medium-close. That does not mean that they should be crowded but rather that a playworker should be on-hand until s/he is content that they will not attack other children, and other children may not need to be re-located.

The playworker's strategy should be one of kindness and positive reinforcement. Children so affected have a right to know that they are loved. However, they may have been so damaged that it might take many attempts and many failures before an over-negative child is able to discriminate between what happens at home and what happens at the play space and begin to be able to appreciate the difference.

The Z1 or erratic door = unforecastable levels or types of stimulation

Play Behaviour(1) + erratic levels of stimulation(1) = confusion(1)

Play Behaviour(n) + erratic levels of stimulation(n) = continuous implementation of unworkable survival strategies = low self-confidence and self-belief

This model is particularly applicable to children whose carers are experiencing difficulties with mental illness, alcoholism and/or drug addiction, and whose behaviour is unpredictable. In this context it is not unusual for a child to ask a carer, 'Can I do something?' And get a 'yes'. Then the child can ask the same question a short time later and get a 'no'. Or worse still, get a 'Yes my darling' first and then a 'What the fuck are you doing now you little ***?!', only a short time later.

Even though one of the main purposes of playing seems to be adaptational, continually attempting to develop strategies for adapting to situations that themselves keep changing erratically would not make biological sense. Children need a level of consistency in order to be able to predict and forecast how to behave in a variety of contexts. Take predictability out of their context and they are forced to conclude that everything is an illusion and act accordingly, i.e., that nothing matters and that nothing they do matters either.

Alternatively, they may spend an inordinate amount of time trying to second guess their carer's reactions to things, devising complex and convoluted strategies to guarantee required outcomes, only to be continually thwarted by the carer's continual inconsistency.

Eventually, if the carer's behaviour is only mildly erratic, children may just avoid them, hoping that by the time they, the child and carer, are in contact again, the situation will have stabilised. Whereas, if the carer's behaviour is widely erratic, incomprehensible or verbally or physically violent, the child may begin to show symptoms of neurosis, increasingly unable to predict or second-guess, in such a fluid and unpredictable situation.

What can the playworker do when 'erratic' children come to play?

Some proposed indicators of an 'erratic' play bias:

- disbelief
- neurotic behaviour
- protection of siblings
- fear of adults
- isolation/withdrawal

- unexpected knowledge of mental illness, alcoholism and/or drug abuse
- imitation of parents
- tiredness
- poor play 'performance'.

More than any other of these extreme groups, 'erratic' children risk being out on the margins, lonely, friendless and neglected. Over-positive children will attract other children because of what they have materially and because of the confidence the positive reinforcement gives them. Over-negative children will attract children similar to them as friends and their confidence will feed from the impact their combined presence brings, wherever they are.

But 'erratic' children have had their trust dented or destroyed. Their reaction is always to not quite believe or trust what is happening because their experience is that it will change again shortly. So, if the playworker says, 'I promise', s/he will not only need to keep that promise on that occasion, s/he will need to keep it many times, before children so affected will experience the synaptic overlay which says that, at the play space at least, things can be relied upon.

In an ordinary, as opposed to a specialist play space, these children will be difficult to work with simply because chronic exposure to erratic stimuli make them very unpredictable and nervy. The playworker should expect tantrums and arguments initially, to be patient and try to build on the reliability and hence the predictability of the space. But playworkers should be warned; unless they are able to maintain the opening hours, session durations, visits, or whatever they promise, they should not build up these children's expectations, or they will actually contribute to the level of damage these children experience.

Having said that, although playing with other, perhaps, non-erratic children will have its difficulties, simply engaging in play that is not continually fragmented by carer's erratic behaviour will, at least, tell these children that the erratic environment is not the only environmental type to exist.

The Z2 or de-humanising door = sensory deprivation

Play Behaviour(1) + low-level stimulation(1) = decrease in behaviour/ increase in imagination

Play Behaviour(n) + low-level stimulation(n) = play extinction + fantasy-driven behaviour

In this context human beings have a similarity with electrical appliances. They need current, i.e. stimulation, to function. From the point of view of the basic human organism, it does not really matter whether that current is positive or negative. What is important is that there is stimulation. If human beings do not get an optimum level of stimulation they cannot function properly and begin to fall into a kind of sleep state induced by this sensory deprivation.

Sensory deprivation experiments on human beings, in Heron (1957) for example, have shown that shorn of the stimulation which keeps them in contact with current reality, human beings hallucinate, sleep and lose all track of where they are. It is a very powerful type of deprivation.

It is likely that a significant group of children is exposed to levels of this type of stimulus deprivation. Shut away, ignored, lied to, battery rather than free range, these children's exposure to diversity and depth of experience will at best be limited, and at worst will be lower than the optimum necessary for them to function as biological entities. At the extreme edge, children may encounter a dream state where behaviour is driven more by fantasy than reality, where the two may begin to merge, leaving the affected child unable to distinguish, for example, between a doll and a human baby.

Serial murderers are often described as lone and secretive players for much of their childhood, bereft of normal extended human social contact, often playing alone, using 'road kills' as their friends. Perhaps there is a link between the dead animals used as toys and the nature of the subsequent relationship they have with their victims (see Hickey, 1991).

Children who are alone and without the stimulation other children get when playing in a diverse and interesting environment are forced to create their own play reality. Where can this come from but from their past limited experience? And what happens to these children if their play is drawn from this limited source for months or even years?

It is not beyond the bounds of reasonable extrapolation to suppose that chronic exposure to such a way of playing would gradually over-ride the existing brain circuitry with affective pathways that rely totally on the child's made up fantasy. The problem might be that the more the fantasy mode is the preferred mode, the more the child's emotions will integrate themselves into it. In other words, the brain will search for an operational norm that incorporates behaviour with affect. If the child begins to associate good feelings with its fantasy world, particularly if it is already associating bad feelings with much of its real world, then fantasy may increasingly become the child's preferred route. This in itself is not necessarily dangerous. But if the child draws violence, blood and death into that fantasy – if, for example, s/he plays at murdering a baby, by 'murdering' a doll – it is not a huge step, if the affect s/he experiences is strong enough, for him or her to try the real thing, if the opportunity to do so presents itself.

This may be the stage that children who kill other children reach. Once involuntarily trapped inside a play fantasy, they may predate on other children. And, unaware of reality and driven by the gratification of affect, may involve them in their violent fantasies. Recent incidents including one at Columbine High in the US and elsewhere lend some credibility to what might otherwise be regarded as wild speculation.

What can the playworker do when sensorily-deprived children come to play?

Some proposed symptoms of sensorily-deprived play bias:

- secrecy
- aloneness
- withdrawal
- whispering to toys and objects
- curiosity with death, dead things, blood and gratuitous violence
- attending to non-existent stimuli
- very persuasive
- decline in social skills
- lack of interest in general play activity
- no friends or friends with younger children
- sexual protocol naïveté
- giving other children scary insights.

In everyday playwork this is uncharted territory. Depending upon the circumstances, sensorily-deprived children may prefer their chosen isolation to the bustle of the play space. If their isolation has been imposed, on the other hand, they may be so damaged that specialist help is needed.

One measure I would use to gauge the appropriateness of any intervention I was contemplating would be my assessment of the child's apparent willingness to interact socially: if s/he was giving signals of trying to join in with the general play space activity, but appeared to be encountering some difficulties. For example, s/he might be trying to talk to other children, but is not easy to understand, talks too quietly, does not make eye contact with those s/he is speaking to, or perhaps may be trying to join in a game, but obviously does not know the rules, or any of the children, is clumsy, or articulates inappropriate violent or sexual examples from imagination.

Then my intervention would be to attempt to make what would unavoidably be an arbitrary initial assessment of her general situation. This would be with a view to developing some form of child/child, child/environment, child/playworker, interactive programme, which would be intended to re-skill the child and help him or her to re-encounter the full play space reality.

This is essentially new playwork territory. And while there must be children who, for a whole variety of reasons, are suffering the effects of sensory deprivation at one level or another, they are not being formally assessed or engaged as such from a playwork perspective, simply because such procedures are not yet in place. However, my intuition is that children who are chronically and seriously deprived in this way, are taken to a psychic space where their original personality is all but lost and where, instead, they become an amalgam of images and related affect drawn from their earlier subconscious experience.

My view is that seriously affected children would pose a considerable danger to themselves, to other children and to society at large, simply because their interface with other human beings is dominated by the images generated by their own imagination and supported by internally generated effects. Such children are to all intents on emotional 'auto-pilot', unaware/numb to the impact of their behaviour on child or adult alike.

Andrew Vacchs, a lawyer in the US, once spoke of what he called 'freezer children', who grew up with little adult contact, or love or affection, whose only real human interaction was with children like themselves, who spent each day sitting on roadside fences or on the curb, staring blankly into space, maybe smoking dope or drinking, unaware of the world passing by. They would remain that way until some internal clock went, 'ding – food time', and only then would they begin to attend to the people passing by. Then they became like sharks, first identifying their prey, getting into the swim to follow it, waiting until the timing was appropriate and then going in for the kill, for money or food.

Vacchs, who worked with young offenders (see Vacchs and Bakal, 1979), said, that all too often, these children, who would hurt somebody without remorse or empathy, when asked what they most wanted in the world, would say, 'A pair of shoes, or a MacDonalds'. They were lost children.

In conclusion

Whilst there is little hard scientific evidence for the theoretical ideas proposed above they do seem to ring true to many of the practitioners I come into contact with when I am training. The implied antidote to deprivation and extremes of stimulation, of addressing them with their opposites, also meets with some agreement although there is no evidence of any strategy being devised to research this further.

However, research cited later, including McEwen (1999), Huttenlocher (1992), Perry (1994), Balbernie (1999) and Zuckerman (1969, 1984), together with my own professional experience, leads me to conclude that children are highly vulnerable to experience in the form of whole environmental stimulation, and that when that stimulation is extreme – whether positive, negative or deprived – the impact upon the playing child is severe.

Every embryonic behavioural filter the child needs to draw upon, whether moral, humane, civilised or legal, is affected by the experience the child is having of such concepts. Experience in this context implies not taught information but that which is absorbed through chronic immersion in situations. The antidote to which I allude is the provision of alternatives in which to also become immersed, providing another template for the child against which to judge its actions and attitudes.

And whilst this proposition may be beyond the means of many play projects in any sophisticated sense, providing for alternatives generally rather than specifically, is relatively easy and can be achieved using the spirals and other tools outlined in Chapter 6.

Chapter 9

Combinatorial flexibility, non-specialisation, calibration and contextualisation

A major reason why play provision has suffered from under resourcing over the years is because it has normally been made for political rather than developmental reasons. In fact play is a very complex phenomenon – as the following chapter confirms – a phenomenon that needs sensitive and informed playwork facilitation if its developmental and evolutionary benefits are to be realised.

Combinatorial flexibility

I first came across the notion of combinatorial flexibility, in the late 1970s in a chapter in *The Biology of Play*, called, 'Play and Learning', by Kathy Sylva. In it, she writes, '[Another] hypothesis of the benefit of play ... focuses on the *flexibility* it affords the player. The playing animal is free from the tensions of instrumental goals and can borrow bits of behaviour from survival patterns such as feeding or fleeing. Loizos, (1967), Eibl-Eibesfieldt, (1967, 1970), and Bruner, (1972, 1974)', she says, 'claim that the essence of play lies in such combinatorial flexibility. Play trains the animal [or the child] to string bits of behaviour together to form novel solutions to problems requiring re-structuring of thought or action. Eibl-Eibesfeldt suggests that some animal play is "scientific research" performed by non-humans.' And finally: 'What is acquired through play is not specific information, but a general set towards solving problems that includes both abstraction and combinatorial flexibility.'

Bruner (1972) threw light on the idea, slightly earlier: 'The flexibility of skill consists not only of this constructive feature, but also of the rich range of "paraphrases" that are possible ... for there is, in a sense, something language-like about skill, the kind of substitution rules that permit the achievement of the same objective [meaning], by alternative means.'

Sutton-Smith (1979) had his own spin on the concept, describing it as responsible for, '... new thought, [leading to] new combinations of thought'. Adding that it leads to '... an increase in the cognitive alternatives available', as well as their flexible management.

Sylva (1977) takes care to differentiate between play and problem solving implying that the difference is in the 'salience of the goal itself. In the latter, the goal is all-important, whereas in play the essential activity is the process of assembling the components.' Whilst Hutt *et al.* (1989) sees combinatorial flexibility as one of the outcomes of what she calls 'innovative' play. 'Play that involves the repetition of certain actions but also introduces some novel elements may be called "innovative", and in such play the child may be considered to be consolidating some skill or knowledge, while introducing some novelty to prevent the execution of such skill from becoming monotonous, as well as perhaps to extend "combinatorial flexibility".'

Sylva (ibid.) also adds a note of caution about the validity of the idea. 'Evidence for the role of play in promoting flexibility is sketchy. The evolutionary data, although appealing, are correlative: the species who most "need" flexibility demonstrate the most play', and then goes to provide 'some evidence for the theory'.

What has this got to do with practical playwork?

If we imagine the child as a young organism surrounded from birth by a huge range of problems, which s/he has to gradually learn how to solve if s/he is going to survive and develop, one question that comes to mind is: 'How does the child go about solving those problems?'

First of all, the child does not see them as problems, but as experiences to be played with. That is, as experiences to be explored, investigated and experimented with.

Initially, these problems are mainly sensory. 'To what does that tactile feeling relate, what is that smell, whose voice is that?' Later, as well as sensory problems, issues around co-ordination, locomotion and so on, also begin to be explored and, as the child's horizons move from its carer, to its living environment, and then to the outside environment, the experiences and the child's means of playing with them become increasingly complicated as the child becomes more skilled. Eventually, the child is normally able to communicate, build relationships, negotiate risk and make sense of the complex realities of being alive.

What the play process does, in this context, is that it brings the child into contact with the world in a graduated sense, which enables the child to start, for example, with very basic information about touch and tactile experiences, until s/he has built a tactile map that helps the child to know where s/he is in his or her surroundings. Similarly, the child builds maps of smells, tastes, sights and noises, each of which helps him or her to have a more accurate fix of where s/he is and what and who else is there.

As I discussed in Part I, just developing knowledge about touch requires the playing child to engage with and absorb hundreds, if not thousands, of tiny pieces of information about different surfaces, different hand movements, different finger pressures, all of which tell us something different in tactile terms. If we broaden this to include all the senses, then we are talking about many different packages of information – tiny insights, reminders and confirmations, about feelings, colours, heights, weights, temperatures, volumes, tones – everything, millions of tiny sensory snapshots of the world around them, which when run together form the child's perception of reality at any given moment.

In very early childhood two main processes are happening. One is information gathering, the other is information processing, both of which, inevitably, have an effect on how the child sees the world. For example, if I start today with no tactile information and by the end of today I have a great deal of tactile information, my view of the world as a tactile space will be greatly changed at tea-time, from what it was at breakfast.

Initially, each tiny experience is totally new, but gradually the child begins to develop first a sensory memory and then other memories, all of which can be drawn on to help the child as it encounters new places, spaces, objects and, of course, new and more complex problems to solve.

Many problems cannot be either perceived or solved until a bank of knowledge has been developed. Each piece of knowledge, like a tiny piece in a vast jigsaw, can then be utilised to discover whether it has any role in the solution of more complex problems, and this is where I think combinatorial flexibility comes into play.

What the term combinatorial flexibility describes to me, is a process of looking at a problem and then scanning one's memory bank for tiny pieces of information that have been learnt, to see if any of those pieces, or if any combination of those pieces of information, might contribute to a solution of a problem.

Children are not born with solutions to problems. Solutions are arrived at through a process of trial, error and elimination. But this process can be greatly speeded up if children have lots of information, always being accessed creatively. Then they will have a vast but current reservoir of unused, but possible combinations of solutions to problems.

In other words, the more a child plays in an experientially enriched space, the better s/he will be at solving those problems and at performing those complex tasks, essential to his or her continued survival and development.

From a playwork perspective, I see the child as an organism that is 'energised' or 'animated' by diversity and variety of experience. That is, the greater the range of experience available to the playing child – the greater the depth, the more exciting, stimulating and interesting the choice – then the more the child will be attracted to play. The more the child is attracted to play the more s/he will become immersed in the experiences available and the more s/he will absorb its individual components. So, the playworker's dilemma is what constitutes an appropriate range and depth of available experiences, what constitutes choice? To some extent this was addressed in Part I, when Play Types and the Playwork Menu (see p. 47) were discussed.

Choice implies access to everything, or at least some of everything. Needless to say, this requirement is instantly breached if some play types are disallowed or if the play environment emphasises one sort of interaction, say social interaction, over another.

So the relationship between combinatorial flexibility – as I understand it – and a good play environment is that in such an environment, the knowledge reservoir, processing speed and potential range of solutions of the combinatorial process is greatly enhanced. This is because the child has free access to diverse experience that it can explore in its own time. It also means, as it does in evolution, that solutions can be different, that there is normally more than one solution to any given problem.

Take for example, the problem of seeing something brightly coloured on a shelf just out of the child's normal reach. Easy, s/he extends his or her reach by standing up straighter or standing on tip-toe, or by finding something to stand on – a book, a chair or a ladder to add enough additional height. However, s/he will only know that if s/he has done it many times before.

A young child is starting from scratch and will have to actually work out what is going on. S/he may try to solve the problem by crying, hoping that someone else will solve it for him or her. S/he may get angry or frustrated. Almost certainly, s/he will return again and again, until s/he has enough of the pieces of the solution and enough of a drive to solve it, to enable him or her to fit enough parts of the solution together to achieve the required result.

Perhaps a better example of the power I imagine combinatorial flexibility to have, is the complexity of driving a car, which calls on thousands, if not millions, of tiny pieces of information to come together in a whole variety of flexible combinations, to make driving possible.

When I am training I sometimes invite playwork students to imagine driving to a meeting on a Friday – a rainy, winter's night – with three colleagues:

> You are driving to a meeting, it is Friday night, it's dark and the roads are busy and it's raining. You are making judgements about the distance of the car in front by the changing size and intensity of its brake lights. You have got your headlights on, you have got windscreen wipers on, you are looking out through the windscreen at traffic in front, which because the roads are crowded, is speeding up and slowing down all the time. You are steering the car using the steering wheel, your right foot is on the accelerator and you are making tiny movements to make the car go faster or slower, your left foot is responsible for the clutch, which you need to change gear, for which you use your left hand, or the brakes, which have to be used cautiously because the roads are wet and slippery. As well as looking out of the windscreen at the cars in front, you also have three mirrors, one just above and to the left of your head and one on each door to tell you the speed and location of vehicles coming up behind you. You have an indicator which you use to inform other drivers of your intended movements to the right and left. You have got the car sound system on and you are changing the stations or putting tapes on instead, you are having an argument with your colleagues, whilst unwrapping sandwiches. You are looking out of the front and the back of the car virtually simultaneously. You are making complex

judgements about the location and speed of traffic, in difficult conditions. Your hands and feet have got several jobs to do and require a great deal of co-ordinated movement to do them. And so on . . .

This is a far more complex example of the same combinatorial flexibility process that eventually solved the problem of the brightly coloured object. It is just that instead of one complex problem there are many hundreds – all occurring at the same time. There is no right way to combine all the skills necessary to drive. There are legal requirements, of course, but the actual process of driving can be totally idiosyncratic. That is because flexibility in this process tailor-makes the solution to our experience – we just have to have the necessary knowledge in an accessible form to arrive at our own solution.

Another way of looking at the combinatorial process is this.

Imagine the brain as a space made up of billions of little compartments – like pigeon holes – into which all the tiny pieces of knowledge learnt go when we are interacting with our world. When we encounter a problem, it makes sense to assume that a solution, or a part of a solution, might lie in what we already know; i.e. in all of these tiny pieces of knowledge. But how can we find out? Evolution has constructed a fantastic tool, which is able to selectively plug into any number or permutation of these knowledge boxes, at any one time, and compare what they collectively represent as a possible solution to the problem (see Figures 9.1a–d).

It is like an old fashioned telephone exchange but instead of having one person doing the plugging, it is like having thousands, perhaps millions, so the process is incredibly fast, as it would need to be. Think, for example, if we were faced with a problem that has immediate survival implications. Immediately our combinatorial flexibility faculties would kick off on a multiple search of what we know. Practice would teach it not to bother with all sorts of information,

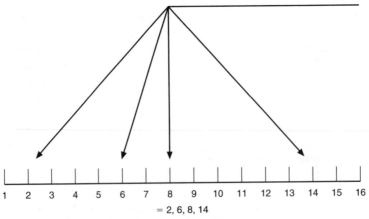

1 2 3 4 5 6 7 8 9 10 11 12 13 14 15 16
= 2, 6, 8, 14

Figure 9.1a Stages of combinatorial flexibility.

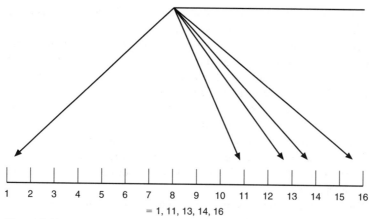

= 1, 11, 13, 14, 16

Figure 9.1b

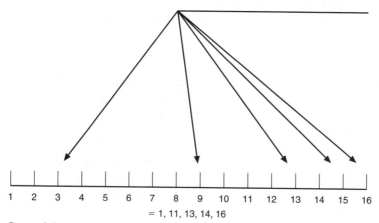

= 1, 11, 13, 14, 16

Figure 9.1c

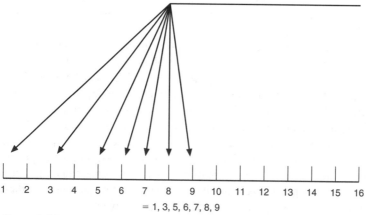

= 1, 3, 5, 6, 7, 8, 9

Figure 9.1d

which we would know to be irrelevant in that context, so the mechanism is quite specific, i.e., it has a rough idea of where to look.

Having accessed the information area where it is judged that a solution to the problem might lie, it tries numerous permutations of boxes – permutations of types of information, permutations of numbers of boxes – until solutions addressing the problem to a greater or lesser extent begin to materialise. (How this might work is not the province of playwork, although some of the questions it throws up are fascinating. Are the millions of tiny packages of information we learn with every single physical and psychological operation we undertake, stored randomly in the brain, are they organised into types of information to simplify the search operation, how is the information located and recognised, i.e., who is the telephonist?)

The problem might incorporate simply working out how to jump over some water; it might be more complicated, like how to escape from a burning building; or more complex still, like locating food.

What I propose is that the process, the skill of combinatorial flexibility, seems to have something to do with three things:

- how we perceive problems
- how we access a vast and increasing body of knowledge as we evolve
- how we explore that knowledge in a way which is both selective and comparative, so that the search process is able to locate permutations that have some relevance to the problem being looked at.

When one thinks how much we know, when one breaks down much of what we do spontaneously – walking, sewing, cooking, driving – into their component parts, how do we know where to look for information to address a problem we may have only just encountered?

As I have said above, we need to know what sort of problem it is, then we need to find where relevant information might be stored and then analyse that information in any number of different combinations, until we find an answer – it is a marvellous capacity.

Its relevance to playwork is considerable. For, if the play space we operate is designed, among other things, to facilitate problem solving, if the children playing there encounter problems when they play, and if the wherewithal for solutions is also there, then children will continue developing the scope and speed of their combinatorial flexibility apparatus as they continue to play.

This does not mean that the play space should be viewed as a problem solving space *per se*. Play spaces do not exist for outcomes but to facilitate processes, and as such must be random as well as diverse. But, if the use and development of combinatorial flexibility *is* an outcome of playing, then we need to ensure that the environments we operate facilitate its development, just as much as they facilitate sensory development, or engagement in imaginative play.

However, the notion of the development of combinatorial flexibility as an essential part of playwork begs the question, 'Would one sort of environment better facilitate combinatorial flexibility than another?' I think the answer is yes! Those environments in which there was graduated access to experience would better achieve this outcome.

For example, on Playground A, I developed an Under-5's area. The age specification is neither here or there, but the idea was that children who came to the playground had an 'initiation' zone, i.e. a zone in which they could become familiar with what a play environment was, what it felt, looked and sounded like.

Similarly, today's children, particularly those who for whatever reasons may be play-deprived at one level or another, would also need access to one or more 'initiation' zones; but it would not stop there. Children who were already combinatorially flexible at one level, could move into other parts of the space which were modified to be even more demanding in terms of its intellectual and other challenges. There is a sense in which this sounds like a model of a school, but there is a huge difference, in that the 'curriculum' would be drawn from all the fundamentals of our biological existence and not just those to do with a sociological analysis of what and who we are. The methodology for learning would be totally directed by the individual child's developmental agenda as perceived by that individual child.

Human beings are systems that operate in conjunction with their environment, as the idea of combinatorial flexibility graphically demonstrates. To operate effectively we need to be more integrated with these other, non-human systems but, at the moment, we appear to be doing everything to separate ourselves further.

Orr (1993) says, 'If we complete the destruction of nature (i.e. if we separate ourselves from the natural world) we will have succeeded in cutting ourselves off from the sources of sanity itself.'

I think we are already some way down that road. However, if children are given access to the best we can give, in terms of a genuine play space, as Harlow and Suomi (1971) and Einon *et al.* (1978) both imply, quality play, in a quality space can overcome play-deprivation and make us more conscious of the natural world.

Non-specialisation

Although originally proposed by Morris (1964), this idea was in the Sylva (1977) chapter too. Quoting Lorenz (1972) she said he had proposed that, 'Man and other species had become specialists in non-specialisation, because they play', and that 'natural selection would favour the most playful individuals in the specialist species for they have acquired more useful information about the potential of the environment and their actions on it.'

Importantly, non-specialisation, which I take to mean being good at many things instead of being expert at a few – having a large portfolio of 'good enough' skills, rather than a small portfolio of 'expert category' skills – is being cited here as being responsible for our continued existence as a species, and that play is central to our continual struggle against extinction.

This makes a great deal of playwork sense and provides a powerful argument for ensuring that children who come to spaces we operate have personal control in accessing experiences that reflect both the planet's and our species' huge diversity. From the perspective that, as individuals and a collective group, none of us knows what is around the corner (as I write Turkey has just experienced another powerful earthquake and the east coast of the US is bracing itself against the most powerful tropical storm on record), we should be continually reminding ourselves of where we are and of what changes are taking place, so that we are continually on an adaptational footing. This should not be at the forefront of our minds, that is not what play is for, but so that the adaptational processes deep within us, perhaps genetic, chemical, molecular processes, somehow linked to our reality and experience, are as up to date in terms of global and species intelligence as is possible.

What non-specialisation means to me is touching every base, having an overview, taking the temperature and checking things out, but doing each of these things from a biological, not a sociological perspective.

When children play what we see is raw biology. But all too often, organisations charged with responsibility for play or children or childhood have an analysis that is social and adulterating in its essence. Saying children need to be socialised at play, that play facilities should be developed to provide employment, that play facilities should be developed to cut crime, or provide child-care facilities. I am driven to enquire, where is the child in this? What about what the child needs?

There is an on-going debate in playwork about the nature of play; that it has two very different but interlocked characteristics. One characteristic is derived from playing now, today, engaging in play that has immediate impact in enabling children to make sense of its immediate context. It is play as something we do as specific individuals.

The other characteristic is that play also has an ever-present influence on us all; that is, play as a transpersonal or species characteristic. Both of these currents run through us simultaneously. They can be differentiated, i.e. we can describe them separately; however, what we must not do is dissociate them. We must not separate them, and facilitate one which is more socially fashionable, but not the other because it might be too primitive. The play experience is a total experience, in which the child moves back and forth between the 'now' and the 'always' state, moving from the immediate individual biological state to the species biological state, and back again, in free-flowing modulations, engaged in a flowing connection between what is happening in reality and what has happened throughout our species' history, information-advising and updating our computations on every level.

This model demonstrates how a part of the adaptational mechanism might work, but more importantly, it provides us with an explanation about why it is so important to ensure that play is not seen just as a mechanism for socialisation, or formal education. In play, children have to be able to move freely between the primeval and the contemporary. Unless that happens, the child's experience is impoverished, but more important, it will not feel right for the child. This genetic connection, this direct line between now and then has to be made. If it is not, then we risk becoming dysfunctional and the connection will probably be made when we are older and far less able to go with the flow, because we will be too aware of what we are doing and try to control it.

I agree with what I understand Lorenz (1972) to be saying. Adaptational intelligence needs a broad brush approach, where children are able to access the widest range of experience when they play, if they are going to be able to analyse the maximum number of situations requiring an adaptational view. The playworker will have realised that s/he cannot teach adaptational interaction and computation; it has to happen spontaneously, i.e., as we play. Each of us is equipped to a greater or lesser extent to do that, that is why we human beings are still here individually and collectively. However, if play continues to be marginalised, if it is always accompanied by feelings of transferred fear, if it is dissociated, i.e., split into its two component parts and one part is left to wither, then as a species we will begin to experience problems at the very root of our perception of civilisation and sanity.

I believe that society is currently making grave errors about where its young should be in its list of priorities and thinking. Rather than being seen increasingly as recipients of services and being smothered by adults' neuroses, children need instead to experience the elements, know the freedom to range, have insights into the lives of other species and take lots of risks. That is a parental as well as a governmental responsibility. It is a species issue for all of us to consider.

For example, in the UK, much of the formal educational process is geared towards specialisation. Everything is constructed to channel children into knowing more and more about less and less. Exam grades are everything. That may be appropriate in terms of specialist jobs markets and status and prestige, but it is a problem on the adaptation front. Money, for example, is no help in terms of biological adaptation. We cannot hire someone to do our adapting for us, we have to do it ourselves. If we cannot, if we are thinking 'superficial society' rather than 'deep biology', then like many other species unable to adapt, we are at risk of extinction. All the effort and sacrifice of our ancestors is wasted because their future stopped with us, their genetic future stopped with us; it is an interesting thought.

Calibration

Calibration is another interesting idea, but it is also a functional reality. It happens to us on a daily basis and the skill of calibration is developed and implemented when we play.

My understanding of the term 'calibration', is that it applies to the measurement of one thing in relation to another.

Much has been written over the years about this subject. Simpson (1976) discusses calibration in the context of mounting behaviour in monkeys, implying that if a child does not put the necessary building blocks together that tell it in total: (a) how to mount and (b) where to mount, then it will not be a player in the procreation stakes. He says, 'It is possible that the infant without the prior experience of calibrating himself – in genital terms – on the relative uniform area provided by his mother could be confused by the sensations coming from a small peer, e.g., a female, and fail to learn to mount correctly.'

What the skill of calibration does, is that it makes it possible for us to have a relationship with the physical environment as we change and as it changes.

Imagine a baby, just beginning to crawl, and in the middle of the room is a chair. This chair has a number of unchanging features. It is a particular shape, a particular weight, it is a particular height, in a particular position in space and so on. These features are fixed. The chair will remain the same shape, weight and height, unless forces external to the chair move it, or change its shape.

The baby is smaller than the chair, it cannot sit on it and cannot move it. The baby will learn these things by interacting with the chair. However, after six months has passed, the baby has grown. Now, in relation to the baby, the chair has changed. The baby can move it. S/he can try to sit on it. But it is not the chair that has changed it is the baby. Every so often the baby will return to the chair to check out the relationship that started by calibrating his or herself against the chair. Now the baby needs to re-calibrate his or herself because things have changed again. In six months' time s/he will have to do it again, and this process will continue until the baby stops growing.

So, one aspect of calibration is learning the physical environment. Children need playfully to explore their physical environment and map it, in terms of a whole range of different characteristics. For example, as they grow, they will need to know how much muscular pressure they need to exert to close doors, turn on light switches and turn on taps. They are not born with this knowledge and unless they are well calibrated, they will be very clumsy, banging doors shut, leaving them open when they thought they had closed them, not turning lights on and turning taps on too full and spraying themselves with water.

The other aspect of calibration is that, as well as mapping the physical environment and re-mapping it as they change, children have to re-map it when it changes. So, if they move to another environment, they have to learn it all over again. For example, part of the excitement of going on holiday is that we go to new spaces, new spaces to explore and map. However, it can be very frustrating when light switches are different and turn in ways we are not used to, or when the hot and cold taps are reversed, or when door handles are not where we're used to locating them.

For the playing child, it is not so much about learning or mapping static or changing spaces, than it is about learning how to learn. Play is about developing the building blocks that make learning possible. So from an early age, as biological players, children need an environment which interests them enough so they will actually explore it and learn how to calibrate it. But they also need an environment which is changing, so that they learn about re-calibration – one reason why a play environment should be in a changing rather than a stagnant state.

I first came across the term 'calibration' in Bateson and Hinde's *Growing Points in Ethology* (1976). In it, Simpson (1976) states, 'I suggest that play may ensure not only the initial calibration of the infant's skills, but also a continuous re-calibration of these skills as he changes in size relative to the fixtures of his surroundings, and relative to his peers, who are also changing size and strength.'

This conjures up the wonderful picture of the child as a biological entity, evaluating a situation as s/he changes in the context of changing surroundings.

One moment the child cannot pick up a chair, then its strength increases fractionally and then it *can* pick the chair up. One minute s/he is smaller than someone else, then s/he is bigger, then s/he might be smaller again. Each of these changes, each of these subsequent re-calibrations, alters the dynamic between the child and his or her environment.

Engaging in the process of calibration not only gives children the skills to be conscious of the relationship they, as physical objects have with every other physical object in our frame, it also has an affective, i.e., an emotional, ingredient that guides how children feel about their physical characteristics. Most of us have seen a baby getting frustrated when it cannot move something. But that interaction is telling the baby that there will be things in the physical universe that it cannot move and it needs to understand that relationship.

Repetition is also an important ingredient both of playing itself and specifically of calibration. Connolly (1973) and McFarland (1973) both suggested that repetition of particular kinds of actions is important in order that complex skills may be learnt. What they may be saying is that complex skills are the sum total of many less complex skills and that for the integration of both the less, and more complex skills into our brain pathways, we need to repeat them many times for imprinting to take place. This is certainly borne out on the playground where children will often do the same thing over and over again and then vary what they do slightly, and then repeat the variation again and again.

Simpson (1976) also re-emphasises the point made earlier about muscular force, what I called muscular pressure. He says, 'The organism may in this repetitive behaviour test the variations in force [muscular force] necessary to perform a particular behaviour.'

He also states, 'there is a point at which early extensive calibration of numerous situations can be termed experience, which can then be extended into new situations, so that repeated calibration in a different environment or set of circumstances becomes less necessary or unnecessary.'

Eye + Action = Calibration(1)

Calibration(n) + Memory = Experience

So if children engage in enough calibration and re-calibration activity early on in their lives, they may be able to navigate new spaces more successfully as they grow up.

Contextualisation

This is a personal variation on calibration and refers to a more psychic than physical version of calibration. Contextualisation is more about gaining a 'sense of place', about having a developed view about where one is in the scheme of things, one's place in the universe.

I began to feel that human beings would need to have some more psychic measure of the world when I found myself engaging with children who came to the playground after they had suffered a bereavement. Contexualisation is a 'What is the meaning of life?' version of calibration and is the way children evolve perspectives and values in later life. Experience tells me that deep play is primarily a feature of the child's play repertoire in middle-childhood and is both an expression of their realisation of the fact of mortality and a way of encountering it in their own world. However, even this realisation is no substitute for the experience of real loss, which tends to throw children into a metaphysical spin, because it requires thought of a kind children are quite unused to prior to this kind of event. When someone disappears out of one's life, it is difficult for most of us, particularly children, to comprehend. 'How can people just disappear?', 'Where do they go?', 'How do they get there?', 'Where is Heaven?', 'How do you know?'

Suddenly, from the secure, or relatively secure reality of the unconscious, children now have all these questions, which those who know everything, i.e., adults, do not have answers to – that is scary and perplexing. It signals to them that death is a big issue and one people know little about, except, of course, that it will come to them too, one day.

Dealing with this new dimension in which people disappear and never come back, where people children love and care about just vaporise, requires a total re-evaluation of what they think life is about and what their priorities in it should be. If this experience is badly dealt with by the playworker it can leave children confused and feeling personally singled out and picked on. It is easy to take life seriously and even easier to take it personally. A child who may have already had a hard time can evaluate the loss of a loved one as the final confirmation that life is pointless and that ideas like concern and respect are meaningless.

The playworker's approach to this type of event in children's lives should be much like their approach to every other aspect of the child's emotional life – to be there, to make sure the child knows that, but not to crowd – ensuring that they do not hijack the child's experience with their adult version of it.

Throughout their lives, children have to make sense of experiences like death, whether a near death of their own, the deaths of thousands in natural disasters or the abomination of other children being massacred. How they deal with both the notion and reality of death as children will determine how able they will be, as time goes on, to deal with it as adults.

The relationship between metaphysical issues and play is an important one, for play is about life in its entirety. This must include the realisation and experience of death for it to be a complete experience.

Hall's (1904) notion of Recapitulation is an interesting one in this context. For what Hall suggests is that play is also a reliving of our ancestral pasts, which must mean, if Hall is correct, that play is genetically programmed and that today's play is actually coded into the genes of today's children to be passed on – with all of the other ancestral information – via procreation. The implication here being that humans not only pass on height and hair colour sorts of characteristics through their genes, they also pass on evolutionary events, of which one would expect death to be a significant part, which would then be played out in the future. As we know, this is the case in a whole range of narratives. Why this might be, I will explore in Part III.

So, perhaps what I am calling contextualisation might be an essential process of review triggered by a connection between external reality and genetically stored long-past events. Death would certainly be a trigger, and other events shared by one's ancestors and one's self could also trigger a similar review process.

Reflections 3

Although the debilitating strain of playwork, and the high levels of transference playworkers are absorbing, is slowly being realised, the pressure on playworkers in the past has been massive. I remember a woman coming to one of our National Meetings and being appalled at how many of us smoked and how many we smoked, too. In the early days a time serving playworker lasted about six months. One of the main pressures is on playworkers' relationships, particularly marriages. It is ironic, that in an area of work which is so dedicated to other people's children, there are so many divorces. I wrote this song just after I had moved out of my home into another house, after my own divorce. The impact of its affect on me is as powerful now as when I wrote it.

> *The kids are OK (1978)*
> The sun can shine or the rain can fall,
> It doesn't really matter at all,
> If it's cold or hot it's a beautiful day,
> It's the rainbow's end if the kids are OK.
>
> Generals can shout orders, soldiers can die,
> Flowers can pray to the opening sky,
> Zen Buddhist monks can show me a Way,
> It's sure to be good if the kids are OK.
>
> I've read books by Camus who died on his bike,
> Seen films with James Dean in and others I like,
> Every person I meet has got something to say,
> Now I've got it too, that my kids are OK.
>
> Most people I know think I'm a bit strange,
> Don't act in ways fitting for a man of my age,
> But I'm just like them and I work for my pay,
> Some of it's in kind see, my kids are OK.
>
> I'm living alone the house echoes a lot,
> For the life that I've had I deserve what I've got,
> In my house there's a window looks over the Bay,
> Through the mist comes the word that the kids are OK. Well, the sun can shine . . .

Sometimes a playworker will know, because of the inevitable effect of circum-stances, that a particular child is almost doomed to a very difficult life. But sometimes that child can demonstrate that however much life kicks them down, they still get up fighting. This Reflection is a snap shot of a child whose life in technical playwork terms was on the borders of extreme negative (=ve) and Z1. As he was growing up his capacity for trust was being continually undermined. What the play space tried to offer was a reliable and positive environment where he was safe – a sanctuary for children who felt vulnerable everywhere else. However, its impact was minimal because of the complexity of the child's external context.

Reflection: Mo the Man

Mo was ten and one of life's born comedians. So naturally I was concerned when he came to the Centre one day, very sad. 'What's up, Mo?,' I said. 'What's the problem, mate?'

'I'm leaving,' he said, but what he meant was he was being sent away. Apparently, he had been caught stealing from a church, and his parents, a very religious couple, had decided to send him to stay with relatives in another country. He was frightened.

It had all blown up the day before when I had seen him running into the play-ground's outside area, hotly pursued by the police. My view of the playground in this context was almost medieval. I saw the playground as offering sanctuary to its children.

We ran outside. 'Excuse me,' I said to a police officer, 'but this is a children's playground, you can't chase children around in here.' I said it politely, I said it simply. But I might just as well have been invisible, they just charged on anyway, along with their dogs. So much for play environments being children's territory!

I needn't have been worried. Mo, like generations of children before him, was fast and agile and knew the area, with all its nooks and crannies, its hedges and walls, its hidey holes and places no adult could reach.

However, even though he had evaded the police, he still went home, and the combination of family shame, and the view that British life was decadent, meant that he had to go away. This was all new to me and I found it shocking, but there was little I could do.

And so Mo disappeared. For six months it was as if he had never been. No one mentioned him, it was like a death without a body.

Then one day, I heard his voice saying, 'It's all fucking bum and dick', he pronounced dick, as deck, laughing at the crudeness of the language as only a ten-year-old would.

'Mo,' I said. 'You're back. Good to see you, mate. Are you OK?' He didn't talk much about where he had been, but the stuffing had been knocked out of him, and the experience seemed to have hardened his little face.

Shortly after his return, with the arse half out of his trousers, he was climbing up the pole of the gibbet swing. I said, 'Mo, be careful, you'll only rip your trousers even more.'

He felt around to where the rip was, and realising he was in trouble again, tapped the area of bare flesh with his hand, and looking at me smiling, said, 'Well, kiss my arse,' which he pronounced 'ass'.

I saw him around for a while, but increasingly he was hanging out with older and much more disenfranchised, and de-sensitised kids than he had until then. He hadn't done time when I left, but that was a while ago . . .

Reflection: missing kids

Although, as a playworker, I was always concerned if children hurt themselves, or if a fight happened, or if one of them got nicked, my real fear was losing one of them. I do not mean if I actually lost one, but rather if one went missing or was kidnapped. This Reflection describes an incident when one of the playground's children, still immersed and playful after the playground had closed, simply forgot to tell his parents where he was going. It demonstrates that parents and playworkers often have expectations of the playworker's role that go far beyond operating a play space and that the limits of one's responsibilities to the children and to their parents are frequently defined, not by remuneration or job descriptions but by commitment to the work and the communities within which it takes place.

The bang on the door was so loud and so frantic that I nearly dropped my dinner.

I was sitting on the sofa, watching television and eating. I'd only been in from work about half-an-hour, and although it was late summer and still warm, it was nearly dark.

'I'll kill those buggers'. I knew that it was almost certainly bound to be some of the more socially minded kids coming to tell me that one of the fires we'd so carefully raked and hosed, so that we'd made sure, without a shadow of a doubt that they were out, had mysteriously burst into flames again.

It happened all the time. There is a fascination with fire that draws children to it like a magnet.

They played with fire all the time when we were open. A small fire, surrounded with bricks and attended by a red fire bucket filled with water. They loved it. I had too, but we were different. I had known what it was we were dealing with.

Every day in the winter my mum or dad had to clean the ash and clinkers out of the fireplace in the living room accompanied by great billowing clouds of dust. And in the frozen evenings we'd made toast and I'd roasted the whole front of my body in its red glow, while my back froze.

Sometimes lighted bits of red hot coal would fall out and onto the hearth, like they did when we lit them in the Tunnel, and I loved to watch the changing land-scape of what I used to imagine as the 'fire kingdom'.

But kids at the playground were a generation of gas central heaters; of oil-fired heating and under-floor electric heating. Fire had been a necessity to us, but to them, it was in every way a toy, and because of that and its inherent danger, it needed looking after.

We cooked on fires and in the darker evenings we'd wave fire brands in the air, but we always made sure that they were out when we left. But almost always, like bloody magic, they burst into life again, and that was when the fire watchers would come around. 'Bob, Bob, there's a fire alight over the Venture, so and so's over there', and on it went. They weren't trying to be naughty, it was more about trying to squeeze that last drop of attention, that last moment of identity from you. It was like sucking an orange that might not be around again for a while. You didn't mean to be greedy, you just wanted to savour it.

I muttered my way to the door. I looked down to stare not at children's faces but at adult waists. I looked up. 'Sorry,' I said, 'I was expecting it to be some of the kids.' The adults were parents of Lloyd, one of the younger kids who came to the playground.

'Bob, Lloyd's gone missing, we can't find him anywhere,' said his Mum. 'We're afraid he might be lost.'

'Can you help us?,' said his Dad.

I said sure, and went to get some shoes on. 'I won't be long,' I called through to the front room, 'One of the kids has disappeared.'

I went outside. It was warm, and where I lived it always smelled of wheat cutting and straw at that time of the year and reminded me of the bale dens we used to make – all darkness and heat and secrecy.

I said, 'Look, if he's just wandered off, he's probably out in the fields near the playground. Why don't you go home for now in case he comes home and I'll do the circuit and come 'round and see if he's back? It won't take long, and if I don't turn any thing up, then we'll have to think about the cops.'

There were a few other people with them and they decided to walk slowly through the estate, which was one of those designer dreams that makes a resi-dent's nightmare. All flying bedrooms, alleyways and garage bays. Dangerous for an adult, but potentially lethal for a child, or an old person. We hadn't had that sort of problem there yet, but these had to start somewhere, and this was ideal.

I left then and headed out the back. I did a wide sweep through the stubble field, keeping low, well back from the street lights, able to see anyone silhouet-ted against them.

I crossed the ditch and moved onto the playing field, stopping to see if I could pick up any noise.

Just the usual summer evening sounds, cars in the distance, dogs, and argu-ments.

I crept through the avenue of bushes that fringed the field and moved out onto the Tip, a rubbish tip that was near the playground, and listened again. Nothing.

The countryside is full of noises, but not normally human ones. We tend to avoid the dark unless we've got a reason to be in it.

I moved on to the road that skirted the Tip and ran alongside the edge of the playground. When I got to the wire, I squeezed through one of the holes and edged my way up the bank. I carefully looked over the top. Not a soul.

There was a string of smoke coming from one of the 'dead' fire places but none of the kids were there. 'Shit,' I wasn't disappointed about not catching anyone, I'd just hoped that he'd be there.

I went back through the wire and walked down the dry road, kicking up dust, past the Cottage, all dark and closed up for the night, and went to see if his Mum and Dad had had any better luck.

I knocked on their door and the Dad answered. 'Hello Bob, come in mate,' he said. I walked into their sitting room and there on the settee was a freshly scrubbed, smiling Lloyd, who having obviously received a worried dot around the ear, was now being forgiven with bread and jam and cups of tea.

'The little sod had gone down the Fair and forgotten the time,' his Mum said, obviously very anxious. 'Thanks for coming out.'

'No sweat,' I said. 'Night Lloyd, night,' I said to his Mum and Dad, and smiled. They might be sods, but there's no sweeter feeling than getting them back when you've thought you've lost them.

Reflection: Piggy Padlock and the Z2 pioneers

In general it is considered bad practice to stereotype or second-guess children who come to any play space one operates. But sometimes, just sometimes, someone will arrive and red-alert just happens instinctively. This was such an episode. As the title of this Reflection implies, play can sometimes take children into realms that are difficult for adults to understand. However, the playworker should be aware that it is not uncommon for human children to engage in cruel and sadistic acts. A training session I ran once explored this area with playworker's own memories of what might be recapitulated experiences. They had cut up caterpillars, speared frogs, shot birds and frightened cats ...

I'd seen these two hovering around at a local arts exhibition, looking at various people and then laughing hysterically, perhaps about something they'd seen or thought. I watched them for a while, just out of professional interest. It wasn't long before I got a taste of what they were about.

Several of the exhibits were together on long stands rather than mounted on the wall, and the two boys, both about 14, were shadowing an elderly woman. She was looking at works on one side of the stands, and they were creeping along on the other side. One, who I later learnt was named Paul, had taken a 'joke' hand out of one of his jacket pockets and was fitting it on to his real hand. The 'joke' hand was much bigger than any normal hand, green flecked with red, in colour, and very gnarled and twisted. A monster witch hand you could buy from any joke shop.

As the woman reached the end of that selection of pictures and pottery, she went to go around the stand, only to be faced, literally, with the hand. Paul had reached the end of his side of the stand momentarily before the woman, and as she had arrived he pushed the joke hand into her face, hard enough to startle her, whilst both of them made a noise which was calculated to make her jump. She cried out and staggered back, but by then they had both disappeared behind other exhibits, perhaps to repeat the process or to leave.

They seemed cruel to me, unable or unwilling to realise the impact that such an act might have on the elderly person. But then, it was only a prank, I'd not done that, but I'd done similar things when I was a kid, playing 'knocking down ginger', and even putting 'penny-bangers' through letter boxes on Guy Fawkes' Night. Children can be cruel. Most adults, if they're honest, if they reflect on their childhood, will be able to recall any number of cringing incidents of cruelty, at least to flies, or wasps, or caterpillars, if not other larger mammals or reptiles. These kids were probably no different and no worse. Simply experimenting with deep play, to see how far they would go before shame, embarrassment or fear of retribution moved them on to other kinds of experiences.

However, that rationalisation didn't make me feel any better, when only a few days later, Paul and Raymond, the other boy, turned up at the playground. Moving through the other children like two sleek tuna or baby sharks looking for someone, or something to predate upon. Not a part of the action, not engaged in the games, but observing, and always giggling, and talking with hand over mouth.

There was a lot to do, so I forgot about them, and then without any warning I realised that, at least for that day, I was the prey. A stone flew past my head and rattled against the wall of the building. It wasn't the first time this kind of stuff had happened. Now and again you have to expect to be the target of someone's revenge on the world, in playwork.

I looked around for the source of the missile. The two of them were hiding on the other side of a small hill, across the space from where I was standing. I walked over slowly and called over to them. 'Here, a minute,' I said, and moved a bit closer. 'Please don't throw stones here, you might hit one of the other children.' As I said '. . . dren' another stone sailed over. Thank God they weren't very good shots. At a previous place I'd worked one of the kids, standing on the roof of the building after we'd closed for the day, caught me squarely around the back of the head with a high-speed clod, just as we were leaving, and nearly floored me.

I moved towards them and they disappeared into a dip on the other side of the hill. By the time I'd reached where they had been, they'd gone through a hole in the wire and were away. However, that wasn't the end of it. Throughout the day they came back, several times, once with a younger brother of one of them. Always the same situation. No conversation, no name calling, no connection, just stones, until I reacted, and then withdrawal. They never hit me and I never stopped them trying. Obviously, it might have been wiser to ignore them and hope they'd go away. But (a) I was responsible for the safety of the other children there, and there were about 60 of them, totally oblivious of all of this, and (b) I doubted totally that a tactical retreat on my part would bring about a cease-fire on theirs. As I said, this had happened before.

I was working alone, and I couldn't close the place, so just hoped that they would get bored. Some hope. There was a sense in which it was a game, but it was the sort of fun you get from vulnerability, from bullying, from knowing that the other person is disempowered. Sometimes, playworkers invite, even ask for, confrontation with children who even at their young age have been so desensitised by their life experience that they can be 'dangerous'. But just now and again, something happens for no rhyme or reason, you don't do anything to make it happen, but like a truck with broken brakes, it just picks up speed and escalates.

By now, the silent stone throwing was making it impossible to operate. I had no help, no support. I couldn't call the cops, that would have destroyed the trust I had with many of the kids who had had bad experiences with the authorities. What to do?

Then I noticed that the younger brother was back, and that he had left what looked like an expensive bike, away from where the three of them now were. I walked towards them, the occasional stone making me duck. When I reached the brother's bike I picked it up from where he had dropped it. 'Come on,' I said, 'Let's stop this, hey?' I looked at the bike. It was, 'Stop this, or the bike gets it' time. Yes, I know it was stupid, but I hadn't got a lot of manoeuvrability. I still had to walk home alone!

They obviously didn't believe me, and several stones came down rattling around me. I gave the bike a little kick, as if to say, 'I'm warning you'. That didn't stop them, so I kicked the spokes a bit harder. And so it went on. I didn't destroy the bike, but I did dent it a bit. But I thought that the younger brother was hardly responsible for what had happened all day, and anyway I had no right to do anything to his bike. Having said that, this show of determination had forced a retreat out of them for a while.

It was closing time now, anyway. And so, as quickly as was appropriate, the rest of the children left to go home and I shut the building and put the padlock on the gates. As I was doing this, a stone hit the cast-iron gates. 'Oh shit,' I thought. It wouldn't have been beyond them to have gone home and told an older brother or cousin about me and the bike, and now they were back, 'team handed'.

Nothing for it but to brazen it out. It was getting dark, too.

As it turned out there were no psychotic relatives waiting to dismember me, it was just playworker paranoia. But as I walked across the park towards home I could hear whispers of, 'Bob, you wanker,' following me, through the evening air.

It was around this time that we got Piggy. Her real name was Piggy Padlock, a name one of the children had given her. Piggy was a beautiful white rabbit with pink eyes and was a massive favourite with the kids. Every day she was cleaned, fed and watered by them, and then was allowed to hop around and eat the grass and weeds that festooned the perimeter of the play area, supervised by one or more of the littlies.

I'd forgotten the bike incident, although its owner, the young brother, must have said something to his parents, as one evening, a few days later, the door went at home, and a man, who introduced himself as the boy's Dad, was standing there. I asked him in, and asked what I could do to help. I explained the situation as best I could, admitting that to even threaten to damage the bike was stupid, but I had a play space full of other children, no help, and three boys trying hard to brain me with stones, did any alternative strategies come to his mind? He was clearly upset. Not with me, but with his kids. I was sorry it had ever happened.

I don't know if he went home and clouted them, or grounded them or stopped their pocket money, I never actually laid eyes on any of them again for years. All I do know is that no more than a week later, something happened which had all the cruel and semi-sadistic trademarks of that original incident at the arts show.

I had arrived at the playground in the morning, as usual, and some of the early arrivals were turning up, when there was a shriek of 'Bob, Bob, Piggy's gone.' Sure enough, when I looked, Piggy's hutch had been broken into and she was missing. Could it have been a dog? Had some of the kids broken in during the night and lost her in the dark? Could she be in one of her favourite places chewing wild flowers and weeds, oblivious to our concerns? We all started to hunt around. Some went over to the allotment area; others looked in the Under 5's; a few went to the construction area where there were piles of wood waiting to be de-nailed; whilst others looked around the stream and the water-play space. No Piggy.

In fact it wasn't until much later in the day that we found Piggy, burnt and suffocated to death. What seemed to have happened was that whoever did it had broken into her hutch, taken Piggy out and put her into our galvanised dustbin, piled grass in on top of her, set fire to the grass and then put the lid back on.

As I said earlier, all children can be cruel and some can act with great cruelty against other species in particular. But I judge most of that to be an important indicator of growing up, a kind of right of passage through middle-childhood. The cruelty stops as children become more conscious of the consequences of their actions and as they begin to identify with the situation of the object of their cruelty.

However, this was no such indicator of middle-childhood. This was done by children or adults, who were lost in a space between reality and fantasy, who maybe thought that they were getting at me, or at the children, but who were, in reality, only engaging in the darkest kinds of imaginings, where the screams of a burning rabbit would simply have been interpreted as background noise to the main event.

Such incidents were so rare, I have only personally come across perhaps three in thirty years, but when they do happen, they certainly cast a shadow over what is normally an enchanted, and enchanting space.

Chapter 10

Democracy, participation, equal opportunities and the child's right to play

The area of play as a human right is an interesting one for playworkers. For, it seems that if we call it a biological need, like breathing, or food, it retains its autonomy and its integrity. Whereas if we regard it as a right, it becomes the target of apparently justified and wide ranging adult contamination.

I do believe that play should be regarded as a human right, in fact I believe the right to play to be the most fundamental right of all. For without the right to play, as Allport (1954) and Amir (1969) point out, all other so-called rights are rendered pointless. However, I do think the meaning of the right to play needs some clarification in this context. Children have a right to play. But having said that, it does not follow that adults have the right to supervise that play and it certainly does not mean that adults have the right to impose their own values on that play.

As I see it, the right to play describes two fundamental rights for children. The first is that they have the right to play *per se*, i.e. to do what their biological play drive tells them. I would argue that they need to be able to do this in order to develop the sub-atomic, atomic and molecular connections which make it possible for them to understand their existence and make some, and hopefully an increasing amount, of sense of it.

At birth, many, perhaps most, neuronal pathways are still waiting to be formed. Playful interaction between the child and its environment begins to supply the basic information, what I call building blocks, for the formation of these pathways. Sutton-Smith (1997) suggests that the more children play, the more neuronal pathways are created, the bigger the brain, and the more of the brain's potential is utilised.

Thus, play must be a human right because it optimises a child's capacity for brain growth, and by so doing, optimises that child's capacity for thought, learning, survival, adaptation and ultimately evolution.

The other fundamental right derived from the right to play is the right to have the space in which to play. Having the right to play without having the right to the territory to do it in makes no sense. Yet there is no guaranteed right to territory; so where is this right to play to be exercised?

In the UK there are a number of choices:

- in the wild
- in the street
- in dedicated unsupervised space
- in dedicated supervised space.

In the wild

By, 'in the wild', what I mean is, outside of what is generally accepted as the built environment – farmland, moorland, national parks, the sea-shore, river banks and so on. Needless to say, many of these spaces are inaccessible to most children, most are also quite dangerous places, unless one has had proper survival training. Others can be treacherous, with deep water, fast tides, unstable sands, cliffs, currents, and so on. Farmland can also be a hazardous place to play, with polluting and toxic chemicals, heavy machinery, large members of other species and sometimes child-unfriendly adults, with guns and dogs.

'The wild', has always been a preferred space for children's play, guaranteeing them, adult-free time. Nicholson's, (1972) notion of the ideal play space was the beach. However, because of the changing face of play, with increasing adult intervention, lack of exercise and the powerful neophilic attractions of television, video and computer games, I suspect that an increasing number of children today would find playing in the wild difficult and demanding.

In the street (the built environment)

The street is also a preferred space for many children, although it is probably less to do with its diversity of experience, than it is to do with its high level of potential social interaction, which makes it particularly favoured by adolescents.

But like the wild, the street can also be difficult for children to navigate. It is massively polluted, and gives many children breathing problems. It is full of traffic, and many children are killed and injured by traffic every year. It is full of other hazards that are at least as dangerous as anything in the wild, including high tension wires, electricity sub-stations, railway lines, machinery, wells and trenches on building sites.

Inevitably children will play out on the street if they can. The street includes their home and gardens and parks. But the problem for children is that although their parents want them safe, and often insist that they play in or around the house, unlike the wild, the street is essentially an adult space, where adults not only have right of way but expect to have total jurisdiction. It is their space and they can be hostile to and intolerant of children who use it to play.

One other factor that makes the street a difficult place for children to play in is the possibility of being abducted by a human predator. I have children myself, and now I have a grandson too, and if ever there was an argument for locking children away in safety, this is it. I cannot cope with the thought of a child going out to play and being found, dead, or perhaps sexually assaulted, or both. And yet, what is the alternative? If play is as important as I am trying to describe, then risking death to play, is a risk that must be taken. If we do not, then our short life on this beautiful planet, will have the scope of a caged songbird, limited by our self-imposed bars.

In dedicated unsupervised space

A solution to the child's territorial dilemma, which has been used for many years, is the provision of dedicated play spaces. Most of us will have experiences of the swing, slide and roundabout play spaces, where the needs of human development were apparently thought to be best served, not by natural features like trees, the elements or by undulating landscaping, but by bent ironmongery, chains, metal sheeting and, sometimes, dangerous moving parts.

Like many others, I had great times on these playgrounds, but stories of amputations and other grievous accidents brought me to the realisation that they may have been there less for what they give children, than what they saved on maintenance for the local government department responsible for them. Over the years, thanks in part to the creativity of the adventure playground movement, this kind of fixed equipment play space has evolved and now timber and other materials are used, along with the ubiquitous and pointless safety surfacing, which protects providers from litigation and children from the risk that is the essence of playing.

But they do give children some semblance of a space to play which is 'theirs'. They also give them somewhere to meet their friends and behave as children, moving from the 'savagery' of early and middle-childhood, to the more socialised individuals of late childhood, without adult help or imposition. However, all too often, these spaces are filthy, vandalised and frequently the haunt of older children, adolescents and even adults. They are rarely fenced so dogs use them as toilets. They are often covered with broken glass and the swings are all too often broken and unusable. So where are children to go?

In dedicated supervised space

We can see from these previous sections that, for many children, supervised space, which is safe from hazards, clean and non-vandalised is virtually the last refuge for the playing child, save the home and garden. For many children, neither of the latter is a real option.

Supervised play space, an adventure playground, a playcentre or an after-school club, can offer children incredible opportunities for access to diversity of experience, self-determination, friends from all types of backgrounds and cultures.

However, the term 'supervised' implies the presence of adults, and this is where the problem I have described throughout this text as 'adulteration' might arise (Else and Sturrock, 1998). What I am proposing is that for many of the children who use them, the supervised play space is not one option, it is the *only* option. The child has no other. This makes supervised play spaces very important to children. They are their sole remaining biological learning ground. This implies that they must be centres of excellence and they must not suffer from adulteration; this is imperative.

Centres of excellence

For some time now it has been recognised that play spaces are compensatory spaces (Hughes, 1996b). That where they are, and what they contain, is intended to compensate local children for the play experiences that are missing in the surrounding area, because of traffic, building density, lack of open space and so on.

In Part I, I explained that we can use spirals and checklists to make comparative measures of available play types, or environmental features to provide us with guidance about what a proposed play environment should contain. For example, if the assessment says that the local home/living environment is flat, the play space needs mounds or access to height; if it says there is concrete and roads everywhere, then children need dirt to play in, to dig in and grow things in.

The supervised play space, has one advantage over the unsupervised play space – it has playworkers. Playworkers, if they are knowledgeable – they know what there is to know about play, and have assessed the play deficits of the local area – can create and upgrade a play space so that it continually addresses children's play needs, as assessed. They will know whether or not they have got it right if the children come and if they do what they, the playworkers, judged they would. In other words, the 'good' playworker is a diagnostic technician, s/he is someone who because of a mixture of experience and knowledge can make informed judgements about what the child, as a young biological organism, will need to meet its developmental requirements. In much the same way as a nutritionist understands the nutritional needs of people, so a playworker understands children's play needs.

This does not mean that all the local children will gravitate to the play space, all the time. A vast number of factors affect children's, as well as adults' behaviour. But what it does mean, where providers recognise the child's right to play and have an understanding of the technical issues that need to be addressed to make a quality presence on the ground, is that it can exist as a resource. And children can be made aware of the existence of the resource, although the final decision about whether to use it or not should always be theirs.

Unfortunately, however technically excellent a play space is, however accurately and sensitively it addresses the needs of the children who use it, its value will be compromised, perhaps lost totally, if it becomes contaminated by the introduction of a non-play agenda, whatever the rationale for it.

Adulteration

This contamination of play spaces and children's play agendas by adults, is becoming known as 'adulteration', after Sturrock (1997). Adulteration can take several forms. Else and Sturrock (1998) cite it as the 'contamination of the play aims and objects of the children by either the wishes of the adult in an urge to "teach" or "educate", simply to dominate, or by the worker's own unplayed out material' (p. 25).

I interpret adulteration to mean the hijacking of the child's play agenda by adults with the intention of substituting it with their own.

Democracy

Inserting democratic processes into the dynamic of a play space is an example of one such adulteration. (Before I begin my discussion, perhaps I should say that, I am a democrat and a supporter of democratic government.)

However, I believe that even democracy has its limitations, and it also has its appropriate environs. Encouraging or manipulating children to adopt democratic processes in play environments is no different, in my view, to expecting them to adopt fascist, communist, Christian, humanist or sado-masochistic practices in play environments. However desirable or undesirable we may believe them to be, they represent an adulteration of the play environment's content, because they would almost certainly not have been present without the intervention of adults (Hughes, 1995: i–ii).

The dynamic in a play space is created by an interaction between children and environment. Obviously, the playworker with all of his or her baggage is a real and legitimate part of that environment. In that context, I would not see it as contradictory, if asked by a child, what his or her political views were, that s/he would tell the child and answer any questions the child might have – honestly and authentically. However, there is a world of difference between the playworker acting as a life resource and the playworker acting as an agent for a particular political ideology.

At its most fundamental level, the play space dynamic is the property of the children, it is nothing to do with the playworker. The playworker is there to facilitate the process, not to dominate it with his or her views. Play spaces are for all children, from all ethnic, economic, mobility, cultural, disability, political and religious backgrounds and it is they who must develop ways of coexisting in these artificial spaces. Certainly the playworker can help this process, by facilitation and occasionally mediating. But if the children are not successful, then it is the mode of provision which has failed and must be thought through again.

It concerns me that, nationally and internationally, adult political ideologies might begin to infiltrate play spaces, posing as legitimate extensions of the UN Convention on the Rights of the Child.

Where children are under the heel of a dictator, or repressed by a military junta, there may be an argument for exposing them to democratic processes whilst at play, although I am undecided. But any play space used for such a purpose would cease to be a play space and would become a school, a place where adults teach children adult ideas. Adult intervention in play should only be made using the strictest of professional guidelines and it is my view that importing democracy onto play spaces would have the effect of breaching such guidelines.

Participation

A similar piece of what is, in my view, inappropriate thinking, is currently being applied to Article 11 of the UN Convention. It states, 'the child has the right to express his or her opinion freely and to have that opinion taken into account in any matter or procedure affecting the child'. There is currently a playwork inter-pretation of this Article that suggests that children should therefore be involved in the design and operation of play spaces. I disagree. Without doubt, children are the planet's play experts, but they are not and should not be expected to be playworkers. The moment children are encouraged to become involved in the design and running of play projects their play process becomes adulterated, i.e. diverted from the random play process onto items on an adult agenda. It does not matter that the agenda is the play space because that is an adult concept anyway. As far as the playworker should be concerned, it is the child's job to play, and the playworker's job is to compensate for any loss of play opportun-ities children experience, by providing the best possible environment for them to play, given current state of knowledge and expertise. Needless to say, if chil-dren involve themselves, without encouragement from adults, then that is their right.

There is one context in which participation is an essential ingredient and that is child-care. There unlike open access provision, children are made to attend by their parents, carers or guardians. They do not have any choice about whether or not they attend, they cannot leave, they are, to all intents and purposes, in custody, until their parents, carers or guardians call again to pick them up.

Here the child's involvement in what is a quasi-play environment – although it might be of very high quality – is critical. If the child is expected to participate in the running of the scheme s/he will at least be able to say whether s/he is happy there, is being well-treated there, and so on. This feedback is both essen-tial to the child's own feelings of empowerment, of feeling that s/he has some sort of control over what is happening in his or her life and to the worker's, who need to know from a welfare perspective whether the children in their charge are suffering.

In a bona fide play space – a space that exists only for the purpose of facilitat-ing play – however, children should, by right, be able to come and go. Although I appreciate that the modern constraints of traffic, etc., have added another layer of complexity to that assumption. Years ago, many children of working parents would have been left to roam the streets, now they are incarcerated for hours a day, for days a week, and for many weeks of the year. It is difficult to know which one is worse. Being left out in all weathers without food or facilities, often in the winter darkness, or confined in a space where everything is run by procedures and standards.

Article 11 talks of the child's right to participate in decisions that might affect them. There are undoubtedly many situations that will directly affect children and in which they have the right to become involved. That is, if becoming involved is seen by the child as an important issue. But in the context of play spaces I think adulteration is occurring. A play project is not school, where teachers, children's councillors and parents may have a legitimate mandate to use that time and space to let children know of their rights. The play space is for play, not for the imposition of an adult agenda, even if it does include information about rights. As I have intimated earlier, if we sanction this form of contamination, it is illogical not to sanction others. The Right to Play in adult-free space, in space uncontaminated by the adult social agenda is *the* fundamental right for children. The contamination of this right by other adult-driven priorities seems to be a denial of that.

Equal opportunities

Here the problem is, whose equal opportunities? Else and Sturrock (1998) identify a similar problem:

> Most playgrounds are situated in areas where there are many cultures in place. The established idea of 'equal opportunity' in playwork has only been primitively understood and should be challenged. As an example, a playground could be seen as meeting this need if it celebrates Diwali as a festival. Our own experience has shown that the play of children from the Indian sub-continent, Hindu and Muslim, uses images, ideas, metaphors, narratives and games that are born out of their particular culture and life-world. (The point we make here is universally applicable to children; we use these particular cultural examples solely to illustrate the point of practice.) The need for containment and return may well reside in the amplification, through the particular culture, of the material being presented. If we fail to recognise this material or terminate or contaminate it with overlaid Eurocentric content, we rupture . . . effective play.
>
> (p. 27)

Should the child from a racist background, who makes racist remarks without knowing what they mean or what potential impact they might have, be denied access to play? Or should that child – simply responding to its play drive – have to endure a talking to, a confrontation, about something s/he is not even aware of? I believe that playworkers have to avoid this superficial judgementalism, unless the child's behaviour, whether it is racist or whatever, is constant, bullying and/or violent. Playworkers should realise that children have to be able to make sense of the world as they see it, as they are learning it, and this applies to all children.

Else and Sturrock (1998) again:

> True equality of opportunity, certainly within the play context, lies in the fullest possible exploration of the child's developing consciousness through the various symbolic and mythic forms it may give utterance to, or create.

True equality of opportunity within the play context is the opportunity to play with other children using whatever language, or perceptions of the world, the child has at hand, learning to gauge, by the reactions of the other children, whether or not a method or mode of interaction is appropriate to his or her needs. Few children want to be friendless, few children want to be avoided or shunned, but it is they who have to learn how, what they say and do, is perceived by other children around them, and make whatever modifications or adjustments they deem necessary. If the playworker becomes involved, and overlays his or her perceptions on the child, then that child will not be able to discover the solution to the problem him or herself, instead s/he will become dependent on the playworker for the way s/he thinks.

It is not enough to recite the mantra of free choice, personal direction and intrinsic motivation, unless one is prepared to adopt it in the most sensitive of circumstances. Playworkers, as difficult as they may find it, must trust that children are equipped to work their way through these issues themselves, with the minimum of adult intervention. It is that trust which makes playwork a tool for development rather than a hegemony of repressive practices and impositions of adult preconceptions, which it has the potential to be.

When I am training playworkers, sometimes they will react to a 'What would you do now?' kind of question, with a response which, although it is portrayed as a joke, implies the use of force, to make a child do something. 'I'd give him a warm ear,' said one of my students. Increasingly I have found myself posing the question to them, 'Would you take the same course of action if the child was, say, 6ft 6ins and weighed 15 stone?' Of course, in general, people would not.

The point I make is that all adults are potential bullies. They know that they can make children change their behaviour by intervening. Sometimes in playwork, this is unavoidable, as I have attempted to illustrate. But in general they should avoid it, particularly when it involves pre-empting children's developing judgement-making processes, by superimposing their own. I cannot stress enough my view that the play space can only be of significant developmental value to the children who use it, if it is allowed to fulfil its function as adult-free space. However well meant, interventions of this kind, whilst they may stop or inhibit all kinds of 'abhorrent' behaviour, contaminate that function and render the space 'adulterated'.

More than democracy, more than participation, more than equal opportunities, the playworker's first motive has to be to ensure that children at play can engage in a developing relationship with the world which is controlled by them. And to be under their control means that playworkers must accept that that includes what children are, from their primeval self, as reflected in Hall's (1904) Recapitulation Theory, to their contemporary self.

Needless to say, playworkers in local government or voluntary sector employment will still have to engage with various policy initiatives, like equal opportunities, irrespective of the ethical implications for the work they do. It is difficult to be sure about the correct course to take in this context.

I have always argued that there are deeper biological forces at work on the play space, which cannot be effectively mediated by the kind of all-pervading policy that equal opportunities, for example, reflects. Play space exists to do a job. It cannot do it if work-space culture is applied, any more than a hospital could do its job if normal house rules were applied.

Chapter 11

Is the play space working?

Over the years numerous criteria have been used to evaluate the success or otherwise of play projects. Some are understandably keen on the 'bums on seats' school of measurement, whilst others rely more on esoteric criteria, like 'It feels right', or 'The children had a good time'.

So what is it that makes a project, a supervised play space, successful?

There is no one criterion that can encapsulate or capture success. Play environments are notoriously fickle entities.

Numbers

Numbers are important, but should be seen rather as a barometer of successfully applied playwork than as a simple measure of success or failure.

If the play space is sited in an area where there are few children, then however good it is, numerically it will not be very convincing. If, on the other hand, it is in an area in which there is a high birth rate and lots of young families, then however bad it is, it will still probably attract a lot of children, simply on the basis that it is somewhere to go.

Assuming that the size of the space and the staffing and resource levels were appropriate, my own numerical ideal would be that I would expect that for half the time the space was open, it would be regarded by local children as significant enough to have a representation of the local child population of between 80–120 children. That is with about one-third of an acre, three staff and an intelligent budget, which catered for consumables, replacements and environmental development.

The other half of the time I would expect usage to be of much more of the 'drop-in' type, where children come to chat, to see their mates, to have a bit of quiet time – a slow period, a more conscious sensory and reflective period.

(As a child I would sometimes use our outdoor swimming pool, three times a day, each session had a personality of its own. My favourite was the virtually empty morning session when the water was clear, the air was sharp and a few of us would relish the luxury of being able to dive for coins and just enjoy the glint of the sun on the water, or the strangeness of swimming in the rain.

The afternoon session was a more classical play period, with lots of other children and involved games of tag, dive bombing and water chase.

Evenings were more mythical. The water temperature had often risen throughout the day and the pool was now populated by lots of adults, who made big noises, big splashes and big waves. We all joined in, but it was their time, more than ours. Needless to say, there were times when we were doing other things and did not go swimming, and there were other times when it was too cold or too wet to go.)

Like that swimming pool, play spaces should not by necessity be seen as spaces that have to have an intensive, round-the-clock usage. The whole process becomes too automated and stops being exciting if it does. I do appreciate the need felt to maximise a resource, but that is not always done successfully by filling it up all the time. As with the swimming pool, children can get very different experiences from the same space at different times. Many factors – space, light, weather, noise levels – affect our perceptions and the resulting value we put on an experience and the benefits we consequently draw from it. It is a very impoverished view that only evaluates anything on the basis of the numbers attending.

However, as I have said, numbers do count. The play space must be being used or else its existence is pointless.

Atmosphere

Another criterion of success is the quality of the changing atmosphere of the space. If the atmosphere is simply changing from dread to anxiety to fear, obviously something is seriously wrong. If, on the other hand, the space feels too well managed, too smooth, too predictable and passive, then equally something may be wrong.

Playworkers have to be clear about what they are dealing with here and what a play space is intended for. Children are not generally dangerous *or* passive. They are lively, argumentative, inquiring, frustrating, micky-taking, scary, beautiful, compassionate, mind-bendingly funny and painfully scathing, and the atmosphere should be a flexible encapsulation of these and many other characteristics. That is when the playworker knows that s/he has freedom in action in the play space. However, playworkers do need to assess this over weeks, rather than days, as the swimming pool example illustrates. Keeping a diary is helpful; writing down how the place feels, assess their own effect, noting the weather, the play types, what might be on TV, will all help the playworker's awareness of what makes the space work and what does not.

The play space should not always be the same. Individual playworker's environmental modification and the children's playful interaction with it should ensure that.

At Playgrounds A and C, the attendance shot up and down like dysfunctional blood pressure. There were manic days, frightening days and relaxed, beautiful days, which in totality were a good example of the ecstasy of variety, no two days were ever the same. If it began to feel a bit flat, we would ask: Is it us, are we getting tired or bored? Is it the children, are they just coming here because it is easy? Is it the space, are we suffering from not being able to see the wood for the trees?

That interrogation would normally lead us to conclude that we had taken our eye off the ball a bit and that we needed to re-engage. It is worth pointing out, as any parent will confirm, that looking after lots of children is very tiring, especially over long school holidays, and the playworker will occasionally lose the plot. The skill is in knowing this can happen and in realising when it is happening, so s/he can do something about it. In my experience re-engagement is often accompanied by an exhilarating feeling of freshness.

The flow of modification

Another useful indicator of success is the existence of an increase in the intensity and frequency of activity by the children during and after modification. Playworkers engage in environmental modification because it increases the level of novel foci available to the children's play drive, and modification should result in an upswing of new activity as a result.

Environments engage children hierarchically. If we create a scale of engagement from, say, 0 to 5, with 0 equalling no engagement and 5 equalling total engagement, the hierarchy would look something like this:

Scale point	Level of engagement	Affect	Locomotion
0	None	Bored	None
1	Minimal	Attending	Extremities/static
2	Minor	Interested	Whole body/static
3	Significant	Enquiring	Moderate mobile
4	Interruptable	Happy/absorbed	Fast and free
5	Total	Invigorated/exhilarated	As necessary

Figure 11.1 The engagement hierarchy.

Earlier (see page 51), I described play as a way of learning by absorption, where the play experience envelopes the child and becomes the child's world, for as long as the experience is 'active'.

Note that it is not until Scale point 4 that I would expect a child to be absorbed sufficiently in a play experience, for any, hitherto, unknown ingredients of that experience to be sensed and retained by the child. So a play environment would have to have a high level of attraction and engagement before it was performing the function for which it is intended.

For, although some children come to play spaces in total play mode, many others have things other than playing in the forefront of their minds. These interfere with the successful flow of their play drive – home, school problems, the potential for being bullied and so on, all play their part as interferers.

Although these domestic and personal issues can act to divert children, their drive to play is very powerful, and good modification can have the effect of deflecting interfering problems and re-focusing children's attention on the activity and affect of playing instead.

Any good play environment will contain an infinite number of 'potential' play experiences, which lie hidden, in the same way different images are a part of the background in many children's puzzles. However, these potential experiences will not be 'activated' unless the child is able physically or psychologically to cross the environmental interface that separates him or her from them. The action of modification provides a physical and psychological catalyst that stimulates engagement and triggers sensory and affective engagement. A high enough level of stimulation will enable the child to continue on his or her own, because interferers have been successfully replaced with characteristics of the play drive instead; spontaneity or intrinsic motivation, for example.

The term 'the flow of modification' addresses that outcome. As modification and the children engage, so an activity transaction begins between them, which, as the child is absorbed, escalates in speed and intensity until the child is able to 'spin off' and engage in activity of his or her own choosing. In this sense, modification is the engine that drives a successful play space, and the degree to which modification can overcome the blocking power of any interferers depends on its own novelty relevance/value as perceived by the children.

Modification is context specific in this sense. To undertake modification without assessing need is nonsensical. The form modification takes, in terms of its scale, its location, its potential for novelty and perceived attraction, given children's current experience, is critical to its success.

The playworker

The final indicators of success are determined by what happens in the physical and psychological space that separates the playworker and the children. What playworkers transmit across that space, how they do it, and whether and how children reciprocate, provide critical indications of the health of the project and of its usefulness to children.

This space has been alluded to in a number of ways over the years. It has some resonance with Winnicott's 'potential space' (Ogden, 1993: 223), and Heidegger referred to a similar idea as the clearing or 'lichtung', (Sturrock, 1997). In reality, it is a *triple interface (3ti)* where three different realities meet – the playworker's, the child's and the environment's, each one projecting its own characteristics onto the other two.

However for the purposes of this text, I intend to restrict my discussion to the interrelationship between the playworker and the child, expressed as *(2ti)*.

As with the scale of engagement, the relationship between these two individual entities is not linear; it is more cyclical, like the spirals. By this I mean that, rather than having a scale of say 0–5, measuring from nothing to everything, on this cyclical scale 0 and 5 are at the same point. Some likely playwork approaches are discussed below.

1 The indifferent approach

I had been asked to meet with a number of adults who were working with children who had suffered indirectly from the Omagh bombing, in August 1998. People were concerned about the most appropriate way to relate to the children in a play context. The idea of good playwork as 'perceived indifference' developed from the notion of distance supervision as described in Hughes (1996b), and from conversations I had with a number of colleagues around that time.

Perceived indifference describes the hoped for effect of appearing to be busy doing other things whilst sensitised to a particular situation, i.e., that although the playworker may give the impression of being otherwise engaged, his or her total concentration would be focused on the children and their 'state'. The rationale being that by using this approach, particularly in this type of context, affected children would feel able to go about their own business without feeling overlooked, that their privacy would be breached or that they would be interrupted, whilst in the full knowledge that if they did need an intervention from a playworker, it would happen.

The inference we can draw is that in a high quality play project, unless conditions dictate otherwise, there is no need for a continual transaction between playworker/child and child/playworker, across the (2ti) between them. It should be implicit from the atmosphere and the playworkers' professionalism that they are there for the children, and they want the children to feel free to play and not feel that need to continually refer back to the them for approval, reassurance or any other form of adult-positive feedback. So their own input into the (2ti) is actually of very high quality, although it is implicit rather than explicit.

So, although the 'perceived indifference' has a (2ti) = 0 on the scale of child/playworker interaction, it is actually an indicator of a high quality child/playworker relationship and denotes a flow, which is primarily child $\rightarrow$ playworker, in direction.

Level of child/playworker interaction	Perceived nature of interaction	Quality of child/playworker relationship
0	Indifferent	High
1	Repressive	Poor
2	Nosy	Poor
3	Functional	Better
4	Enthusiastic	Good
5	Controlled Authentic	High

Figure 11.2 The relationship between the playworker and the child.

2 The repressive approach

Adopting this approach probably means that the playworker is either frightened of the children, or of the context. I include it because I think that most playworkers do find themselves in this mode from time to time – tiredness and feeling unsupported are probably the main causes.

For example, my employers on one of the projects I operated said that, if I was assaulted in the course of my work, they would not prosecute my attacker. It was not so much their refusal to prosecute that made me feel deflated. It was that by saying it, I felt valueless – that they just could not care less.

However, the playworker should be under no illusions. S/he must prepare for times when it feels as if it is just the team and the children – an oasis in a jungle – when nobody else wants to know. As well as looking after a large number of children, playworkers may have to deal with violent men and women walking onto the project, drunks, people urinating in front of the children, boy racers driving at speed through or adjacent to the project, police with dogs charging in chasing a runaway, frightening everyone half to death, violent parents, older brothers and sisters, even irate religious leaders, without any realistic support from any source. It can be madness, and when playworkers feel alone and unsupported, it is hardly surprising that they get grumpy from time to time, when it all gets a bit much.

My own experience of the repressive approach is that it is very transitory, passes quickly and happens to most workers from time to time. And whilst incidents like those I have mentioned do happen, they are balanced, if not overwhelmed, by the positive nature of the work.

During the repressive approach, a playworker might catch him or herself in survival mode, saying 'don't' and 'no' far more than s/he means, simply because being there is not engaging and energising him or her. Then it is a bad space to be in. It feels bad for the playworker and is obviously not good for the children either. The play space might be the only refuge they have, the only place they have a name other than 'Oy', the only place they can go without the fear of being hit or humiliated, so it is debilitating for everyone when it happens.

Even mildly repressive interaction manifests itself as low quality child/playworker relationship. If children come to the play space to play and because the playworker feels insecure or vulnerable find their play being continually interrupted, or controlled by the playworker, it will be a disempowering and frustrating experience for the children, and they will probably react badly.

Rather than the high quality interaction implicit in the previous category, the interaction here will be low quality, scoring $(2ti) = 1$ because it denotes a flow that is mainly playwork $\rightarrow$ child, in direction.

3 The nosy approach

Playworkers fall into the trap of the nosy approach – what is called 'infantile toxicity' in Else and Sturrock (1998) – when they think they are one of the children. When they unwittingly force themselves into children's conversations, or into their spaces, and when the children are either too polite or compassionate to ask the playworker to go away. Neither repression, in this context, or nosiness are particularly adulterative, because they are short lived, but nosiness is intrusive, can be dominating and has to be resisted.

A lot of play space activity is intimate and private. This should not just be an illusion on the part of the children, it should be a reality – i.e. playworkers really should respect the child's space. Children do not want to be overheard when they are interacting and negotiating. If they want to do it in front of a playworker they will. If playworkers are just passing through, they will not mind that either, but to try to become a part of what is going on between children can be an embarrassing distraction for them.

Ideally the relationship between the children and the playworker should reflect a recognition of the children's *and* the playworker's integrity. Because this category does not differentiate between a playworker being friends with the children, but not being one of them, I regard the nosy approach as poor with a $(2ti) = 2$ score, because it denotes a flow that is mainly playworker $\rightarrow$ child in direction.

4 The functional approach

The functional approach describes the occasions when the playworker is working well, but going through the motions rather than allowing him or herself to be drawn into what is going on. Like the repressive approach this might also be a sign of tiredness or, worse still, of burn-out. Even the best playworkers get to this point. Probably the worst aspect of this mode is that modification slows down or drops out of the work programme. The children are fine and the playworker is fulfilling all of the legal obligations, etc., but the dynamism, which is normally the result of the dynamic between the playworker, the children, and the space, is lost to some extent.

This is a mode that needs monitoring. It can be short lived, but it can be a sign of losing interest or needing support. This category describes a better quality relationship between the children and the playworker on a day-to-day basis than either the repressive or nosy modes and scores $(2ti) = 3$, because it denotes a reciprocal flow, child $\rightleftharpoons$ playworker.

However, if the functional approach is being caused by tiredness or worse still, lack of enthusiasm, it could soon decay into a poor $(2ti) = 1$ relationship instead, because the flow could change from one which is reciprocal, i.e. $\rightleftharpoons$, to one which is playworker $\rightarrow$ child in direction.

5 The enthusiast approach

The enthusiast is born, not made. S/he is the animator. S/he cannot stand and watch, but is neither nosy nor repressive. The enthusiast, like an inventor, has child-like characteristics that both children and adults find infectious. S/he is constantly making things happen, finding things that can be used, doing things and engaging in banter with the children.

However, the enthusiast can run the risk of presuming ownership of the space, in a way that no other playwork approach will.

For example, for the playworker, whose (2ti) = 0, the (2ti) represents the playworker as the confident 'loner', as someone who feels s/he only needs to play a servicing role in the interactions between the children. In many circumstances this will be the ideal compensatory response, where a play space is provided, because of a recognition of the need for an interesting space for children to play.

For the playworker whose (2ti) = 1 or 2, his or her (2ti) represents either a lack of confidence in, or understanding of, the playworker's role. Because of this, both modes represent a negative, rather than a positive, input from the playworker. For although they recognise that the play space is the child's space, as does the (2ti) = 0, they are too present, too in the children's faces to be making a high quality input.

Perhaps the major flaw with the (2ti) = 4, playworker is that the play space itself reflects an extension of their need to play. Not like the (2ti) = 2 playworker, where the children themselves are mistakenly perceived as playmates, but where the space itself is perceived as personal territory and where structures and other play space characteristics may be jealously preserved and guarded against marauding children.

Although often a 'great' playworker, the (2ti) = 4, is more leader than facilitator, is more gang leader than playworker and as a result can become a source of dependency because s/he is so strong and has a tendency to take over.

I have known several (2ti) = 4 playworkers over the years. They have been practically minded, almost genius inventors and improvisers, with a huge talent for motivating children. But they still fall short of the ideal, simply because although a large part of their (2ti) is reciprocal, $\rightleftharpoons$, there is still too much of a tendency for the flow to be in the playworker $\rightarrow$ child direction. Perhaps one reason for this is that they do not value either analysis or reflection of what is actually happening enough to step back and conclude that it is less about what they want and more about what the children are driven to do.

One veteran who springs to mind sees play in quite simple terms and sees her function as a catalyst in the context of construction and other interactions. I understand the viewpoint, but as my IMEE acronym implies, there is more to playwork than what is reduced from our own personal feelings. Like the rest of us, children operate on many different intellectual and psychic levels, and providing our own level alone, however resourceful it may be perceived initially, is limiting rather than liberating in the end.

Having said that, if every play project was operated by (2ti) = 4 playworkers, it would ensure that children who attended those play spaces would have access to very creative and inventive minds and high quality playwork. And whilst play spaces operated by these individuals are not as subtle as those operated by playworkers whose (2ti) scores 0 or 6, they often normally provide very visible examples of good playwork practice, particularly from the perspective of modification. So, even though the actual quality of their intervention may not be as high as some, the visible impact of their playwork is considerable.

6 The controlled authentic approach

Perhaps the major difference between this mode and that where (2ti) = 0 – the controlled indifferent playworker – is in the outcome of their analysis of compensation. The perceived indifferent approach only works well in two situations. Where children are confidently engaged with one another or their environment and only rarely need an intervention from the playworker, or where children are highly traumatised and may need a covert, i.e., indifferent presence initially, rather than one that is interactive.

However, like the 'enthusiast', the playworker who is 'controlled authentic' is in the thick of things but the balance of input is always biased towards the children and their needs. So at worst, the nature of their (2ti) is $\rightleftharpoons$, and, at best, it is in the direction of child $\rightarrow$ playworker.

This mode is both facilitative and empowering. It is facilitative because it allows for children who have lost some of their skill to interact playfully. That is, it recognises that many children are dysfunctional to a greater or lesser degree because freedom to play is very limited in some circumstances, and that some children are losing interactive skill and physical motivation.

It is empowering, because the controlled authentic playworker will be looking for signs of improved confidence, or an increasing desire to retake the initiative and – perhaps, unlike the enthusiast – will unselfishly relinquish any control and pass it back to the child, by stepping back, or moving on from that interaction.

The difference in the quality of the (2ti) space, between the perceived indifferent and the controlled authentic approaches, is dictated by differences in how they express their concern for the children. The former is implicit and the latter explicit. The concern expressed in the former is perhaps quieter and more reserved than the latter, who may be a more joyful and personally expressive person.

The children, in knowing they are cared about, either by the freedom they are given or by the quality of the interaction they share, are secure and able to engage in whatever play type their own drive wishes. This means that the play space is truly compensating for the absence or loss of wild, adult-free space.

Conclusion

Most playworkers are amalgams of several of these modes and manifest them at different times. Certainly I have been scared and repressive and feeling out of my depth; I have been the nosy child and the tired functionalist. Part of me wishes that I had been the enthusiast but that would have required a level of ingenuity and creativity to which I regrettably cannot aspire, although I have had the privilege of knowing playworkers who did.

Summary of Part II

Part II is unavoidably more esoteric than Part I, dealing as it does with more complex and contentious issues at the root of what playwork may or may not be. It attempts to look inside the player's head and to imagine, with the help of respected texts, what might be going on. It also wrestles with the notions of constructs and the impact of environmental stimulation on the child.

In Chapter 10 it explores the child in the play space in the context of the other children who may inhabit it too, and expresses concern about the potential 'adulteration' of children's experience by the adult's input. Although this chapter may appear deliberately provocative, it is not intended to be so. The fears expressed by me are genuine and the result of many hours of reflection. I remain deeply concerned that in our attempts to protect and support we forget the nature of the world children are entering and the true, rather primitive nature of children's play.

The thrust of Chapter 11 is that the playworker, like the child, is an amalgamation of factors, some good, some not so good. In the final analysis it is up to the playworker and the rest of the team to monitor each playworker's practice and provide supportive but analytical feedback about the quality of what they do.

Part III

Evolutionary playwork and reflective analytic practice

What you are doing for children is as necessary to changing things in their favour as rebellion is to politics and storms to the physical world.

Paraphrasing Thomas Jefferson, who drew up the American Constitution in 1787

Chapter 12

The idea

At the beginning of Part I I wrote, 'Evolutionary playwork is a new and developing discipline. As yet it has no agreed theoretical or practical base', and even though in Parts I and II, I have tried to 'capture' my own playwork feelings, insights and experiences, I still feel that a comprehensive articulation of what playwork is and does is some way off, although some new developments in thinking are undoubtedly underway.

However, what the two previous Parts do hopefully demonstrate is that there is a great deal more to playwork thinking and practice, than familiarity with a small amount of what has become known as 'underpinning knowledge', and the ability to implement equal opportunities and child protection policies.

However, becoming better informed and more investigative about playwork still does not appear to be the general thrust of what is happening in the training and education offered to playworkers in many settings. Recently, for example, I saw the breakdown of an 'introduction to playwork' course offered by a large local authority. The primary focus of the course was on different modes and rationales of intervention into the child's world. Play and playwork were only peripheral ingredients, whilst the ubiquitous equal opportunities, together with behavioural management, health and safety, child protection and first aid, were the dominant features.

One can appreciate that fear of litigation might be partly to blame for this peculiar emphasis, but I cannot imagine a course on anaesthesia or particle physics being so strangely weighted. Certainly from the perspective of civilisation and legality, playworkers like everyone else, have an obligation to be aware of their legal and other constraints and requirements, but this information can be provided in other ways. I cannot imagine a ten-week maths course, where maths figured for a day or a week and the rest of the time was devoted to issues that although important were peripheral to maths itself. A student might be forgiven for concluding that the tutor did not know much about maths.

Playwork, the craft of appropriate intervention and modification in children's play, has by definition, to be a huge area of thought and practice, because it involves the interaction of two of the most complex entities we know, the human child and the environment it which it plays. And yet, as I write, although I know many playworkers who provide 'good' environments for children, and who do everything they can to ensure that their intervention is appropriate, it is impossible for them to know whether or not they are being effective, from a playwork perspective. Simply because we neither have the theoretical models nor the practical confirmation of what being effective means to make that possible.

Playwork needs a great deal more thought and research about what it is and what it does before it can claim that it has anything more than a holding role for parents or a distraction or entertainment role for children.

Personally, I want playwork practice and thinking to play a major part in informing us all about the priorities we can choose to have and the kind of society and community we want to live in. I believe that playwork has a great power for good for our species and for the habitats we share with every other living thing. However, it will never exert this role unless it can demonstrate to non-playworkers that it has a unique perspective on life that others perceive as desirable and valuable. This will not happen until we demonstrate a greater depth of thought and analysis of practice than we currently do. And this will not happen, in my opinion, unless thinking and striving to understand are seen as a vital and essential part of what being a playworker entails.

This means that playworkers need to spend a part of their time focusing on and analysing all of those areas of playwork which currently remain unexplored; and that is most of it! This means that playworkers, as an integral part of their working day or week, are going to have to do what children do daily in playing, when they launch themselves at the future. Playworkers are going to have to learn to take psychic as well as physical risks, to step into the unknown, into the void, in order to begin to understand what it is we are engaged in, and what it is we are doing. Then it will have to be written down, made sense of and then exposed to the criticism of appropriate peers. Only then will it constitute a legitimate development in playwork.

Reflective analytic practice is the process through which I believe we can achieve that end. Unless we begin, what will inevitably be a difficult and demanding personal and professional journey, playwork will remain an intellectually impoverished discipline.

The essence of reflective analytic playwork (RAP) is that by deep reflection on the literature, on what we see and know as playworkers and by analysis and synthesis of what that reflection exposes, we can begin to answer a range of important questions. For example:

- what is happening when children play?
- what is happening at the interface, where child and environment meet?
- what is in what I do, for the children?
- what does my practice exist to change?
- why do I do what I do, in this way?
- what difference do I make?
- what are the effects of play-deprivation and/or inappropriate play experiences?

By so doing we move our general thinking on from what is primarily a contemporary social or sociological interventionist analysis, which has little or no grounding in the literature, to one which is informed by a kind of timeless biological thinking.

However, I feel I should emphasise the effort, rigour, discipline and focus that need to be brought to bear and the depth to which individual thinking needs to go, from my own experience, before a view which is transcendent of our current general position regarding the role and importance of play can even begin to evolve. It is not enough peripherally to explore ideas. RAP requires that we take ourselves to the limits of our knowledge and experience and this can be a painful, difficult and frightening process. (It should also be noted that RAP requires a far deeper level of immersion in thought than the other reflective tool, IMEE, that is outlined in Part I and in Hughes (1996b).)

So this, Part III, is an attempt to capture some of the thoughts and illusive ideas that have been sparked off by my own journey from an interventionist style of practice, rooted in the imperatives of social engineering, community development, child-care, crime and social exclusion, to one in which playwork is alternatively defined more in the context of play as a mediator of physical and psychic well-being; as a maximiser of children's developmental potential, and as a facilitator of adaptive and evolutionary skills.

The original term 'reflective analytic *playwork*' literally evolved out of a series of long telephone conversations between Gordon Sturrock and myself, over the winter of 1996–7. The conversations were generated by attempts to begin to develop an embryonic understanding, from a playwork perspective, of some of the processes underlying the development of sectarianism in Northern Ireland – I was working on the issue in Northern Ireland at the time.

Neither of us was particularly clear about the implications of such a term, but we suspected that it could be used to describe a process that involved playworkers reflectively immersing themselves in playwork at such a depth, that new and important insights regarding the mechanisms and motivations behind it would begin to emerge. I was studying for a Master's Degree in Playwork Development Studies at the time and was actually engaging in this kind of thinking process on a daily basis.

Two useful definitions that helped us as playworkers to better understand how sectarianism worked were the immediate result of the discussions between us, but the longer term benefit was a realisation that deep reflection on the problems of playwork is very productive and enlightening.

The power of RAP seems to rest upon a combination of three things:

1   the ability of the playworker to bring his or her contemplative and regressive skills to bear upon a 'What if this was happening/or had happened to me?', kind of problem
2   the ability of the playworker to locate, digest and study material relevant to this problem from the literature

3   the ability of the playworker to craft an analysis of the two, producing either a practical playwork solution or greater clarity to a difficult theoretical area.

If, for example, we are attempting to better understand an event or incident prior to the application of a playwork strategy, the child's observed or related experience is first reflected on, then it is put into a personal frame where the playworker asks, for example, 'How would I have felt/what would I have done', in a similar context, creating a form of paradigm shift?

This requires the playworker to go into what I would describe as a contemplative and regressive mode. To do this the playworker must undergo what I have called immersion, approximating what Meares (1993) calls 'being lost in thought'. 'Immersion' in this case means allowing oneself, through focused concentration, to become sensitising to an imagined scenario to such an extent that one feels surrounded by it, or by a part of it. Some years ago, for example, I attempted to imagine what it was like to be a child climbing up through the branches of a tall tree. I tried to imagine the scene actually unfolding through the child's eyes, from the child's physical perspective. The result was an extraordinary regressive period, during which recall of what felt like 'real' tree-climbing experiences from my own childhood, began to come to the surface of my consciousness (Hughes, 1993).

One remarkable aspect of RAP is that it can have the effect of opening up long-forgotten sensory and affective childhood play events, which in themselves – particularly from the perspective of a playworker – can be fascinating. It is, however, equally remarkable that these emergent episodes and their imagined approximations can be utilised to enable the playworker to experience a real or imagined equivalent experience to that which the child has undergone. *Not in the cockpit with the child, but certainly flying in parallel!*

RAP works best if the playworker concentrates on imagining being in an approximate situation to that of the child. Obviously, we are not that child, in that situation, and at best, we can only approximate her or his experience, particularly when it is not an experience we have ever known first hand.

The problem the playworker may be trying to clarify or solve could be as complex as any in medicine, or science, but as we do not have a vast number of case histories or appropriate measuring instruments, we have to find appropriate means of making informed guesses at what might have happened to the child instead, and then add our own empathic input to personalise it, arrive at a playwork diagnosis and hopefully a practical playwork solution.

We *do* have the advantage of being able to access an increasing amount of scientific data that are relevant to our needs and, so, our emergent episodes or imagined approximations can often be supported by findings in the literature.

Needless to say, the only child we can truly access (and only then with practice) is the memory of the one we were, and even then the only reactions to similar events we might be able to recall will almost certainly be masked and distorted by the passage of time. However, the combination of reflection and analysis, including the literature, does provide us with useful results, which however primitive, give us some limited guidance regarding what might be happening to a particular child in a particular space, or when particular phenomena occur.

Although the actual term 'reflective analytic practice' was only born in 1996, I was using the process of 'problem immersion' as a device for helping me to understand what I interpreted as the effect of environments on children's play, as early as the mid 1980s, following my work with Hank Williams. Then it was intended to help in the development of a theoretical model for play which, it was hoped, would make sense from the playwork practitioner's perspective. I have continued using the process ever since.

Chapter 13

Reflective analytic practice
Some examples

What follows are several different examples of some of my own results from RAP, together with some contemporary commentary on them. Several of these examples are unfinished or incomplete – sketches or doodles rather than full blown portraits or mindscapes – whilst others attempt to provide, if not a comprehensive analysis of a particular area of interest, then at least a 'best shot' at doing so.

They are ideas, and should not be read with the intention of obtaining answers, but should be seen, rather as attempts at making explorative journeys. I offer them in the hope that reflective analytic practice will serve as a useful tool that will, along with the efforts of others, enable playwork theory and practice to evolve further.

RAP Example 1 (c. 1989)

Built environmental effects on instinctive and intuitive play outcomes – some reflections

Human beings exist at both conscious and sub-conscious levels, and play behaviours reflect each of these levels. They are:

1   Play that is driven by conscious need, which I will call instinctive play; for example, rough and tumble, role play, logical play and calibration.
2   Play that comes from sub-conscious need, which I will call intuitive play; for example, fantasy, symbolic and deep play.

Instinctive play encourages children to engage in those features of the environment that will enhance their ability to survive in the here and now. It shows them how to cope with the present. Whilst intuitive play encourages children to engage those ingredients of the environment that will enhance their capacity to understand the most esoteric and spiritual aspects of life. It shows them how to shape the future.

In ideal circumstances playing would create a balance between instinctive and intuitive play behaviours, producing knowledge and skills relating broadly both to conscious and sub-conscious needs in equal amounts. However, there are circumstances in which an imbalance between these instinctive and intuitive play behaviours might occur naturally. Some children may simply be more instinctive or more intuitive, for example.

Having said that though, it feels to me that if the environment in which these children play can offer them an optimum range and level of experience, then their own internal biasing will not necessarily be of a negative nature.

However, it is not the suggested naturally occurring imbalance between these two play forms which is the focus of this essay. What is, is the potential imbalance in the 'whole' environment in which children have to play and its possible effects upon the natural imbalance.

I can think of four main scenarios of environmental imbalance:

Type 1 Over-positive (Note, this category was later called 'indulged')

An environment in which the range of experience is biased towards the positive. Where children only feel fulfilled, happy, optimistic, successful and secure.

Type 2 Over-negative (Note, this category was later called 'desensitised')

An environment in which the range of experience is biased towards the negative. Where children only feel pain, sadness, anger, revenge, fear and failure.

Type 3 Unpredictable (Z1) (Note, this category was later called 'erratic')

An environment containing erratic and destabilising levels of stimulation, where the creation of behavioural strategies is continually being undermined by changes in the environment.

Type 4 Low-level (Z2) (Note, this category was later called 'dehumanised')

An environment where the level of available information is below the optimum, in which some children might find themselves turning inwards as a compensation for the lack of stimulation in their external environment. These environments all exist in the real world and access to them is therefore a real possibility for some children.

What I am proposing is that some of these environments will have a profound and perhaps detrimental effect on some of the children who play in them and not on the others. This is because some of these environments actually reflect or respond to the nature of the specific play types referred to above and react, for example, to physical or dramatic behaviour almost to the exclusion of any other.

For example, because they exist as a series of tangible events, over-positive and over-negative environments will have an amplifying or inflating effect upon a child's conscious condition and thus on his or her instinctive play behaviour.

Whereas, because they only exist as intangible events of emotion and mood, unpredictable and/or low-level environments will have an intensifying effect upon the child's sub-conscious condition and thus on his or her intuitive play behaviour.

If this is so, then children who play in, for example, over-negative environments, and whose personal play preferences are instinctive, would run the risk of becoming more violent than otherwise.

Part of this effect can be shown to some extent in the work of Harlow and Suomi (1971), Einon *et al.* (1978) and Zuckerman (1984), who demonstrate a resulting tendency in those affected by chronic negative input, towards anti-social and violent behaviour. However, although there is no recorded initial preference for hostility in the subject in these studies, I would suggest that a combination of preference and environmental hostility might well enhance the original environmental effect, yielding an offensively violent person.

Although I know of no data relating to the effect of over-positive environments on behaviour, it is conceivable that the instinctive child who had, for example, unlimited access to consumer goods, might have his or her preference inflated by that environment. Preference and access might lead to a defence of this over-positive space, which could eventually lead to violence, although, in this example, the violence would be motivated by defence rather than the offence of the over-negative child.

Biased environments like these may be a problem for us all. However, I suspect that they are particularly insidious for those of us whose play preference is the real world, creating in those affected the potential for behaviour ranging from negative and positive extremes.

The combined potential effect of the unpredictable or low-level environment, and intuitive play behaviours taking place in it, gives cause for even greater concern. In order to develop behavioural strategies, human beings seem to need a consistent and reliable input of information provided at an optimum level. If either of these criteria cannot be applied, then serious problems arise for those who are affected. To all intents and purposes we are talking about the effects of sensory deprivation or sensory confusion and, at worst, a kind of dehumanisation.

Suomi and Harlow (1971) speak of bizarre behaviour; McKinney *et al.* (1973) of psychosis; Rosenzweig *et al.* (1962, 1971, 1972) and Bennett *et al.* (1964) discuss changes in brain size and activity and Heron (1957) talks of hallucinations.

What seems likely is that playing in unpredictable or low-level environments is dangerous for all humans. I contend that it will, however, be of greater danger to those whose behaviour is more internally driven in the first place, if, as I suspect, its effect is to further internalise that behaviour, into fantasy, neurotic and sociopathic behaviour – turning the child into a major participant in life horror movie.

The argument for the widest possible choice in terms of accessib.~ μιαy experiences has always been strong on experiential grounds. If these reflections have any substance in reality, they provide an additional impetus for the need for choice, variety and alternatives in play to be made available by the playworker. (An appropriate shift in the emphasis of social policy, towards providing the resources for good play provision wherever there are children, would not only make playwork more effective, it would enable adult communities to have a more holistic perception of their children – viewing them as biological organisms, as well as social entities.)

Commentary/discussion

The environment has been a constant theme throughout my time as a playworker. Initially, I only saw it as benign, although sometimes difficult and demanding in terms of its terrain and obstacles. But the combination of the scientific literature, my childhood and professional experiences with children and my developing ability to project myself into an imagined situation, made me realise just what insidious power some environments have.

I like the idea of different play types not just having different experiential functions, but having totally different roles in terms of consciousness. However, my idea that some play types engage the sub-conscious and some the conscious, has been somewhat superseded by evolutionary ideas informed, in particular, by Ken Wilber's, (1996) writings. Writing today, I would probably still suggest that the primary role of some play types, e.g., rough and tumble, may be to enable the development of survival skills, but for others I am tempted to see their role as evolutionary and transcendent, rather than simply informing the sub-conscious, which might be a retrograde step in the role of play in evolution.

It is interesting that some of the play types or processes mentioned here do not appear in the Taxonomy I devised seven years later.

The notion that the environment, particularly the indulgent environment, could have such devastating consequences, was quite a shock. Naturally, I had experience of children who could not only do no wrong, but who never knew what it was to want, or wait, who were loud, rude and bullying. But even the possible connection between being immersed in this pampered space and the genesis of emotionless violence, was frightening and made me doubt the authenticity of my own conclusions.

This is not to say that indulged children become sociopathic. It is more subtle than that. Rather, what I am implying is that the nature of the environment we play in changes us. And that, when a number of ingredients come together, i.e. chronic parental indulgence, effortless gratification and, say, chronic adulteration, a perception of the world may be developed that begins to include disdain, lack of respect and violence experiments.

What is also interesting is the idea that indulgence *and* neglect can both result in similar violent outcomes.

The most depressing outcome of these postulated environmental types, however, is the one I label Z2. The advent of the opportunity to shut oneself away for hours on end, in a world that is totally controlled either by manufacturers or personal whim, with tapes, CDs, mobile phones, computer games, leads us to prefer this escape to the more difficult and demanding world of unpredictability and apparent loss of control. This feels like a more de-humanising route, with low levels of stimulation, which may increasingly move children into dream and fantasy states, where, as I have mentioned earlier, the line between reality and un-reality may become blurred, and where perversion and cruelty are behavioural norms.

RAP Example 2 (c. 1998)

Play and individual neophilic potential matrices and the evolution of consciousness

I believe that every child, at birth, perhaps even at conception, is endowed with the potential to pass through stages of development in turn, to reach their optimum personal developmental level. However, like a seed with the potential to produce a flower or a tree, conditions need to be appropriate for any of this to happen, for each stage of that flower's or tree's development to be reached and then transcended into the next developmental stage.

However, because each human being is different, each may have their own personal formula for appropriate conditions for developmental transcendence to happen. Morris (1967) described human beings as neophilic, i.e. as fascinated by the novel and new. This caused me to reflect on the possibility that each of us might have a personal neophilic matrix, a genetically determined formula of types and intensities of sensory stimuli, appealing to us alone.

If this is so, and we are all in possession of an 'individual neophilic potential matrix' (INPM), that is, a matrix of stimuli and groups of stimuli that reflect our individual personality and which appeal to us specifically, then development or evolution on an individual level may be a function of the drive behind that INPM. This would be the play drive, plus the range of compatibility of our INPM to be found around us in our individual neophilic context (INC), i.e. in the play environment.

It could be stated thus: that only when $INPM \equiv INC\infty$ can individual development or evolution of our consciousness (EC) be ongoing and, only then, when our INPM is at maximum or optimum drive (od).

i.e.

$$INPM (od) + INC\infty = EC > EC\infty$$

In other words, if the play drive, operating through the INPM, encounters a context that has an infinite number of combinations/permutations of stimuli, which match facets of the INPM (i.e. INC∞) then evolution of consciousness tending towards infinity, or what Wilber (1996) calls Stage/level 8, would occur.

$$INPM \ (od) + INC\infty = EC > EC\infty > EC8$$

Level 8, in what Wilber (1996) calls the 'Great Chain of Being', is the Ultimate level of consciousness to which human beings can transcend. He refers to this Ultimate, using the name 'Atman'. From a developmental perspective, I suggest that the potential to be Atman or any of the other stages in the Great Chain, rests with the individual; it is a kind of sub-conscious or internal aspiration, whereas the potential to actually become Atman and the other stages in the Great Chain rests either within the totality of that environment with which the individual may come into contact, or within the interaction between the individual and that environment, that is, real transcendence is a function of both internal and external, i.e., play environmental, factors. I think the latter, so,

$$Drive + INPM + INC = EC$$

or,

$$Power + Individual \ Potential + Environmental \ Potential = EC$$

We can use the analogy of an INPM being a tram with a certain size wheelbase, and say that in an infinite number of available tracks there were only a limited number of them suited to the wheelbase of this particular tram. Then for the tram to reach destinations, i.e., different EC stages, either in a lifetime, or ever, would be dependent upon the level and duration of that tram's power and the level of possibility of it accessing appropriate tracks to make forward movement possible. Movement without the appropriate track to move on could result in deviation or stalling. This may also be the case with the play drive. i.e., the play drive active in an inappropriate context, where the child could not encounter any compatible neophilic connections, resulting in distress or aberrant, malfunctioning or malformed play patterns.

My view of an INPM is of a multi-faceted key where each facet and any combination of facets and the sum of the facets – the individual key itself – can access physical and psychic environmental features and release affect or effect or both. The drive activates the INPM, which accesses the INC in the form of an identifiable but individually modified play type. EC would then depend upon two variables:

1   the efficacy of the play type to access the INCs it exists to access
2   the concentration of those INCs within the playing environment.

The potential for evolution is released when features of the INPM access compatible INC features. The released potential exists in the form of a realisation, insight, skill or building blocks of that feature. Only when sufficient building blocks make sufficient bigger blocks etc., to facilitate transcendence, can an evolutionary movement be made. Whether evolution (in the context of consciousness) is gradual or incremental, I have no opinion on. The problem being that until one is aware that it has taken place the process is unconscious and therefore not available for analysis!

I have chosen the term INPM because we are all different, all interested, attracted by and to, different things, and yet apparently we all evolve or have the potential to evolve through the same stages, in the same order. The idea of an INPM means that, in the knowledge that none of us can access everything – and it would render us extinct if we tried – what the INPM does is limit the necessary search area for each of us to reach the next state in EC.

The INPM's structure in this is, for example, at Stage 1, only certain receptors are activated and we learn from experiences, where the activated receptor key contacts a similar keyhole in the INC. When the activated receptors have found sufficient connectors in the INC, an evolutionary stage is complete and other new receptors are activated, enabling new connections in the INC.

The old receptors are still active and may still dominate connections (this depends upon the nature of the INC to some extent). However, old receptor connections will not contribute further to EC. Only the newly activated receptors will do that. This suggests that the INPM is a very complex phenomenon, perhaps a metaphor for the personality itself, or even the evolving soul.

So, to summarise, we have the play drive, put into our own unique context INPM, manifested in play types, accesses events/experiences that are compatible to it, which then energises the INPM until a stage in EC is complete. For example:

Energy from drive $\rightarrow$ INPM $\leftarrow$ Energy from event/experience
$$\downarrow$$
Critical mass from the combination of bio-energy and awareness $\rightarrow$ $\rightarrow$ EC

Commentary/discussion

The primary question here is: what is the relationship between children's play and the environment in which it takes place? In this example, I am suggesting that the relationship is a function of three things:

- the sensory/affective attraction that environment holds for any particular individual
- the efficiency of that child's play drive
- the 'fit' between the child's neophilic needs and the neophilic content of that environment.

Some suggest that children will play anywhere, citing the Holocaust as an extreme example. My experience is that they certainly might try to play anywhere, but if the space in which they are trying to play is sterile, then the drive to play will eventually be extinguished.

It is also true that different spaces are preferred by different children. Some like water, some hate it, hence the idea of an INPM. Even when certain spaces are preferred by some children, there is still no guarantee that they will play there if they are tired, distressed or hungry. The drive to play has to be powered up, and satisfying the child's basic needs is fundamental to this. Children who are hungry, or frightened or exhausted cannot play, or certainly cannot sustain what is a very energy intensive activity, for any length of time.

Another notion implicit in this piece is the child's play as the key and the neophilic environment as the keyhole. During my own playwork I have seen examples of this individual 'fit' on numerous occasions – children attracted only to construction, or arts, or family or games with rules. Of course, we can suggest that this is more to do with social and socialising factors, but nevertheless, because children come from ancient biological stock, it could be that as we cannot integrate the whole universe into our psyches, we have evolved with different environmental preferences, the sum of which still enable us, even with these differences, to survive and flourish. Presumably because, although they are differences, they are not so different within the parameters of natural selection, to render us extinct.

It is interesting that I have moved from the symbolism of the word to mathematical symbolism to articulate these ideas. I think this is because the idea of neophilia and the INPM, and the combinations and permutations of stimuli that they imply, require me to think in terms of large numbers and complex calculations, rather than in what might be regarded as the more creative symbolic modes of letters or pictures. There is something vast about the nature of each individual child, back into the embryo of human consciousness, interacting with every aspect of the environment they live in or near, in a playful, exploratory and experimental way.

It is numerically incomprehensible to me to imagine the diversity of these INPMs for each child. It almost makes the term 'species' meaningless in this context, and yet there must be some commonality of experience within the concept of the INPM, which might, for example, be found under the basic headings of the Playwork Menu of Senses, Identity, Concepts and Elements. Breaking these four headings into component parts would eventually yield a huge number of potentially totally different experiences. Our sense of smell alone can distinguish between many, many types and intensities of perfumes, odours and smells, in an infinite variety of contexts.

The function of playwork is to ensure that diversity is available and accessible and that its individual manifestations are continually changing. A play space cannot have fixed characteristics if it is to serve its purpose. Of course, some environmental aspects will be subject to perceptual change by the action of a child's imagination. So a swing or a slide are not by definition useless, simply because they cannot be changed or replaced. They are, however, fixed in most other play contexts and are not as useful in terms of diversification as natural materials in a constantly changing context.

The serious side to this argument is the relationship between diversity and adaptation. How much experience of playful diversity does a child need before it is equipped to adapt – how much diversity is enough diversity? How much diversity do we need experience of, to enable us to move house, family or even country or climate?

I feel that it is enough to know that there is a relationship between environmental diversity and adaptation, at this stage in the unfolding of evolutionary playwork, and to work simply to ensure that play spaces contain an ongoing contribution to an input of the universe's diversity. That, at least, ensures that children are having some access to some diversity. In the context of a lot of home environments and play provision that will be a marked leap forward in itself.

RAP Example 3 (c. 1999)

Play and neuronal over-capacity

The most recent work of Sutton-Smith (1997) and Rosenzweig et al. (1971, 1972) on notions of brain plasticity, Huttenlocher's (1992) neural over-capacity of neonates and Sylva's (1977) Bruner's (1976) Hutt et al. (1989), and Sutton-Smith's (1979) concept of combinatorial flexibility, suggests a powerful model of play's pivotal role in the processes of human adaptation and species evolution.

Linking what he describes as play's 'amazing' diversity, to Gould's (1996) notion of variability – which he suggests is 'the central characteristic of biological evolution' – and what Edelman (1992) describes as an 'associatively quirky process', Sutton-Smith (1997) suggests that because of brain plasticity the human brain will retain what he calls its potential variability. The child, because the over-capacity of neurones at birth – by at least a factor of 2 when compared with the neuronal capacity of a human adult, according to Huttenlocher (1992) – will be more effective if he or she are exposed to the diversity of experience through playing.

Sutton-Smith (ibid.) argues that play's role could be in the 'actualisation of brain potential' – making connections real, rather than possible: 'its function being to save ... more of the variability that is potentially there, than would otherwise be saved if there were no play.'

The thrust of Sutton-Smith's view is that the human child is born with a huge neuronal over-capacity, which if not used will die. And that 'quirky, apparently redundant and flexible responses to experience', i.e., play, result in the uptake of this over-capacity, thus ensuring its continued participation in future brain processes, avoiding problems that Gould (1996) suggested were associated with 'rigidification of behaviour after any future successful adaptation'.

However, it is in an almost throwaway remark, that Sutton-Smith (1997), citing Kotulak (1996), provides us with one of his more important insights. In it he states: 'an over abundance of cells and synapses is produced and the brain has to use them to make itself work'.

From the playwork perspective this is a very interesting statement. How does the brain use this over abundance to 'make itself work'?

Does play create a Sub-Operating System (SOS) for cerebral evolutionary software?

I envisage this 'optimisation of experiential potential' as being facilitated by a psychic net of pre-actualised neurones and synapses, sensitised to 'catch' a 'sensory meteoric shower' of basic information both about its content and context.

As the information is 'caught', two things happen. One is that, as information is processed by the child's brain, so it becomes synthesised into it and the brain's subsequent complexity and capacity is increased by that transformation. The other is that, as the brain's relative complexity increases, so the range and sensitivity of the metaphorical net increases with it, thus enabling increasingly greater amounts of information to be trapped and processed.

One is attracted to the metaphor of the creation of a basic Software Operating System in a computer – Bateson and Martin (1999) use scaffolding as a similar metaphorical device – which, by providing the interface between the hardware, the physical substance of the computer and sophisticated software, enables increasingly complex computations to be undertaken.

If play does provide a metaphorical cerebral equivalent of an SOS, i.e., an interface between brain and behaviour, which captures and incorporates radical operating mechanisms essential to processing larger and more complex packages of information, then this not only highlights play's vital importance, but provides an explanation for the apparent invisibility of its outcomes. This suggests play provides a sub-system for operating 'evolutionary software', without which other systems, dependent upon it for their basic operation, would become inoperative.

Taking this assumption as read, not only would it further highlight the importance of play, it would also throw light on the potentially devastating potential for play-deprivation resulting from adulteration, by everything from traffic, poverty, predatory adults, overcrowded housing, poor community relations and, above all, conflict.

Commentary/discussion

Although he draws from a wide variety of sources, I have to pay tribute to Brian Sutton-Smith for drawing our attention to the neurological literature again. For the playworker it is an incredibly fertile area. What I understand Sutton-Smith to be suggesting is that, although children are born with a huge neuronal over-capacity due to the brain's characteristic for plasticity, this over-capacity only becomes actualised when children play, i.e. it only becomes useable and relatively constant when it has been used in playful episodes. It is only when cerebral material has been run-in, using play, that it can be used for other purposes. Otherwise it remains 'virtual' and is eventually lost.

Huttenlocher, the author Sutton-Smith cites, takes this a stage further. In one study (Huttenlocher, 1990) he suggests that there is what he calls a 'sensitive period' for neuronal plasticity to occur, which in human beings begins sometime between birth and four to six months and lasts to between six and seven years of age. At which time, so Sutton-Smith implies, this material attenuates if it is not actualised. The conclusion has to be drawn that there is a relationship between play and plasticity, simply because play is all that children choose to do, during that period. I do not imply that that is all they do, only that is all they choose to do. There does seem some evidence that plasticity and choice of actions are related.

In another study, this time by McEwen (1999), it is suggested that stress is responsible for negative plasticity, where instead of growing, the brain actually shrinks. If this is so, then the relationship between positive plasticity, where the brain does grow and the child's consent is likely. This would imply that, if behaviour were not play specifically it would have to be at least playful.

However, the part of this example of RAP which I found fascinating, from a reflective point of view, was what this knowledge did to my own thinking. Suddenly, the picture of a psychic or cerebral net came into my mind, together with the notion that, fundamental, universal knowledge, has to be caught at the beginning of human life. The sensitivity implied by this metaphorical net gives us an insight into the nature of play. That it is a state that changes our everyday relationship with the world into one which is highly sensitive to certain incoming stimuli. The world does not discriminate between those who are used to being exposed to stimuli and those who are not. The world is the world but, learning to learn in this context, suggests that human children are sensitised to a hierarchy of incoming information. What I am suggesting is that if a child's neuronal material has to be actualised by playing, then actualisation must take place in a particular sequence for neural processes to be constructed from it. Building blocks enabling actualisation, in whatever form it takes place, and the more complex processes that follow actualisation, have to be constructed at the interface between neural matter and incoming stimuli.

My suggestion is that, at the start of the process of actualisation, the child's brain is only sensitised to incoming stimuli A–C. It is only when stimuli A–C have finished their building block work that the brain becomes sensitised to incoming stimuli D–G. This 'graduated sensitisation' will also allow actualisation, or the actual form that play takes during the actualisation process, to become increasingly complex, until the total neural system is up and running, and play's position in the child's behavioural repertoire becomes, perhaps, less necessary to its survival and more important to its evolution.

RAP Example 4 (c. 1999)

Recapitulation and the evolution of consciousness

Sutton-Smith (1997) states, 'My theory would be that play, as novel adaptation may have developed as a fuller imitation of the evolutionary process, in which the organism models [or imitates] its own biological character.'

The concept of recapitulation, alluded to here, was originally pioneered in 1904 when G.S. Hall, the educationalist and developmental psychologist, wrote, 'the best index and guide to the stated activities of adults in past ages is found in the instinctive, untaught and non-imitative play of children' – the term 'non-imitative' implying an absence or distancing of adults.

His theory, which was later expanded by Reaney (1916), proposed that play was a re-enactment of that individual's forebear's transmitted activities. What I understand by this is that the essence of each forebear's past is encapsulated in her or his genes and passed on through the process of procreation, to be played through by the next and future generations.

Thus, as Reaney states, childhood could be 'divided into play periods that correspond to our species' "various evolutionary stages"', i.e., the animal, savage, nomad, pastoral and tribal.

Regarded by Schwartzman (1978) as 'influential', Hall's Recapitulation Theory provided a template upon which models of 'unilinear stages of development' were evolved further by, for example, Freud (1918), Piaget (1951) and Erikson (1963).

However, from a playwork perspective, it was not until transpersonal psychologists, particularly Wilber (1996), began to provide a less latent theoretical analysis of processes similar to the recapitulation phenomenon than that provided particularly by Reaney, that recapitulation could take on any more than an 'interesting' theoretical mantle.

For, although Reaney's interpretation is a manifestation of unilinear development and demonstrates a progression from ape to modern civilisation in classic Darwinian mode, it has no overt function. By that I mean, to paraphrase Bruner (1972), 'knowing that, is not the same as knowing why'.

What Wilber does is to overlay an idea similar to that of recapitulation, with a scholarly analysis of the evolution of consciousness and by so doing, he invigorates Hall's notion with a depth and importance that encourages a synthesis of the two ideas, into one with evolutionary significance for play.

Although Wilber (1996) also analyses evolution as unilinear stages, his emphasis is on the evolution of consciousness itself and, because of this, his stages reflect that perspective. He maps our species' evolution from a historic 'ground zero' – what he calls the 'ground unconscious' where he suggests the human being was fused with the environment – to the now of the present day, where, having passed through stages that reflect some similarity with Hall's (i.e., the reptilian, typhonic, mythic, and what he describes as membership stages, the latter of which is an encapsulation of the period of the major ancient civilisations) he reaches an approximation of our current dominant evolutionary peak. This he describes as egoic, where human beings are increasingly conscious of themselves as individuals, rather than as members of a group or culture.

Importantly Wilber (1996) describes this process in terms of a transcendence from one stage to the next, where his view of recapitulation starts from the simplest point, the reptilian or uroboric stage and gradually evolves into an increasingly complex view of being, with its own new problems and solutions. He states, 'each stage of evolution transcends but includes its predecessor ... each stage of human evolution, although it transcends its predecessor, must include and integrate [it] in a higher unity'.

If Wilber's model is then compared to Hall's, a major difference between the two ideas emerges. Hall's model describes a process of 'playing out', perhaps an exorcism of the child's ancestral past, i.e. a necessary 'ridding' of the past to join the present, where the child's perceived identity may only incorporate that present. Whilst, in Wilber's model, the playing child retains and incorporates each evolutionary stage into the next, rendering it an amalgam of its evolution rather than a derivative of it. 'Each of these levels continues to function and continues to live', coupled with a drive to move on, even though each new stage has its own new fears and perceptions.

This analysis may provide the child with a perception of self more amenable to homeo-stasis and well-being, because, having played through and incorporated each evolutionary stage, the child would be at ease with an identity, which included echoes from other ages.

From a playwork view, this is an important model. Playworkers attempt to facilitate play. But without a clear biological, developmental, evolutionary explanation of play's role, on which to develop and evaluate practice, both practice and provision irresistibly become driven by adult social and cultural imperatives, child-care and juvenile crime reduction, rather than the fundamental need of the young to experience 'unfettered' play.

Playing 'up to speed'

What the Wilber and Hall models provide, is an embryonic biological articulation of what playworkers often observe in practice. One that enables them to revisit practice from a fundamental developmental orientation, from a perspective which is biological, rather than sociological, in its essence.

The synthesised Hall/Wilber model of play, called perhaps 'evolutionary-recapitulation', if applied to the playing child, also casts fresh light on the question, 'Why do we play?'

At birth, no human child knows either where or when it is. By that I mean, its geographical location could be Lima or Lisbon and its chronological location could be anytime. One reason children play may be that if early play contains a high level of recapitulated material, and if recapitulation means recapping individual genetically recorded evolutionary stages, playing, if the environment as Nicholson (1972), Moore (1986), and Hughes (1996b), suggest, is appropriate, will enable each child to play itself, 'up to speed', if we use each evolutionary stage as a metaphorical gear.

The child, in playing in any particular evolutionary stage (and in so doing, intuiting, via cues, that the way it is relating to its environment indicates that it is not yet synchronised with the present) continues to play as stages unfold.

It does this until its play begins to take on a more considered and conscious form, in which the play drive modified by a feedback loop, signals that the child has reached the limits (not limitations) of its own evolution (the present) and moves from a recapitulation (i.e., a 'past' mode) into a new 'present and future' mode.

These analyses serve to provide brief examples of playwork thinking on the importance for children to experience holistic and free-ranging play. However, for children subsumed in conflict, for example, we can begin to appreciate that the drive to play, and play's possible natural evolutionary manifestations, may suffer some restriction and mutation of play forms as a result, causing children great psychological difficulties. Wilber (1996) predicts that 'failure to integrate [each stage] into the next, will result in neurosis', the consequences of which could be catastrophic.

Commentary/discussion

Again I have to thank Sutton-Smith, this time for reminding me about Hall's Recapitulation Theory. Here Hall's Theory is used in conjunction with Ken Wilber's scholarly work on the evolution of human consciousness, to explore what I am going to call, 'recapitulative play', or play that is a physical manifestation of the genetic echo passing up through the generations by children as they play.

As with the previous example, I was surprised by what this information did to my own views. I had long thought that play's adaptive power enables children to be born anywhere on Earth and still, within reason, be able to adapt to the climactic and cultural conditions in which they found themselves. However, it had never crossed my mind that the human child may need to undergo a genetic recap via the recapitulation process, in order to have some idea of who it was in the context of where it had come from historically. There are interesting questions about whether the genes of current generations of playing children are filing away experiences of the child's present, to pass onto future generations, via recapitulative play.

One could be forgiven for asking why children need to go through the recapitulation process at all. Much of our history is written down or past on via oral tradition, and we know more or less where we come from, all the way back to the early Palaeolithic period, and the present and future will almost certainly be recorded in increasing detail. So why does our psyche – if indeed it does – undergo recapitulation?

I can think of one answer. Whilst records are of great benefit to learning, they do not give most of us a tangible link with our past. Axe heads, old documents and buildings, cave drawings, stories of hunting and gathering and of warding off monsters, do not convey the same intensity of meaning, of identity with, of being a part of, as actually doing these things naturally without being prompted. With recapitulative play we have a physical and psychic manifestation of the direct link between the playing child and the lineage of its ancestors right to the beginning of time. In other words, without recapitulative play, all human life starts and ends at the start and end of each individual life, whereas, with recapitulation, the notion of continuity, of 'evolutionary confirmation', of *hands held through time*, is very powerful.

When I am training playworkers, I sometimes ask them to envisage themselves as at the apex of a pyramid, of generations of their own ancestors. Without them we would not be here, and because of them, we represent the most advanced – in the sense of time, anyway – version so far.

Human life only contextualised in the here and now seems a bit pointless to me as a playworker. Play has existed, and we as a species have been conscious of it, at least since the time of Plato and Aristotle. So this powerful medium has been a behavioural priority for us for many generations. Given that, perhaps it is not so strange, after all, that unconsciously, we recognise its importance in continuing the link between our species' present and its extraordinary past.

It is not uncommon, as I suggest in RAP Example 8, for play types that may have links with recapitulation to be disallowed in supervised play provision – fire play, rough and tumble and deep play, to name three. My fear is that contemporary political correctness and parental paranoia, may act together to deny many children access to experiences that are essential to the enactment of the recapitulative process and, as a consequence, those children may be damaged. For, if recapitulative play exists to enable us to manifest our direct links back to our beginnings, the reason for this may be that it is important to our psychic health. The down side being that if we do not do it, then our psychic health is seriously at risk. We all need to know who we are and recapitulative play gives us access to one representation of that area of knowledge or experience, without which we may be left to flounder, a piece of the jigsaw, so freely available, denied.

RAP Example 5 (c. 2000)

What follows are four examples of RAP from research undertaken in Northern Ireland (see Hughes, 2000). They attempt to explore the impact of thirty years of war on children's play in urban Belfast from the perspective of chronic adulteration – whether that be adulteration by adult involvement in children's games; the saturation of the play space by adult stereotypes; the limitation of ranging, choice and mastery by fear of death, injury or sectarian abuse from adults; or by the impact of high levels of close proximity violence caused by adults.

A Play types deprivation and substitution and the continued perpetuation of sectarianism

Much of inner-city Belfast is a series of very tight-knit communities whose identities are determined along traditional Protestant/Unionist/Loyalist or Catholic/Nationalist/Republican lines. Areas that relate to either tradition are segregated from one another, either by main roads, motorways or 'peace-lines'. They can normally be identified by the flags seen flying in them, by the colours their kerb stones are painted, or by the murals that decorate many gable ends. These segregated areas, under fire from paramilitary groups, the army and police, were, and are, dangerous places for children. As a consequence, over the years, many children have played close to home, drawing their friends from that local community.

For example, when I asked, 'Did you have any friends from the other [Catholic or Protestant] tradition?', eighteen of the possible twenty-one responses for early childhood were 'No'; sixteen of the possible twenty-one responses for middle-childhood were still 'No'; and of the possible nineteen responses for late childhood, twelve still answered 'No'. My own experience of these areas, is, as 'G' says, that they are 'close knit . . . everyone knows everybody' and this closeness is reflected in the high level of social play urban Belfast's children engaged in throughout the 'Troubles'. This included street games like skipping, chaseez, hunts and churchy one-over; social locomoter games like sports and swimming; role-play, like doctors and nurses and, later, sexual and mischief games.

This tendency for social play – rather than, as Hughes (1996a) suggests, a balance between all fifteen play types – is mirrored in both communities, with games often having exactly the same names even though their exponents never meet!

Burman (1986) wrote of one of the possible transmission mechanisms for sectarianism: 'Exactly how parents in Northern Ireland achieve this has not yet come under close scrutiny'. However, social play in this context seems to have often involved adults and it is the amalgamation of the following elements:

- the tradition of adult involvement in children's play
- the 'close knit' nature of communities
- the bias towards social play
- little or no input from the other tradition.

I believe these factors provide the play equivalent of a synaptic neurotransmitter. In reminding us that 'we should study the variations within play in such detail as may allow us to speak more confidently of their functions than we have to date', Sutton-Smith (1997) draws our attention to the fact that the impact of such a social play bias is not yet understood.

However, given the endemic nature of sectarianism, the above four factors, comments like 'F's, 'sometimes your parents have a habit of influencing you' and the fact that, 'Everybody's Mummy was out [playing]', it is difficult to see how play, in this context, would not have acted as a medium for the transmission of sectarianism. A vivid example of sectarianism at play is supplied in Duncan (1977), reporting that, during Bernadette Devlin's school days, she often skip-roped to this song,

> St Patrick's Day will be jolly and gay,
> and we'll kick all the Protestants out of the way,
> If that won't do, we'll cut them in two,
> and send them to hell with their red, white and blue.

Protestant children countered with:

> If I had a penny, do you know what I'd do?
> I would buy a rope and hang the Pope
> and let King Billy through.

The suggestion I make that parental involvement in children's play may act as a sectarian transmitter is not intended to be offensive. But if, as I asserted earlier, play creates a sub-operating system, in a context in which sectarianism is endemic, then its contamination of children's play would be unavoidable. We can only imagine the shrieks and laughs when the above songs were sung, and the approving meta-communication – smiles, winks and other subtle cues – the singers would have received from adults already long affected, further reinforcing this insidious indoctrination of the young. Austin (1986), in Cairns (1987b), comes to a similar conclusion, saying, 'What this investigation revealed is that the [school] playground is a place where Northern Irish children learn not only to be boys and girls but also to be Protestants and Catholics' (pp. 128–9).

Cairns (ibid.) underlines the potential of adults to transmit sectarianism: 'children have already been subjected to sectarian indoctrination before their school life even begins ... In other words ... the greatest pressures of all to take sides come from the child's own family.... The family is one of the main channels for the transmission of cultural attitudes and values' (p. 122).

However, this is not to apportion blame. It is my belief that the transmission of sectarianism through adulterated play is such a powerful biological mechanism as to prove irresistible to every child within its sphere of influence. This is to say that, in close-knit communities, sectarianism, like racism, provides an 'obscene normality' in which its transmission, via reinforced verbal and body language and meta-communication, guarantees its presence at the cradle and in the play of children. Cairns (ibid.) appears to feel similarly, saying, 'It is important not to impute malicious intent to the adults of Northern Ireland in their attitudes and behaviour'.

Possible mechanism

Closing down the play environment		Play Types Deprivation Substitution		Feedback loop of compliance and/approval		The false self		Propagation of sectarianism
	$\rightarrow$		$\rightarrow$		$\rightarrow$		$\rightarrow$	

Hughes and Williams (1982) suggested that play experiences normally take the form of a benign,

interaction(1) $\rightarrow$ feedback $\rightarrow$ evaluation $\rightarrow$ interaction(n)

loop. However, when conflict closes down the play environment, this loop may, in certain circumstances, be substituted by others. For example, when those circumstances include:

- adult involvement in children's play
- a 'close knit' sectarian community
- a bias towards social play
- little or no input from the other cultures or tradition

sectarianism is able to be integrated into a child's play behaviour because of the imposed substitution of a compliance/approval loop, by the adults, i.e.,

Invitation(1) $\rightarrow$ Engagement $\rightarrow$ Compliance $\rightarrow$ Approval $\rightarrow$ Invitation(n)

Unable to engage in its own choice of play activity, the child is encouraged to engage in social play with older children and adults. In engaging with the game, the child is expected to comply to the game's rules. Compliance gains approval, non-compliance results in rejection. In sectarian games, as in the skipping game above, the rules are the same. Compliance, including what Sturrock and Hughes (1998) term 'the demonisation of the other', results in approval, ranging from subtle meta-cues, e.g., a smile, or a wink, to co-opting applause and verbal reinforcement, which convey feelings of belonging. What Wilber (1996) terms 'membership'. Non-compliance, on the other hand, results in exclusion and rejection and may leave the child, and even its siblings, friendless and vulnerable, so the albeit unintended pressure to comply is considerable.

The normal play loop contains no external intervention except that devised by the child. For example, the choice to repeat an action or not, is always under the child's control. Whereas in the adulterated loop, the child's control is substituted by that of the adult. Once the child enters this loop, s/he is contaminated.

In time, this 'erosion of choice and control', creates in the child a false-self, composed of a narrow and sectarian life view, which, because of the limitations imposed by the conflict and the adult community, becomes increasingly absorbed into one culture. The result is a child with a false identity, without

insights into the other tradition, except those which s/he has been taught and whose resulting negative perceptions are reinforced by the songs, icons and symbols of local cultural membership. Over time, the child's life-world becomes increasingly constructed by what Sturrock and Hughes (1998) call, 'pernicious narcissism', an inward looking sectarian perspective and, like the football supporter, s/he begins to derive much of his or her self-esteem from the successes of the home team over the opposition or the 'other', in the form of sectarian interactions or outrages.

However, I stress again, it is unlikely that either today's, or yesterday's adults could have resisted the transmission of sectarianism and sectarian identity through their play, any more than their children can through theirs; it is a truly vicious cycle.

B   Saturation by adulterating images and the development of SPNs – Stereotypical Play Narratives

No one will ever know the combined total of paramilitaries, secret agents, police and army on the streets in Belfast over the period of the 'Troubles', although it may have run into many thousands. 'They were a part of your life,' said 'P' and, needless to say, there are many references to the army in the interviewees' recollections within this study.

And, although there are only a few references in these data to children engaging in paramilitary narratives, other evidence, notably in Hughes (1997, 1998) does describe children engaging in mock paramilitary shootings, assassinations and punishment beatings and, more recently, making a mock bomb from scrap materials, in an after-school club. As Einon (1985) implies, children have always absorbed adult roles into their play narratives. However, when those roles are frightening or disempowering and impact on the children themselves, then reference to simple imitation or role play does not suffice as an explanation for their inclusion. We should remember, as reported in Smyth (1998), that from 1969 to March 1998, nearly 400 children, aged 18 and under, have been killed in Northern Ireland.

Belfrage (1987) alludes to the scale and intensity of army activity, for example: 'I was raided 59 times', said one of her interviewees with young children. Anecdotal evidence speaks of gun-fights between paramilitaries and the army during a family funeral where several children were present. Children have seen their siblings and parents gunned down, or blown up, before their very eyes. One can also imagine children in either community, overhearing descriptions of the most gruesome attacks on others and having trouble sleeping, not able to articulate what they are imagining, able only to exorcise it through their play.

Those who carried out shootings and bombings, who raided houses and fired baton-rounds, were, throughout the thirty years of the 'Troubles', the brothers, sisters and parents of playing children, who inevitably heard and internalised the experiences that they related. 'R' gives one example, saying, 'And where maybe over in England they would sit and talk about, "Ah! did you see the match last week?" [here], they're sitting in a pub and they'll say, "Do you remember such and such a time? That was a good hit. You shot a soldier or whatever." You sit and you think about things like that.'

Out of my own experience as a playwork trainer in Northern Ireland, it is difficult for me to believe that such reminiscences, descriptions of operations, hate-filled opinions about whole communities, experiences of anything from a car bomb to a shooting, would not be talked about in front of children or overheard by them. Particularly in a context where sectarian remarks are made by 'well-adjusted' individuals as a matter of normal conversation, although as Smyth (1998) points out, perhaps, not in mixed groups. If the adults did not discuss these issues in front of their children, as Bar-on (1993) describes, in Smyth (ibid.), 'even silence about traumatic events contains information which children pick up'.

Certainly children did play at military and paramilitary roles. 'P' describes the lengths that his group went to in their search for authenticity. 'We had our own sergeant and our own general, and our own HQ, and we had parades and all the rest . . .' 'R' relates that he and his friends also imitated the army. 'You used to sit and watch the way they would have took up positions at corners . . . used to wonder what they were doing,' and 'S' talked of his, 'fascination with the real life Action Men, with their guns and sticks'. 'M' spoke of her interest in the soldiers. 'You were just fascinated by wee soldiers sitting there. We used to follow them around the streets,' and 'K' remembered 'dressing up like a soldier', and 'D' said, 'I remember playing soldiers, boys and girls . . .' However, my interpretation of why they did so, given the context, is that circumstances made it impossible for them not to. In short, their play was an effect of adulteration, creating what I have called previously, in Hughes (1997a) Stereotypical Play Narratives.

Possible mechanism

It is likely that there will be two distinct manifestations of SPNs within the child population of urban Belfast.

SPN (1)

The first, SPN (1), is generated as follows. As the combination of the 'Troubles' and sectarianism were closing down children's normal play choices, their play ecology was being increasingly saturated with military images and experiences. Children are fascinated by the unknown, a characteristic called 'neophilia', by Morris (1967) and they would have been attracted to this new military phenomenon. Two interviewees actually said they were 'fascinated' by soldiers. The combination of this saturation, a play environment increasingly bereft of choice and the children's neophilia, would have had the effect of leaving only one play choice for many children, i.e., playing soldiers.

However, there was also another factor at play. Because of their own role, the soldiers were not necessarily perceived as fascinating for long: 'eventually he got the ball and stuck his bayonet in it,' said 'R', and 'S' spoke of playing 'mock riots against pretend soldiers', and 'K' fired his catapult 'at the jeeps'. The effect of the soldiers' physical domination of the children's space and the constant danger they represented would have caused children to experience powerful negative emotions that would only be relieved by taking control of the hated image, i.e., by imitation. For one way of retaliating, one way of regaining control, although not without its own dangers, would have been to pretend to be soldiers themselves.

SPN (2)

For other children, subjected to terrible and 'toxic' adulteration, although their play would not have been able to be so focused, such imitative behaviour would still have been necessary therapy. Being present at atrocities, seeing ambushes – 'K' spoke of 'two IRA shooting at Peelers (RUC)' – experiencing explosions – 'P' said, 'the gun fire and the bombs . . . your whole system jumped' – or over-hearing detailed accounts of 'hits', assassinations, or mutilation, would have subjected children to violent trauma. Lyons (1974), in Smyth (1998), reported that 'serious affective disorder' was suffered by 92 per cent of those witnessing a bomb explosion. The requirement for secrecy in some circumstances would have further exacerbated the child's need for release. What would have been the child's reaction to the real and imagined images, that would have inevitably followed the words and deeds s/he had witnessed or overheard? The fear and help-lessness that some children must have felt would have needed to have been compensated for by action, action having the consequence of reversing the affect experienced by the child. It would either be that, or s/he would rapidly deteriorate, locked in a spiral of nightmares, with all of the accompanying negative affect.

In this context, the only choice would have been for the child to take control of its imagination by enacting events, by actually taking on the mantle of his or her tormentor, as human beings have done through the ages, as a way of coping with their fear. Acting-out the source of its 'shadow'; by dressing up as the perpetrator, by speaking like the assassin, and pretending to do what s/he did, perhaps even extending the experience beyond the known, offers a potent affective antidote to fear and helplessness.

However, SPN (2) is a more disturbed and solitary narrative than SPN (1) and much less bounded or constrained. And, whilst engaging in it might act to release the child from its nightmares, there is a real risk that, in so doing, s/he becomes confused between what Jennings (1995) describes as 'the two realities'. The child is so obsessed with the resultant deepening violent imaginings, s/he eventually takes them to the point of 'actualisation', because of the feelings of power and of mythical potential, which playing them out generates. The transition from benign enactment to violent fantasy for some of those most terribly scarred is another possible consequence of thirty years of militaristic adulteration of children's play. We only have to look to the gun culture of the USA for confirmation.

C   Range, choice and mastery deprivation and mental mapping deficits

Closing down the play environment	→	Ranging choice and mastery deprivation	→	1. Range growth deficits 2. Range development deficits	→	Mental mapping deficits

Ranging

Of the twenty-one people interviewed, only two reported that their ability to range freely during either their early, middle or late childhood had been unaffected by the 'Troubles'. Of those whose ranging has been affected, six said that their ranging had been affected throughout their whole childhood period; six reported that ranging had been restricted during early and middle-childhood; four said that ranging behaviour had been restricted during early, middle or late childhood; and three said ranging was restricted in early and late childhood. The chronological development of ranging restriction, as the 'Troubles' began and then escalated, is also interesting. Sectarian bullying and attacks, bombing and shooting, danger, military vehicles, fear of abduction, segregation, army barriers, paramilitaries, soldiers, stone-throwing, rioting, traffic and strangers, were all cited as causes of restricted movement.

Hart (1979), Moore (1986) and Parkinson (1987) suggest that ranging is both a complex, 'fluctuating phenomenon' that is an essential element of play behaviour and that, if restricted in some way, could 'delay or block development'. Moore (ibid.) says of ranging:

> this is a crucial limiting factor on children's experience of the environment. Every child needs equal access to opportunities for asserting her or his individuality through interactions with the environment. The potential for interaction exists at all levels of range experience, depending on the availability of adequate resources, the absence of physical constraints, and the degree of freedom accorded by parents.

From the data generated by this study, it is reasonable to suggest that the ranging behaviour of many of urban Belfast's children was severely restricted throughout the 'Troubles' period.

Choice

Restricted ranging would affect children's choice of play experience too. For, if their living environment lacked trees, water, architectural diversity, books, or other children, for example, and access to spaces containing them was denied, then the child's life-world would be impoverished. Access to diversity of play experience was affected throughout the 'Troubles' period. Of the twenty-one people asked, 'Could you do what you wanted, how you wanted?', nine said their choice was restricted throughout their childhood, four said their choice was restricted in early and middle-childhood, three said their choice was restricted either in early, middle or late childhood, and only five said their choice had not been restricted at all. Those who said that their choice had been restricted cited, 'being hemmed in by snipers, the 'Troubles', IRA/Sinn Fein, and the army', as being responsible.

'A' articulated the restriction she felt. For example, she could not play where she wanted because of the intensity of stone-throwing and rioting. She could not do what she wanted, because, 'You'd only come home crying'. 'C' also picked up on this theme. 'You didn't get out of your own district,' she said. 'L' agreed, 'There were places you couldn't go . . . if you wanted till. You had to stick till where you knew and people knew you . . . Just not being able to go where I wanted.'

Mastery

The emphasis on social play, discussed above, betokens another serious deficit in terms of play experience for children in Belfast over the 'Troubles' period. For, although some of those interviewed played war and soldiers, which might have entailed using the 'non-street, non-house' environments, only two referred to mastery play, defined in Hughes (1996a) as 'an urge to master the environment' and 'a feeling of being in control', in a more direct sense. One spoke of 'adventurous play', in the wild, and one of going 'camping'. Like restricted ranging and choice, this may be a critical play deficit resulting from the 'Troubles'. Citing Pearce (1977), Hart (1979) and Cobb (1993), Thomashow (1995), alluding to mastery play in middle-childhood, states, 'this is the time that children establish their connections with the earth, forming an earth matrix, a terrain symbiosis which is critical to their personal identity'.

Mental mapping deficits

My concern is that the combined effect of severe restrictions on ranging behaviour, experiential choice and mastery play, over much, if not all of their childhood, has affected children's basic mental mapping skills. The development of what Moore (1986) calls a child's urban geography is dependent on two processes, which he describes as 'range growth' and 'range development'. The former relates to the assimilation of new territory as it is discovered. This is the spatial ingredient of mapping and describes a ranging requirement that would have been very difficult to develop in the sectarian and militarised context of Belfast during the 'Troubles'. The latter describes the depth of experience children gain in these new territories over repeated visits. What Moore (1986) describes as the 'motivational pull', and what I would term 'neophilic attraction', after Morris (1967).

However, if children were unable to range or engage in mastery play, i.e., dig, build, light fires and play with the elements, but had instead to 'play in the street where my Mother could watch me', their knowledge of where they were, both in a wider and deeper ecological sense, would be seriously diminished. This could have longer-term implications for feelings of security and 'a sense of place', in other locations. Hart (1999) partially agrees, 'Only if a child's range was severely curtailed to the point that they never travelled outside on foot, could I imagine it affecting their basic mapping abilities'. However, he goes on to say, 'but it would of course affect their specific knowledge of their whole community ... this has serious implications for their sense of membership in a larger community.' Cosco (1999) is less circumspect, stating that, 'Mental mapping is a product of the notion of a well-established "corporal scheme", with the characteristics of orientation, position and direction in space.' She continues, 'the child needs exercise and movement to develop each of these parameters. To achieve an appropriately developed mental spatial map, the individual needs a well-established body scheme. If children do not explore, physically, actively and mentally, these representations do not develop and the spatial mapping abilities lay unrealised.'

It is true to say that this phenomenon could happen anywhere, and that children's development of mental mapping skills could be affected by several factors, including restrictions caused by dangerous roads and over-strict parents. However, my contention is that the 'Troubles' have added another and significant dimension to the potential for this form of deprivation, which could have had such a restricting influence as to leave those affected permanently unable to move location, or travel to areas that are not predictable and familiar.

D   Violation of the play process and stress-related neurochemical and neurophysiological mutation

Closing down the play environment	+	Sudden violent propulsion	OR	Sensory deprivation	→	neurochemical neurophysiological mutation	→	1. Violent behaviour 2. Withdrawn behaviour 3. Fantasy-driven behaviour

The 'Troubles' had two other major effects. The first was that, as the military situation closed down the play environment, access to diverse play experience was restricted and this, in itself, may have had the effect of sensorily depriving children, although Petrie (1996) is sceptical. Fear itself may have had a similar effect, by driving some children indoors to play. Certainly, there was a small but noticeable tendency for some participants to engage in solitary play, as the 'Troubles' progressed. For example, 'D' states, 'I was supposed to go out that night but I had the fear that built up in me'. She also said she had become, 'Very security conscious'. Notes I made following some interviews remarked that, 'All [of today's] participants seemed quiet and withdrawn'. 'P' is reported to have said, 'I was into training. I would spend time upstairs maybe with a small set of weights or something to keep my mind busy, to keep my mind off . . .' He also said he was 'more vigilant'. Toys that participants used increasingly included those with solitary applications, e.g., TV, computers, games consoles and ham radio.

However, the second and more serious effect would have been the sensory jolt and resultant reality shift children would have experienced if playing when gunfire, explosions, or other intrusive events occurred. Immersing in, and exiting from, a play narrative should be a gradual process, which Meares (1993) likens to becoming 'lost in thought'. The double shock of a sudden and violent propulsion from an internalised play state to a violent adult reality caused by these intrusions would be hugely traumatic. This could perhaps result in children avoiding playing altogether, or taking control by fantasising, simply because, as 'P' said, 'Your whole system jumped, you came out in a cold sweat,' when, as 'R' said, 'They just come in and kick your door in.'

The impact of environmental impoverishment on plasticity and levels of neurotransmitters is well documented (Rosenzweig et al. 1962, 1972; Bennett et al. 1964; Zuckerman 1969, 1984; Rosenzweig 1971; Ferchmin and Eterovic 1979; and Huttenlocher 1992). However, recent studies also highlight the effects of stress, trauma and low levels of stimulation on brain development. Balbernie (1999) states:

> A child who has been traumatised will have experienced overwhelming fear and stress. This will be reflected in the organisation of his or her brain, as neurochemical responses to fear and stress have designed it to survive in that sort of environment. By the same token, [a child] who is not being stimulated, by being . . . played with, and who has few opportunities to explore his or her surroundings, may fail to link up fully those neural connections and pathways which will be needed for later learning.

> (p. 17)

Perry et al. (1995) also suggest that trauma in childhood has the effect of influencing the child's brain physiology:

Children exposed to sudden, unexpected, man-made violence, [are] at great risk [of] profound emotional, behavioural, physiological, cognitive and social problems.

(p. 17)

Gunner (1998) reports that the brains of traumatised children develop 'hair trigger' circuitry, for stress reaction, because of high levels of cortisol, which 'increases activity in the part of the brain involved with vigilance and arousal.' However, Gunner continues, 'high levels of cortisol also directly effect the hippocampus', and 'children with disorganised attachment . . . have a permanently higher level of cortisol' (p. 18). Balbernie (1999) also suggests that another adaptive response that can be activated by fearful situations is what he calls 'the dissociative continuum – the freeze or surrender response'.

In Part II, I suggested that out of five environmental play scenario effects, four resulted in children being confused, withdrawn, fearful, fantasy driven and dissociated, but always over-ridingly violent.

The playworker's concern is that the resultant effect on children of trying to play in conditions which combine extreme violence with play-deprivation, would be similar to the changes in brain structure and neurochemistry cited above. The consequence of this would be children who show symptoms ranging from confusion to dissociation, underpinned by violence. This view has some support from Perry (1994), who stated, 'the very neurobiological adaptations that allow children to survive violence may, as the child grows older, result in an increasing tendency to be violent'. 'J' described a play environment where violence by one tradition on the other was always legitimate, a situation that can only deteriorate further if these predictions prove correct. 'If you were known for being from the Protestant side you would probably got a hiding from someone. So I just stayed clear of 'em. 'Cos if you'd ended up getting to know 'em, a Catholic, they could easily turned 'round and set you up. Make [you] think that you're friends and then just turn on you.'

In such a complex neurological/pharmacological soup, forecasted outcomes other than violence are rare and intervention that enables large numbers of children, both to successfully play-out trauma and re-engage with a reliable normality, in secure child-centred space, is clearly crucial.

Commentary/discussion

These are different examples of the simultaneous impact of play-deprivation and external environmental conditions. The above four analyses took place during 1999. In early 2000 I was doing some training for Hackney Play Association with a colleague, Jess Milne. The subject was Play, Playwork and Child Development. During the two-and-a-half day course two embryonic assessment models began to evolve whilst we were dealing with the impacts of play-deprivation and other external affects. The first was a stimulation pendulum

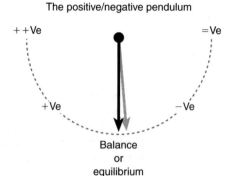

Figure 13.1 The environmental stimulation pendulum.

which gave a visual representation of how adult and environmental influences could swing the child's stimulation input from an optimum state, i.e., Balance or Equilibrium, to – depending upon the nature and level of the stimulation – a ++ve (over-positive/indulged) position, or a =ve (over-negative/desensitised), position. See Figure 13.1.

The second, which occurred during the same period of training, was a rudimentary matrix which included not only the indulged, desensitised and balance states, but also the Z1 (Erratic), and the Z2 (Dehumanised) states as well. This made it possible to visualise the complexity of some children's stimulus input, which could include permutations of any of the boxes. See Figure 13.2.

The simultaneous impact of play-deprivation and external environmental conditions

If one judges that the problem for the child is rooted in play-deprivation; then which play type(s) is the child being deprived of and how would one provide access? If, on the other hand, one judges that the problem source is an external

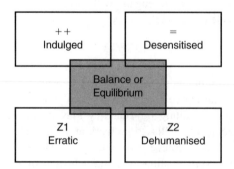

Figure 13.2 The environmental stimulation matrix.

factor; which ones are causing the problem? Of course, these are very rudimentary tools, but they begin to give us a place in space from which to refine our judgements.

If, for example, we are working in environments in which we are encountering violence, we can make judgements relating to its source being predicated either in indulgence (type $++$ve stimulation), or in one or more forms of abuse (type $=$ve stimulation). Knowing this may take some of the inevitable effect out of our own judgements and allow us to be more circumspect and decentred, seeing children as damaged or experiencing difficulties. This means that our diagnosis will hopefully culminate in an intelligent and sensitive appraisal of what action to take. In the case of these two extreme types of stimulation, access to the opposite gradual re-balancing experiences might help the child. Over-positive children may benefit from a negative input. Over-negative children may benefit from a positive input.

Equally, if we are encountering children who are neurotic, lacking in confidence or withdrawn, we might judge that they may be experiencing type Z1 stimulation (erratic or inconsistent) and may be in need of a level of reliable stimulation. Whereas, if we are encountering children who are more fantasy driven, we might judge that they might be experiencing type Z2 stimulation (sensory deprivation) and may be in need of a stimulation input which breaks the fantasy cycle.

However, we may also need to be able to discriminate between internal and external factors. Is the issue one to do with the impact of different types and levels of external stimulation, or is it to do with the quality of the child's play experiences? If we judge that it is to do with the former then we have dealt with that above, for now. If, on the other hand, it is to do with play-deprivation, unless the level of play-deprivation is total, i.e. all play types have been eradicated, then we need to make judgements regarding which play types are chronically absent from the child's experience and give the child access to them. When I say 'Give the child access to them', I mean that literally. This is not an exercise in the adult domination of the child's ludic ecology. Rather it is an attempt to 'fly in parallel' and give the child playwork support. So the term 'access' means that experiences are given a proximity near to the child's behavioural orbit. Whether the child chooses to access the experience is up to the child. Ethically, we can go no closer.

So, whether our embryonic diagnosis brings us to conclude that child A needs access to one or more play types, or whether it leads us to conclude that child B would benefit from rebalancing experience, or from more consistent stimulation, or from fantasy cycle breaking stimulation, or both, what happens is dictated by the child, as it should be.

If this sounds a bit like engineering or worse, like electro-convulsive treatment, that is not my intention. We have many damaged children coming to play environments, who have suffered every form and intensity of deprivation and abuse. We have children who, simply because of circumstances, find themselves more comfortable with violent, aggressive or fantasy driven behaviour. I believe within what is written above is the germ of an approach that will enable those children to access another reality and make choices about who they want to be: it has to be their choice. Any other way would be adding to the abuse.

I am aware that this is controversial, but I am also aware that it is only a theoretical postulation. And, although ethical guidelines would have to be written anyway, I would imagine, in the short term at least, that the ideas rooted in the relationship between stimulation theory and play types will remain a training tool to enable playworkers to be observant, reflective and analytical. Perhaps in the longer term, it will become a method of enabling the playing child to access potentially curative experiences for the range of difficulties I have attempted to describe.

RAP Example 6 (c. 1999)

Playwork philosophy and practice – a personal view

Early playwork thinking (pre-1975) was, as far as I can remember, based on a set of commonly held, intuitive beliefs. Some are listed below.

Original core values

That playwork would give children:

1   love and security
2   new experiences
3   praise and recognition
4   responsibility
5   a sense of self
6   knowledge of their own integrity
7   respect
8   informed choice
9   connections with the past, present and future.

By the early 1980s, there were many more playworkers, and these beliefs had evolved into a set of core values which informed a developing sociological analysis of what play was, and therefore what playwork was. Many aspects of this model are still common currency.

Sociological analysis

Outcomes	**Practice**
Citizen	Interventionist
Well-rounded	Predeterminist
Socialised	Pragmatic not idealistic
Tolerant	Value-driven
Democratic	Multi-culturalist
Happy and having fun	Management of behaviour
Clear cultural identity	
High self-esteem	

The weakness of such a model was that it appeared to be drawn from, and dependant upon, an adult social agenda. One which although it emphasised tolerance, child-centredness and empowerment, was rooted in high levels of intervention, behavioural management and adult preconceptions of, for example, morality and risk.

Weaknesses	**Outcomes**
Cultural cloning	Colonisation of the child's play space
Adulteration	Damaging to health and well-being
Specialist (see Lorenz, 1972)	Extinction/disabling
No Deep Play (see Hughes, 1996a)	Loss of identity
Aims adaptation to follow funding	Practice was based on social/political
Not derived from the literature	imperatives

During the early 1980s, a theoretical base for playwork was also being developed, using the original core values to guide its ethical and practical parameters. It differed from the sociological model in the following ways:

- it was derived from the scientific literature; in particular, the psychological literature
- it avoided social analysis by focusing instead on the child's needs as a biological organism
- it was intended to facilitate children's biological rather than their cultural development
- it addressed assessed deficits in children's play experiences from a compensatory perspective
- it was more about how and why play happens, than it was about that play happens.

Biological model

Outcomes	Practice
Evolution	Diversity
Adaptation	Non-adulteration
Flexibility	Environmental modification
Calibration	Stimulation theory
Balance	Applied definition of play
Mental mapping skills	Immersion in play types
Survival/development skills	Responsive to meta-communication

The weakness of this model was that it could be seen as irrelevant to contemporary social policy needs, that it was just navel gazing and unlikely to attract funding or political backing.

Weaknesses	Outcomes
Unpragmatic	Requires seismic shift in perception of self and child
Unrealistic	Requires seismic shift in content and delivery of knowledge
Politically naïve	Litigious culture/democratic government
Tenuous data links	Psychobabble
Reductionist	Dehumanising

The 1980s and early 1990s saw steady developments in each of these approaches. The sociological model was favoured by many playworkers. It made sense in terms of their own practical context and it made sense from a funding perspective. It gave them a vocational qualification and it gave them a kind of voice, but its weaknesses were that it was not grounded in evidence, it was dominated by an adult agenda, it was highly interventionist and it left playwork vulnerable to external exploitation.

Having said that, it was a model which, for all its flaws, did influence political thinking and brought important issues, for example, special needs, equal opportunities, Article 31 and children's participation, to the fore. However, some of its machinations are currently suffering what I can only call a qualitative and field credibility crisis, in particular the NVQ.

Many playworkers found the theoretical model too complicated and conceptually difficult to articulate, and it only gradually evolved, informed by theoretical inputs from the field and the work of a variety of academics including Bruner (1972), Sylva (1977) and Lorenz (1972), and later, Sutton-Smith (1997), and scientists in the fields of sensation seeking, sensory deprivation and the neurosciences. By the late 1980s, it was describing a playwork curriculum and a complex stimulation theory of playwork. By the late 1990s, its language and concepts had begun to permeate all aspect of playwork thinking, training and practice.

So where is playwork thinking positioned now?

My personal view is, although the sociological analysis is still regarded as the ideas reservoir the majority of playworkers are most comfortable with, that situation is rapidly changing. Acceptance of a theoretical model rooted in the ideas of environmental modification and a biological/evolutionary construct of the child is growing throughout the field. I think many playworkers are unhappy with contemporary developments and are looking for an analysis based upon evidence that will robustly describe the benefits of playwork to parents and politicians.

Playwork is also beginning to explore its role in the neurological development of children and is also evolving a diagnostic and curative case.

Here are three examples of ideas currently being explored.

1 Playwork and its role in human evolution.

In his book, *The Ambiguity of Play*, citing Huttenlocher's work on brain imaging technology, Sutton-Smith (1997) implies that children under ten years of age, have twenty-times (see note) the potential brain capacity of adults. This 'over-capacity' is linked to human evolution, because it enables the human brain to retain what he calls its 'potential variability'. Sutton-Smith suggests that this over-capacity will be more effectively utilised if it is exposed to the diversity of experience through playing. He also argues that play's role could be in the 'actu-alisation of brain potential' – making connections in the brain real, rather than possible – 'its function being to save ... more of the variability that is poten-tially there, than would otherwise be saved if there were no play'.

Thus the human child is born with a huge neuronal over-capacity, which s/he can 'actualise' by playing, enabling its participation in future brain processes.

This reinforces the view that play is spontaneous, child-driven behaviour that needs to occur in environments of maximum diversity.

(*Note.* The literature is rather ambiguous about the precise figure. Hutten-locher's research implies that the multiple is at least 'twice' as much as the potential brain capacity of adults, whereas, Sutton-Smith's figures imply a much higher multiple of many thousands, which could indicate a printing error. Although the multiple of 'twice' is itself highly impressive, I have used the multiple 'twenty', to indicate that it could be much higher.)

2 Playwork and the alleviation of play-deprivation symptoms.

The term 'play-deprivation' at its most extreme, describes a chronic lack of sensory interaction with the world, a form of sensory deprivation. Its effects are only currently being evaluated and may be catastrophic.

Studies on other species, particularly by Suomi and Harlow (1971), recorded aggression and social incompetence as outcomes of play-deprivation, whilst Smith *et al.* (1998) state that children, especially from 'economically disadvan-taged backgrounds showed less frequent and complex fantasy and socio-dramatic play'. However, it is recent studies in Romania, Switzerland and the US, which provide the clearest insights into the potential impact of play-deprivation.

The problem of play-deprivation (see also Huttenmoser and Degan-

Zimmermann, 1995; Chugani, 1998; McEwen, 1999), caused by the negative impact of certain levels and ranges of environmental stimulation, has long been a factor in playwork's theoretical development, see Hughes and Williams (1982) and Hughes (1988, 1996). Increased knowledge and research in this area will hopefully enable us to help children who are play deprived, and suffering problems ranging from autistic and neurotic, to psychotic-like symptoms.

3   Playwork, plasticity, neurophysiology and neurochemistry.

As early as 1962, neurological researchers were aware of a phenomenon known as brain plasticity. What this means is that the brain's size and the intensity of its internal chemical activity is related to the nature of experience and the nature of environment to which the individual is exposed (Rosenzweig et al. 1962, 1972; Bennett et al. 1964; Zuckerman, 1969, 1984; Rosenzweig, 1971; Ferchmin and Eterovic, 1979).

Zuckerman, for example, suggests that, '[Environmental] stimulation and behavioural activity act on the neurotransmitter systems in a brain-behaviour, feedback loop'.

The playwork implication being that, if children play in what are called 'enriched environments', their brain growth and neurochemical activity will increase. If, on the other hand, they play in what are called 'impoverished environments', their play will be limited and may even stop, and brain growth and activity will decrease accordingly.

This last point is taken up by Zuckerman (1984). Again referring to extreme levels of neurotransmitters, caused by environmental impoverishment, he states, 'inappropriate levels of neurotransmitters were reported to be responsible for an organism [which] is unsocial or aggressively anti-social'.

Recent studies also highlight the effects of stress, trauma and low levels of stimulation on brain development. Perry et al. (1995), Balbernie (1999) and McEwen (1999) suggest that trauma in childhood has the effect of influencing the child's brain physiology.

The playworker's concern is that the resultant effect on children of trying to play in impoverished conditions, which may combine extreme violence, abuse and/or physical neglect with play-deprivation, would be similar to the changes in brain structure and neurochemistry cited above, with similar outcomes.

The thesis of these three examples being that there is a growing body of evidence suggesting that, when children access good play provision operated on biological principles, not only can they experience the fun, diversity, risk and freedom, characteristic of such environments, they can also:

• develop up to twenty-times (see Note, p. 217), the brain capacity of many of their adult counterparts, which has important change and adaptational implications for our individual and collective futures. (Central Government Ministers are continually talking about how we need to be able to adapt to a changing world.)

- overcome the problems associated with the crippling effects of various forms of play-deprivation, which has important personal and social health implications. (Central Government is continually talking about how we need to be able to save money in the NHS.)
- avoid the prognosis of a violent lifestyle resulting from trauma, abuse and the insidious effects of stimulus and behavioural impoverishment, which has vital personal and social implications in the context of health and crime. (Central Government is continually talking about how we should be able to live in a safe, violence-free environment.)

The depth psychologies

As well as these theoretical developments, another new influence is also making its presence felt, namely the role of the depth psychologies in helping us to better understand play and the role of the playworker in facilitating play. Work by several playworkers, including Rennie, Sturrock and Else, has provided a very powerful analysis of the importance of the effects of play-cues, intervention and adulteration on the mechanisms of the playworker/child interface. They are also exploring the role playwork might have in assisting a better understanding of ADD, ADHD and dyslexia.

Northern Ireland

Adulteration has also been explored in another context, i.e. that of children playing in areas of conflict. Recent work in Northern Ireland (for example, Hughes, 2000) has identified a particular form of adulteration, as a highly potent mediator of play-deprivation. Adulteration as a result of ethnic conflict is cited as having a role in the perpetuation of sectarianism, adult domination of the child's play narratives, loss of mental mapping abilities and of having a negative effect on brain structure and neurochemical activity. Each of these effects has serious implications for how playworkers work, particularly in custodial contexts.

New language

Theory and practice derived from these more recent developments is giving rise to a new language to describe what playworkers think and do, so that they can communicate better with one another and the non-playwork world. For example, a whole raft of new terminology has begun to appear in playwork's consciousness – not as one might expect, terms like New Apprenticeships, SPRITO, Child-care strategy, Welfare to Work, OFSTED, NVQs, outcomes, QCA and all the other Government paraphernalia that makes us appear to be a new branch of the Civil Service – but rather terms such as:

Adulteration
Stereotypical play narratives (SPNs)
Flexibility
Adaptation
Imaginal play
Metalude
Ludic ecology
Play frame/return/decay
Reflective analytic playwork
Evolutionary playwork
play-cues
Play types
Containment
Neurochemical mutation
play-deprivation

Terms that describe a growing understanding both of the play and the playwork phenomena with which we study and work.

Finally

Although, from time to time, different issues like safety and child-care, for example, have had the effect of undermining some of playwork's core values and have facilitated several unhelpful re-interpretations of playwork's *raison d'être*, playwork theory and practice is continuing to evolve. Increasing its potential effectiveness in ensuring that children not only enjoy the right to play, but that that experience touches what Wilber describes as their deep structures, as well as the culturally moulded surface structures we have tended to focus upon in the past.

The evidence strongly supports the view that children have to play to make sense of who they are, what they are and where they are, to help them to evolve and to keep themselves sane and balanced. In the future playwork will have a diagnostic and curative role in helping children whose play has become a manifestation of the problems and negative experiences they have undergone.

Theoretically at least, no time in history has been so difficult for children to engage in the most simple, and most powerful acts of playing, and so children's evolutionary potential is not being maximised. They are still suffering the debilitating effects of play-deprivation and a violent lifestyle is still the unavoidable path for many of them.

Playwork thinking and practice can only go as far as research, development and resourcing allows. The scale of the problem is enormous. And, paraphrasing Perry (1996), a solution requires, 'nothing less than a transformation of culture'. Radical changes in social and political attitudes to play and its importance, need to be made. Addressing these factors is a huge challenge.

Commentary/discussion

This compressed chronology hardly does justice to the strength of feeling I have about the sociological analysis with which playwork has been plagued since the early 1980s. In my view it has not only been an irritating distraction, and an irrelevance, it has held, and is still holding, the development of playwork up, because of its total contamination by the adult agenda.

If, as I believe, playwork is a compensatory response, then it is responding to a weakening, and in many cases a loss of play experience in the child's repertoire. The loss to which I allude is not economic or political, it has nothing to do with citizenship – not in any direct sense – rather it is molecular, it is atomic, it is neurochemical and neurological, and it is psychic and spiritual – about the human condition in a general biological sense, rather than in a specific geographical or political/economic context.

I suggest that playwork (not childcare, or early years or youth work, each of which exists for other perfectly valid reasons in their own right) exists to maximise the facilitation of adaptive potential. It is based upon the realisation that play, as far as human beings go at least, is synonymous with food, oxygen and water, rather than football, democracy or gender issues. It is a fundamental, a basic essential. And to be deprived of play is to be punished unforgivingly by genetic and cellular revenge. The Huttenmoser and Chugani material are at least powerful indicators that that is so.

Of course it is difficult for any of us not to get drawn into the socio-political agenda, wherever we live. Issues matter to us as adults and as parents, but we can exercise our concerns at a biological level as well as at an economic or party political level.

Towards its end, this chapter stresses the educational, health and crime/social exclusion benefits of a good play provision strategy. The foundation of any biologically successful society has to be rooted in the priority it gives, and in the way it treats, its young. In this context, in many countries, we do this well. But the price we expect our children to pay for society's support, as Cairns (1987b) suggested about Northern Ireland, could be accurately described as tantamount to abuse, if children's individuality, their own integrity is at stake.

If children have always played, there is a vitally important biological reason for it, or it would have disappeared through natural selection thousands, if not millions, of years ago. One reason which makes sense to me is that, as well as maximising diversity of experience to help each of us to adapt to change, it acts to maximise diversity in adult society, by providing it (society) with a continuous supply of non-rigid thinking, an essential for adaptive potential. That is, thinking which has evolved from spontaneous and goalless, i.e. non-specialist, interaction with planetary diversity, rather than from planned, goal driven and specialist interaction with the locally predictable, i.e. thinking which is a manifestation of the non-adulterated individuality which can only result from the challenge, freedom and personal responsibility which are implicit characteristics of playing.

Whilst this may be viewed as inconvenient by those who are attempting to plan and legislate, it nevertheless provides them with an incredibly rich seam of creative, yet still contextualised thinking, which can only be of immense value to any human organisation wishing to survive and adapt to changing conditions and circumstances of any kind.

Currently, it seems to be viewed as easier to see play as an addendum to social policy directed at parents, than as a policy area in its own right, or even as a value underpinning all policy. Nursery education, early years and child care, are examples of this. To me that is crass short sightedness.

If we make play experiences available and accessible to children, if we provide the financial, land and training resources needed for provision, if we think about provision as compensatory and as developmental, then parents will still be able to go to work, as they would if there was globally available child-care, but the emphasis would be on the child's developmental needs and not on the adults'. That would not only be a remarkable water-shed for child-orientated social development, it would also demonstrate that adults do not have to lose out simply because society begins to put its children first.

It does not take a rocket scientist to deduct that many of the individual and collective problems which exist in all societies are rooted in the early childhood experiences of their children. Really good play provision and playwork, and that has to mean play provision and playwork which has been far more appropriately resourced than that which currently exists, should be able to make a major contribution to addressing and combating those problems, through work based on a recognition that the context which most effectively stimulates learning and facilitates well-being in children, is play. Many great educationalists, including Froebel and Montessori, appeared to be convinced of this (see Bruce (1994) for example).

RAP Example 7 (c. 1997)

Towards a technology of playwork

Introduction – The job of playwork

We know that as commerce, transport and housing eat up space, as cars, animals and predatory adults render the streets unsafe, and as parents opt for pre- and post-school childcare, so children will increasingly be forced into artificial spaces to engage in play.

The playworker's function is to compensate for the loss that children experience, both as social animals and biological organisms, as their freedom to range, to interact spontaneously with the environment, to explore and experiment and learn the skills necessary for their survival and normal development, is curtailed by the relentless march of the adult world.

The playworker does this in what are often tiny, poorly resourced, bleak spaces by finding ways of ensuring that the children who come to the playground, playcentre or club are able to play in as diverse and natural a way as possible.

As a drive manifested in what we know as play behaviours, play is as old as human beings themselves. It is linked to the development of virtually every aspect of what makes us intelligent, human, flexible and adaptable and is known to facilitate most of the building blocks that enable us to travel to the moon and create information technology.

It is a complex phenomenon, which does not always sit well with our pre-scribed stereotypes of behaviour, or of children. For in their post-birth struggle to establish themselves and gain a sense of place, children have to interact with the world in ways that enable them to have a detailed understanding of where they are and what the implications of that are for them.

These interactions must, therefore, by necessity include the whole menu of known human behaviour – daring, violence, imagination, creativity, symbolism, prejudice and so on. A menu which, by its very nature, will not always meet with contemporary desired aspirations.

So, because there is this misfit between

- what children do/are driven to do, on the one hand, and
- the realities of artificial play provision, on the other,

the playworker is forced to make critical judgements, which must genuinely facil-itate quality play. They must also recognise the constraints imposed by the artifi-cial nature of the space in which play is taking place, and that is no easy matter.

Making these judgements requires incredible skill. It requires a judgement, which, in itself, needs a level of knowledge and insight that would befit any other complex vocation, like medicine or engineering.

Whether we get these judgements right is to a great extent dependent on the training we receive. Behaviours as complex as calibration and combinatorial flexibility need to be at least understood before we can begin to create the con-ditions to facilitate them.

What is clear is that we need to have a detailed understanding of what play is, and what it is for, and then incorporate that knowledge and experience into play-work training. If we are to equip playworkers with the skills and tools they will need to help children to have as challenging, interesting and useful play experience as most of us will have enjoyed, this task must be undertaken.

The contemporary scene

As a professional, freelance playwork trainer myself, I do not have many opportunities to see other trainers at work. However, feedback from colleagues and my attendance at the NPFA's Playwork Education and Training Advisory Group Meetings do give me some insights of what is currently being offered as an appropriate curriculum. This is an example:

The Children Act
Health and Safety Legislation
First Aid
Disclosure Procedures
Assertiveness
Teamwork
Equal Opportunities
Programming Activities

Figure 13.3 An appropriate training curriculum for playworkers?

If this is accurate, and this list constitutes the core of what most student play-workers are being given to equip them to do their job, I am gravely concerned. For, with respect, inputs like these alone can only result in a training equation that manages at the same time to be both breathtakingly simplistic and virtually irrelevant as far as playwork is concerned.

Playwork Training = Supervision + Legislation + Procedures

Figure 13.4 A playwork training equation.

This training equation gives a bleak view of how we might facilitate something as awesome, complex and as developmentally important as play. It is selling children short.

Perhaps sadder is its blandness. It could be describing basic training for almost anything. There is nothing there to highlight the uniqueness of children, play or playwork. Nothing to argue why playwork should not simply succumb and be subsumed into care, youth or recreation, in line with current pressures. Why bother, if all playwork is, is the implementation of an apparatchik's check list of how to avoid litigation and confrontation?

I believe – and there are others too – that it is essential that playwork offers both a curriculum and methodologies in its training, demonstrating its unique role. Not to head off the ever present, the predatory and the colonising, but to ensure that play in all its diversity is always an option for children, a free choice, a quality alternative to the life-threatening road and railway track, or the brain numbing nature of much of what is commercially available.

I know it rankles some when this is said, but if playworkers do not undertake this role, who will? Playworkers are technicians who implement a system which, by tying together means and ends, provides children with the best that our know-ledge and experience of play can offer. However, the success of that system is dependent first of all upon the worth of the people out there implementing it and that, in turn, depends upon the quality of the training they receive in the first place.

Playwork tools and their use

If the training model summarised in Figures 13.3 and 13.4 is not sufficient to produce playworkers with a high enough quality of knowledge and experience base, what models would be more appropriate and why?

This is a very difficult question to answer. Not because the information is not there, but because no permanent models exist currently, except perhaps variations on Figures 13.3 and 13.4, at least in my experience.

My own training models change on demand, and according to several variables; like how long the course will be and the experience level of the students. But I always try to include what I regard as the absolute bottom line for competency and this will include a mixture of the list below.

- Philosophy – why playwork exists and what it exists to achieve.
- Knowledge – what play is and why it is important.
- Experience – the role of a playworker including ethical considerations.
- Quality benchmarks – examples of how quality judgements can be made.
- Deprivation indices – ways of generating data about play-deprivation and environmental impoverishment.
- Case studies – to encourage students to be analytical and reflective.
- Personal inputs describing the student's own experience and insights.

Figure 13.5 The 'bottom line' for competency.

Generally, I try to put these into the form of a process which has a beginning, a middle and an end. If I formalised this into curriculum headings it would probably look like this.

1   What are we trying to achieve and why?
2   What do we know already?
3   Collecting useful data
4   Undertaking environmental modification
5   Developing strategies for intervention
6   Evaluating practice and applying qualitative checks and balances

Figure 13.6 More appropriate curriculum headings.

This would include the following sub-headings:

Heading	Sub-headings
• What are we trying to achieve and why?	Social, biological, ethical values
• What do we know already?	Intuition, Memory, Experience, Evidence (IMEE)
• Collecting useful data	Environmental audits, play-deprivation indicators
• Environmental modification	Playwork Curriculum, Play Types, Loose Parts
• Intervention strategies	Values/IMEE and audit and indices data

Figure 13.7 Curriculum sub-headings.

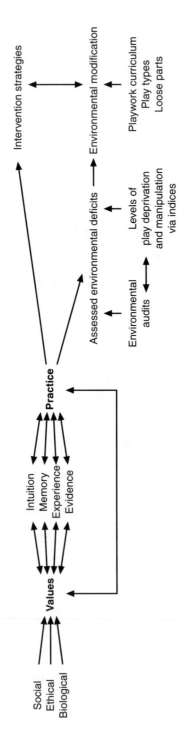

Figure 13.8 A new training equation.

These, in turn, would be represented by a new training equation which, above all, demonstrates that playwork is an evolving discipline in which practice and underpinning belief continually update each other in a cyclical process of evaluation and feedback:

The absence of evaluation and feedback mechanisms is one of playwork's most impoverishing flaws, both in practice and in training courses. Practitioners, in general, do not have a culture of observation, keeping records and analysing practice, except in the context of accident books and diaries. Training courses invariably do not upgrade and synthesise current knowledge/practice in the light of any new developments. This needs to change.

Let us turn our attention to the headings and sub-headings in Figures 13.6 and 13.7.

1 What are we trying to achieve and why? Playwork's social, biological, ethical values

Vital to the development of a competent playworker in my view is that they have a clear philosophical foundation. I have worked with playworkers for twenty-five years now, and many of them have never had a clear idea of why what they do needs doing. Without that foundation they find themselves buffeted about in every financial and political storm, changing their terms of reference to suit the next grant aid form or next fashion.

Note: Useful discussion of values that cast light upon playwork's philosophical base can be found in Chapter 5.

Perhaps the greatest benefit of having a clear values statement is that not only does it tell playworkers where they want to go, it also helps them to judge whether what they are actually doing is going to get them there. However, that does not always work.

I have been to many playwork organisations which have stated values on the office wall and that is normally the last reference I have seen to them. The reality has been that they articulate gentle values, that are often implemented in a much harsher reality.

The lesson is that having values is vital but they have to be implemented and that is particularly important on play projects with real children.

2 What do we know? Intuition, Memory, Experience and Evidence (IMEE)

Between my own knowledge as a trainer/practitioner, the field's collective wisdom and the life experience of individual students I am working with, there is normally a great deal of knowledge and experience of play and play provision already present in the training sessions I run. I devised the IMEE process to draw this out when I was drafting *A Question of Quality*. Simply put, IMEE is two processes in one.

First, it is a way of drawing out of the three participants, the trainer, the field and the student, much of what they know, have experienced and felt about play and making provision. This is done through discussion, exercises, problem solving and lecturettes.

Second, it presents students with the start of a quality assurance process by engaging them in an analysis of their knowledge, experiences and feelings. It begins to get them back in touch with what it actually means to be a child playing and what it means to be a child playing in a space in which they are operating.

It does this using a non-judgemental and quite vulnerable format, one where student and tutor alike first explore their intuitive reactions to situations. They access their childhood play memories, discuss the implications these data have for their practice and then put this in some sort of formal context by juxtaposing it against the 'evidence' from the literature.

It is very interesting for students to explore their prejudices, their personally possessed view of what play is, what constitutes a good experience and what quality is, only to find out that Bruner, a psychologist, agrees with them or that Loizos, an ethologist, described the same experience.

The sadness I feel with Figures 13.3 and 13.4 is that they lose, perhaps *disregard* is a better word, the links between the children and their play, the playworker's and their play and the academics and their play.

The amalgamation of intuition, feelings and images, practical strategies and ideas, and academic analysis generated through IMEE, provides students with a whole range of personal, professional and academic benchmarks, against which to test their practice and make judgements about it. This is particularly the case when exploring risky and cruel play practices.

3   Collecting Data – Environmental audits and play-deprivation indices

If playwork is an inexact science, then collecting data must be the most inexact part of playwork. Yet I think it has considerable value to the field and to students in the longer term.

I have long believed that the piecemeal process of placing fixed equipment, or an adventure playground, playcentre or club into an area, without making an appropriate assessment is nonsensical. It is the kind of 'Aspirin-will-cure-all' syndrome and only serves to diminish play and play provision in everyone's eyes.

Play provision can come in an infinite variety of forms and I think we need to be helping the field and our students to make judgements about which forms most appropriately address which needs.

The question is, 'How do we measure need?' Obviously socio-economic indicators will give us an idea of the conditions children will be living under, but we need measures that will give us a more accurate view of the quality of play children are experiencing, if we are to tailor provision to their developmental needs.

I suggested at the beginning of this presentation that playwork is a compensatory discipline, which means that it tries to compensate for the play experiences children do not normally get. Obviously some of these are pretty obvious and were summarised by Drummond Abernethy, on several occasions, when he worked for the NPFA, and included fire play, constructing dens and having gardens.

However, others, like that of social interaction, lack of manipulative interaction, lack of mastery play, and so on, are not so obvious. These and other deficits can be easily identified by using simple checklists of play-enabling and play-disabling features in the environment, or by using evaluation spirals, to test for particular play forms, or to collect data on aspects of the children's behaviour which are judged to be the result of deprivation or manipulation, the level of violence, for example. Obviously, these are not truly scientific measures, but they do give us and our students data for the judgements we make.

Without the use of more sophisticated methods of creating benchmarks, like these for a start, practitioners will always be open to being over-ruled by management or politicians, who may know little or nothing, but whose arguments carry more weight.

4   Environmental Modification – The Playwork Menu, Play Types and Loose Parts

The rationale for environmental modification and the use of the Playwork Menu, Play Types and Loose Parts is well documented in *A Question of Quality*. But, briefly summarised, each ingredient provides a benchmark, a standard against which practical judgements can be compared. In fact each of these ingredients, is given the name, 'Comparitor', for this reason.

The Playwork Menu invites both playworker and student to ask: 'Does what I am thinking of providing enable the children to access their senses, explore their identity, develop a comprehension of concepts and experiment with the elements?'

Play Types refers to the fifteen play types identified from the literature. Assuming that each of them is of equal importance in helping the child to access information and experience, this Comparitor asks, 'Are each of these play types catered for with space, props and with supervision, as in the case of deep play and rough and tumble, in particular?'

Loose Parts refers to the recognised need for play environments to contain any number and combination of loose materials, which children can move around, manipulate, use as props, and use to change the environment. They are a formidable ingredient for enabling children to engage in play.

5   Intervention strategies – Values/IMEE and audit and indices data

Although I have included values, IMEE and indices data as benchmarks for developing intervention strategies, and that is rightly so, this is probably the most difficult of all areas of practical playwork for which to legislate.

Just recently, I received information about yet another training course on dealing with challenging behaviour from children and adults. It is obviously an area that exercises us all. Hopefully, one can see how students might be better equipped to make judgements about how a play environment should look and feel, from, for example, the environmental modification material, or how the issues around safety and hazards might be dealt with from the IMEE and Values material, but intervention is a vexed question.

There can be no definitive answer to the questions 'How and When to intervene?' There are simply too many variables.

Personally, I have always been a minimal interventionist both in terms of interrupting the children when they are playing and being in control if they are being disruptive.

Certainly if, as a playworker, you are experiencing difficulty and you are scared, it is easier and more manageable to have the 'three strikes and you are out' kind of intervention policy, where the playworker falls back on old response strategies to deal with violent, damaging or racist children. I just feel we can do better than that. I feel that we are making some progress in understanding from what basis to intervene. One development is in the area of values; i.e., when is it appropriate to intervene?

There is the now famous intervention example, which has since entered the annuls of playwork folklore, posed initially by Stephen Rennie, one of the Leeds Metropolitan University lecturers, which demonstrates the dilemma. Stephen asked a group, 'If you noticed a child carefully cutting up a worm into 10 mm pieces, what would you do and why?'

As one can imagine, the group at whom this was aimed came up with a wide range of responses, from, the child is being cruel ('How would you like it if someone did that to you?') to incredulity ('What on earth do you think you are doing?').

However, as Stephen pursued the point, by asking the question 'Why?', the members of the group, reminded that most children – including themselves when they had been children – have a very vicious streak, began to accept that in this case, intervention might only be appropriate if the child was seen to be doing this on an obsessional basis, when it might be judged as a manifestation of psychosis. Here they were guided by their playwork values base.

I thought this was a bizarre enough example of the problem of intervention, until, whilst training in Ireland and giving the worm question as an example of the problem, a playworker there said it had reminded her of something she used to do with worms when she was a child. Apparently, she used to dig up worms, so she could wash them and then put them back into the ground! Obviously, the lesson here is that any playworker intervention should be tempered by observation first, as this case demonstrates.

In the context of violence or disruption, recent work undertaken, again in Ireland, with volunteer and professional playworkers demonstrated that creative intervention strategies based upon a knowledge of the child's circumstances and an understanding of the dynamic of behaviour adults find threatening or difficult, especially with children who are showing symptoms of ADD or ADHD, can be devised and valued by workers.

In this study, scenarios relating to real experiences of disruption, interruption, fighting, threatening behaviour, tantrums, destruction and abuse were analysed and strategies developed over a weekend. The recommendations included using a more strategic and decentred approach on the part of playworkers, where situations potentially requiring intervention could be analysed and controlled in much the same way as a doctor might when viewing a difficult patient. Assessing the situation through the filter of professional experience and knowledge was felt to be much more appropriate as a strategy than just banning or disciplining. Without this reflection and analysis, the temptation to forget the point of the exercise in our desire to protect ourselves must be considerable. However, we do need to remember that a play project without conflict is probably not doing its job.

From a training perspective, inviting students to explore scenarios and make intervention judgements will develop important skills and help them to feel much less vulnerable in situations that most adults would find difficult and demanding. However, as I indicated earlier, we should not see intervention as a purely negative tool. Playworkers are often invited to intervene if they can recognise the invitation.

A playworker working with withdrawn and isolated children should, as a matter of professional judgement, be able to recognise when the child is sending them play-cues. My reference to ADD earlier is a case in point. I understand, from Sturrock (1997), that these children often get caught up in a negative behavioural cycle simply because other children do not recognise their play-cues.

Cues reflect the classic literature descriptions of play. Meta-communication – the play face, sometimes accompanied by exaggerated movements or gullumphing, behaviour which is clearly out of context, eye contact and all sorts of comic expressions, can all be attempts by children to make contact.

At my last full-time play project, young children would frequently begin a game of chase between the workers, older children and themselves, using most of the cues I have described. Recognising them meant that any intervention or participation on my part was invited; this was very important both ethically and strategically to me.

Implications for playwork education and training

So what does this say about playwork education and training and the lessons we might learn from the perceived current situation? There are six important implications I would like to highlight.

1   Playwork education and training models that are based mainly on legislation and procedures should be radically rethought. Trainers should be expected to take a more play-based approach in future.

2   The emphasis in all playwork education and training courses should be on providing the experience, knowledge, tools and techniques necessary to enable playworkers to provide a constantly improving service to children.

3   Service providers should allocate resources towards playwork R&D, specifically to facilitate the technical development of tools and processes to make playwork judgements that are based more on data. These developments should be reported and published.

4   There should be more opportunities, i.e., conferences, to put playwork rationales and education and training developments under the microscope.

5   Those who commission education and training should try to standardise the structure of core inputs. Practitioners could use a more formalised and realistic study period like a day release for up to two years.

6   There should be at least one on-the-job teaching/research playground, or play project in the UK.

Commentary/discussion

More than anything, this chapter was a plea for more professional and more rigorous debate in playwork. Debate, that is, about play and about playwork themselves. It seemed that the field was always happy to discuss what I called 'issues' – and others called 'values' – relating to social policy and legislation, but to get a discussion about combinatorial flexibility, or environmental modification has always been nigh on impossible. This unavoidably resulted, in subjective, even dogmatic stances, being taken by some playworkers, as parts of this book demonstrate. And dogmatism is probably as unhelpful to the development and effectiveness of playwork as is a bias towards an analysis derived from social policy issues and the current legislative framework.

Having said that, over the years, the playwork field has consistently put the national training cart before the horse, devising complex delivery systems for national training in advance of agreements relating to training needs.

What does a trainee playworker need to know to do his or her job effectively? What does an Assistant Playworker, or a Senior Playworker need to know? What does a Playwork Manager need to know? These questions go right to the root of playwork. What is playwork and what does it exist to change? Without clear agreement on our response, particularly to these last two questions, it is difficult for us to move forward.

The other interesting emphasis of this chapter, is playwork's perceived need for measuring instruments and research and development budgets. It is probably the chemist in me, but I have often felt the need to be able to measure things in playwork, to quantify, to measure change in terms of volume or density. Perhaps this is because the unquantifiable, almost undefinable nature of play drives me toward something more tangible, something I can hold. Possibly others in the work feel the same, and this is why so much effort has gone into, and is still going into, NVQ work and other projects.

Wilber (1996) talks of our current history as the 'subtle period', and perhaps that is the key to measurement. Perhaps research into the impact of playwork has to be conducted in a more subtle manner; that what is glaringly obvious is being masked by our preconceptions and expectations of what children are, and of what children do. Perhaps we need to look more closely at subtle variations in children's play behaviour, in their use of play types and meta-communication, to identify clues to development, adaptation and well-being.

My intuition is that we will have measures which result in evidence and findings which are tangible and valued, one day. When this happens, it is more a function of will than it is of ability. Research and development cost money, and those who fund provision find it increasingly difficult to do that, let alone find money for research.

Optimistically, one final plea from this chapter is for more playwork material to be written down and published, and increasingly this is happening, albeit slowly.

RAP Example 8 (c. 1999)

Uncensoring play – towards an evolutionary perspective for facilitating recapitulation

> Sometimes I think this whole world is one big prison yard and some of us are prisoners and the rest of us are guards. Lord, Lord, they shot George Jackson down. Lord, Lord, they laid him in the ground.
>
> Bob Dylan

In 1904, the educationalist and developmental psychologist G.S. Hall wrote, 'the best index and guide to the stated activities of adults in past ages, is found in the instinctive, untaught and non-imitative play of children.'

This was the basis of his theory of recapitulation. The theory, which was later expanded by Reaney (1916), proposed that play could be viewed as a re-enactment of an individual's forebear's transmitted activities, i.e., that the essence of each forebear's past and present, a kind of life summary, was somehow encapsulated into the player's genes and passed on via procreation, to be played out by the next and future generations.

This 'life summary' could be 'divided into play periods that corresponded to our species' "various evolutionary stages"', e.g., the animal, savage, nomad, pastoral and tribal (Reaney, 1916).

More recently, a similar, although transpersonal model of recapitulation has also been developed.

The evolution of consciousness

In his book *Up from Eden*, Wilber (1996) has provided us with another slant on recapitulation, elevating it from the Hall/Reaney basic model, to a developmental matrix, which underlines the potential evolutionary significance of the phenomenon. For, although Wilber sees recapitulation as a life-long, transpersonal process, rather than an individually specific childhood experience, there is, nevertheless, a remarkable resonance between the two ideas.

In *Up from Eden*, Wilber maps our species' evolution from a 'ground zero', what he calls the 'ground unconscious', to the present day. Having passed through stages which possess great similarity to Hall's evolutionary development, he reaches a stage that is an approximation of our species' current evolutionary peak.

His stages include what he calls the uroboric, the typhonic, the magical, the mythical, the membership and the mental egoic. Unlike the Hall/Reaney model, which on the face of it is almost too predictable, Wilber's stages describe characteristics which are a more accurate reflection both of the human condition and of the content of children's play. For example, his stages refer to our long interest in magic and spirituality. He acknowledges that humans are sexual and violent organisms. He explores the notion of leadership and citizenship in the membership stage, by looking at ancient civilisations like the Mayans, Greeks and Egyptians. He also reminds us that, like these other characteristics, ritual has also always featured strongly in human nature.

But importantly, from the perspective of playwork and recapitulation, he implies that every one of us passes through a speeded up version of these stages during our own development, in much the same way as the Hall/Reaney model.

By overlaying the Hall/Reaney stages with Wilber's, as in Figure 13.9, we have a series of defined stages of what Hall called bio-psychic growth, that he says recapitulates biologically and psychologically. We also get a more authentic picture of what may actually be displayed during recapitulation. For example, some episodes of recapitulation will certainly be closer to Wilber's 'Lord of the Flies' model, than Hall's 'Five go Camping'.

Wilber describes his view of recapitulation in great detail, seeing it as a transcendence from one stage to the next, like Jones (1993), and evolutionary mutation, where our species gradually evolves through increasingly complex forms of being, each with their own problems and solutions. The Hall/Reaney play periods model is a microcosm of this same process.

This view seems to be supported by Sutton-Smith (1997). He states, 'play . . . may have developed as a fuller imitation of the evolutionary process, in which the organism models [or imitates] its own biological character'.

However, Wilber does sound a note of caution about the delicacy of recapitulation: 'each stage of human evolution, although it transcends its predecessor, must include and integrate [it] in a higher unity. Failure to do so, equals neurosis' (Wilber, 1996).

WILBER →	Ground Unconscious	Reptilian Uroboric		Typhonic	Mythic	Membership	Egoic →
HALL →			Animal	Savage	Nomad	Pastoral	Tribal →

Figure 13.9 The Wilber/Hall/Reaney model.

I interpret this to mean that recapitulation is a totally hermetic biological package, which if tampered with, will have negative health and evolutionary consequences for those affected.

What might recapitulation be for?

Two interesting ideas come to mind.

- One is that it enables us to play ourselves up to 'contemporary evolutionary speed'.
- The other is that it enables us to integrate our present into our personal recapitulation process.

PLAYING OURSELVES UP TO 'CONTEMPORARY EVOLUTIONARY SPEED'

At birth, no human child knows either where or when it is. Its geographical location could be Lima or Lisbon and its chronological location could be anytime. It does not know where in its biological/historical/cultural continuum it is. So how does it locate its current evolutionary peak?

Hall and Wilber imply that we are all an amalgam of our total individual and collective histories, struggling to mutate into our evolutionary future. I think this mutation is able to occur because we are driven to play ourselves up to contemporary evolutionary speed, via the process of recapitulation, which itself might facilitate a whole series of mutations.

By this I mean the following. Imagine that, to survive and develop in 1999, we need to be able to operate at a level of complexity represented by 100 kph, and that at birth we are actually operating at a relative level of 0 kph. Let us also imagine that the first stage of recapitulation represents 0–10 kph. By playing through Stage 1, we make it possible to move on to Stage 2, which is, say, a more complex 10–20 kph. Stage 3 is 20–40, Stage 4, 40–60, increasing in complexity all the time, until we reach our current optimum complexity of 100 kph, the present. When we reach the final stage, with no new stage to recapitulate, this is our current evolutionary position. Now there is potential for genuine original development, i.e., recapitulation is replaced with evolution.

INTEGRATING OUR PRESENT INTO OUR PERSONAL RECAPITULATION PROCESS

The other role for recapitulation may be that it provides the mechanism for the actual integration of the child's present into the recapitulative potential it will pass on. That is to say, the actual act of recapitulating ensures that the recapitulation process is extended by each generation, by adding on the present, thus making our present the past. By actually playing now, the information is coded, to pass on to the next generation in the appropriate form.

Gould (1996) seems to support this, saying, 'Biologically, play's function is to reinforce the organism's variability in the face of rigidification of successful adaptation', i.e., play's primary function is to maintain our species' evolutionary momentum and behavioural diversity, when the process might otherwise falter. It could be through the biological power source of recapitulation that, as individuals and as a species, we continue to evolve.

Uncensoring censored play

From my perspective as a playworker, what is most significant about Hall's and Wilber's models, is that they both assign great significance to the expression of play types that many in the play world would regard as unacceptable, and which many of the current generation of children are being prevented from engaging in.

Hall talks of the instinctive, untaught and non-imitative play of children and Wilber alludes to much the same phenomenon. This is the wild-play children normally engage in when they are adult-free.

But over the past decade or so, in many after school clubs, playgrounds and other play schemes, for reasons ranging from safety to citizenship training, there has been a gradual but relentless attack on certain of the types of play children naturally manifest.

I am concerned that the deficit caused by the lack of experience of these less accepted types of play may leave the children affected, disabled by this 'experiential censorship', increasingly unable to respond to the adaptive demands of climatic, cultural and other changes. This occurs because the flexibility of response implicit in engaging in these types of play, with I believe vital evolutionary significance, will not have been incorporated into their cerebral processes. I am thinking particularly here of rough and tumble play, communication play, deep play and mastery play (see Hughes, 1996a).

So here we have a playwork dilemma. What is playwork for? Is it to facilitate processes many agree are vital for human survival, development and ultimately evolution, or is to provide a 'socialisation enclosure' within which certain play behaviours are categorised as acceptable or unacceptable by legislative 'apparatchiks'? (Potential censors should remember that each of these types is very complex, and that they do not necessarily exist to perform the most obvious function their names imply.)

Rough and tumble, for example, often called 'play fighting' is rarely about real fighting and, is more often, according to Baldwin (1982) 'precisely the cause of social bonding', consisting as it does, of 'players experiencing generous levels of positive reinforcement and little adverse stimuli'.

There are also other considerations that cause me concern. Wilber implies that not allowing the play types that frequently occur in the recapitulation process could have consequences for the mental health of those deprived of them. Equally, not providing an appropriate backdrop for these play types could have similar consequences.

Orr (1993) for example, observed that, 'the human mind is a product of the Pleistocene age, shaped by wildness that has all but disappeared. If we complete the destruction of nature, we will have succeeded in cutting ourselves off from the sources of sanity itself.'

So wildness in the play environment, as well as the opportunity to recapitulate therein, may be another pre-evolutionary essential.

Visible signs of recapitulation seem to occur mainly in what is known as middle-childhood, the 6–10 period. Emphasising again the importance of recapitulation, Thomashow (1995) writes of the period of middle-childhood, that it is, 'the time of place making, in which children expand their sense of self, a time that children establish their connections with the earth, forming an earth matrix, a terrain symbiosis which is crucial to their personal identity.'

What I infer from this, is that there is a relationship between recapitulative play in appropriate environments and well-being. And this proposition would not only be in-line with Wilber's assertion that 'failure to integrate each stage ... equals neurosis (Wilber, 1996), but reaffirms the position taken by Else and Sturrock (1998) that, in the play space, what they term the 'ludic ecology', 'lies a means of healing trauma, neurosis and psychic ill'.

What are the playwork practicalities for facilitating recapitulation?

Although this area of playwork practice is virtually unexplored and my input is inevitably quite rudimentary, facilitating play that appears to be connected to the recapitulation process is relatively straightforward, although it would probably not meet with general adult consensus at this time.

Personally, I would provide two things:

- the props to make recapitulative play authentic
- what Melville (1996) described as 'permissions' – implicit knowledge that the play area is a space in which children can, as of right, explore and experiment with materials, processes and ideas, which would normally not be appropriate in any other space (Abernethy, 1977, 1984).

For example, for play to be authentically recapitulative it would need to contain elements of the instinctive, untaught, spontaneous and non-imitative play of children of which Hall spoke. It might include some of the elements included in Figure 13.10.

Obviously these are more a representation of my own recapitulation experiences than those of the current or future generation of players. However, they serve as examples of what might be useful for recapitulative play and what may be being censored.

- Archaic/mythic and shamanistic ritual
- fires for warmth, cooking, burning and games
- changing identity using paints, masks and body decoration
- large group events, like tag, wide games and other mock battles
- den/cave building
- all aspects of deep play
- growing and preserving food
- using weapons – bows, catapults
- rearing other species
- tactile sand and earth interfacing
- creating magic and illusion – the magic tower
- story telling, song, music and dance
- tracking
- making and flying things, e.g. kites
- recognising the behaviour of animals, birds, fish, reptiles and insects
- knowing trees, flowers and other plants
- iconic play – e.g. designing and flying flags, making coats of arms, etc.
- playing with water
- using tools.

Figure 13.10 Elements of the instinctive, untaught, spontaneous and non-imitative play of children.

Conclusion

Darwin is cited by Gruber (1974) as saying, 'Survival depends upon the organism remaking itself. Variation and novelty are not chaotic or unrelated to the organism's past'. It is variation and novelty that is being censored out of children's experience.

The play world has taken upon itself the responsibility to protect and promote the child's right to play. If we are to really live up to that responsibility, by choosing flexibility rather than rigidification, then in the context of denying children access to experiences of fundamental importance, of tampering with one of evolution's hermetic packages, we should heed Arendt's words, when she says, 'what I propose therefore, is very simple: it is nothing more than to think what we are doing' (1958).

Commentary/discussion

Although this piece may appear to be more about Wilber, Hall and Reaney, what prompted it was that I had learnt that some playworkers were deciding what the play content of the lives of children they worked with should be. If they did not like rough and tumble, because it mimicked real fighting; if they did not like children using certain words because they might have been construed as racist or vulgar; if they did not want to see children playing, 'bang bang you are dead' type of narratives, because they, the playworkers abhorred war toys; then rough and tumble, communication play and imaginative play were banned. That not only incensed me as a parent and grandparent, it worried me professionally.

Whose needs is someone who dictates the content of a child's play meeting? What is a play space for if not for play? Surely not for socialisation, we have home and school for that.

However, the big issue around banning certain kinds of play is the impact it might have on the evolutionary process itself. At a time when people all around me are becoming evolution literate, reading Jones, Wilson, Dawkins and above all, Pinker, I am loath to put more than a playwork toe in the evolutionary water. However, as I have intimated within this chapter, play does seem to have some kind of evolutionary role, and playwork does have a responsibility to facilitate play. The corollary being that if play, in its totality, is not facilitated, then evolution, in all of its totality – whatever that means – will not be facilitated either.

Evolutionary biologists would probably be frustrated at such a statement, because evolution happens, it is not facilitated. And yet climate, the availability of food, disease, the absence or not of predators, meteors, comets, earthquakes and floods, have all impacted upon evolution. So perhaps that is what I mean, that play has impacted upon evolution, and by definition, so has playwork. Jones (1993): 'it seems that social (and economic) changes have produced many of the genetic patterns seen in the world today. ... Society drives genes, rather than genes driving society.' The impact I judge censorship may have will be the creation of unease, of disquiet in the body of the child. By that I mean in its deepest essence, perhaps in its genes. Most children expect limitations on behaviour at home and at school, but not limitations on play. Censorship might have the effect of discouraging children from some play types, because they believe them to be wrong. Such an effect would impoverish a child's experience and developing life perspective. In fact, such playwork would act against ideas which underpin playwork itself, because it has the effect of limiting experience and closing down choice. Lorenz (1972), in Sylva (1977), should have the last word. 'Natural selection would favour the most playful individuals, for they have acquired more useful information about the potential of the environment and their actions on it.'

RAP Example 9 (c. 1999)

Does playwork have a neurological rationale?

If we are ever going to be able to provide evidence for the claims we make for our practice, then the need for testable playwork theory has probably never been more urgent. However, it is probably also true that playwork is only now reaching the level of maturity needed to do this on any significant scale.

Without a convincing theoretical base and the development of credible research programmes, it is unlikely that playwork will ever attract the research resources necessary to demonstrate the impact of playwork methods, on facilitating quality play experiences, and on helping children who manifest dysfunctional play.

The past thirty or so years have seen numerous brilliant hypotheses published relating to the benefits play affords the player, many of which themselves have yet to be tested, but typically it has been rare to encounter a parallel hypothesis that demonstrates how playwork practice might be used to both facilitate and maximise those benefits for children.

I think immediately of play as a mechanism for the development of identity, of flexibility, adaptation and calibration.

One issue that comes to my mind that deserves further investigation, is whether connections can be made between the playwork practices of environmental modification and facilitating freely chosen play, and brain growth and neurochemical activity.

My story begins twenty-one years ago in the psychological library at Cambridge University. This was when I first discovered some of the material I want briefly to explore now.

In 1978, I came across psycho-pharmacological data which proposed a triangular relationship between neurochemical activity and brain growth, activity and environment. Immediately I saw the parallels at least in terms of the language, between the subject of this research and playwork, and suggest that it is reasonable to propose that by simply replacing the word 'activity' with the word 'play', and 'environment' with 'play environment', a triangular relationship between brain growth and neurochemical activity, play and the play environment could also be proposed, at least in theory.

Of course the association I suggest might be spurious or simplistic, and I am not a psycho-pharmacologist, but if theoretical comparisons can be made, this may be a fruitful area for future playwork research.

Playworkers are aware that play is often described as a freely-chosen interaction between the player, in our case children, and the whole environment, in our case the play environments we create and manage. They will also recognise the notion of a two-way transfer, in which the child affects the environment and the environment affects the child.

However, what has not been explored or researched by our field is the effect of this transfer (whether created by a drive or by reactions to sensory stimuli), on the neurochemistry and neuroanatomy of the brain of that playing child. Long established studies of other species show a powerful relationship between the nature of the environment and the development of brain and behaviour.

Rosenzweig et al., for example, suggested in the early 1970s that rats kept in an enriched – what he called a 'lively' – environment, showed distinct changes in brain anatomy and brain chemistry when compared with animals kept in an impoverished – or what he called a 'dull' environment.

The Rosenzweig team had already made similar claims as far back as 1964, when they suggested that the kinds of changes in brain as demanded by learning theories, could actually be brought about by exposure to experience, implying a real link between brain size and activity, environmental type and behavioural interaction with that environment.

What they suggested was that, depending on the nature of the experience to which rats were exposed, so a phenomenon known as 'plasticity' occurred. What this meant was that, with use, the brain expanded, without use, the brain contracted – both in terms of its size and its internal chemical activity.

This relationship between behaviour, environment and brain was also highlighted in 1978 by Ferchmin and Eterovic, who, when discussing the mechanism by which brain development might be brought about by environmental stimulation, cited the work of Cummins *et al.*, who suggested the hypothesis that, 'the development of some neurones can be described as environment dependent'.

However, Ferchmin and Eterovic proposed an alternative explanation of their own, that 'processing a wide variety of stimuli coupled with motor feedback is necessary [for environmentally stimulated growth]'.

Interestingly, what Cummins is implying is that experience does not necessarily stimulate brain growth *per se*, but that because some neurones are environmentally sensitised, it is they that will grow in receipt of stimulation. Ferchmin and Eterovic's alternative offers that brain growth as a result of environmental stimulation is a whole brain phenomenon, which is the outcome of an interaction, what they call motor feedback, between in this case the rats, and an enriched environment containing a wide variety of stimuli. In fact they may well both be right. For whilst Ferchmin and Eterovic's proposition is supported by the work of the Rosenzweig team, Cummins' proposition, that some parts of the brain are particularly sensitive to environmental stimulus, is borne out by more recent work.

Ferchmin and Eterovic go on to say of their whole brain growth proposal, 'this is the equivalent of re-stating that learning, if complex enough, will trigger a trophic, or nourishing, i.e. growth, response'.

Although the debate relating to the actual mechanisms which bring about anatomical and chemical plasticity may still rage – the idea that some sort of relationship existed between experience, what I am calling play, and plasticity, had been established.

By 1984, the relationship between activity, environment and brain chemistry was also being extended, suggesting that complex learning – which I take to mean the result of an interaction between increasingly complex behaviour and a complex environment – and the activity of brain chemicals, was also being established.

Zuckerman's work, and that of other leading pharmacological pioneers, demonstrates the central role played by brain chemicals, both in activating behaviour and in regulating it.

Zuckerman states, 'Preliminary studies have related norepinephrine, a brain chemical known as a neurotransmitter, and enzymes involved in its production and degradation to human sensation seeking' – or what we might again call play. He continues:

> 'A model is suggested that relates mood, behavioural activity, sociability, and clinical states to the activity of these neurotransmitters, and to other

brain chemicals. Stimulation and behavioural activity act on the neurotransmitter systems in a brain-behaviour feedback loop. At optimal levels of the activity of these systems, mood is positive and activity and sociability are adaptive. At very low or very high levels of certain brain chemicals however, mood is dysphoric, activity restricted or stereotyped, and the organism is unsocial or aggressively antisocial'. (p. 413)

What this is suggesting is that there are optimum levels of stimulation and behavioural activity which produce brain chemical levels which result in good moods, normal activity and sociability.

e.g. Using the symbol $\varnothing$ to denote an optimum state, what this is saying is that,

$$\varnothing \text{ environment} + \varnothing \text{ activity} = \varnothing \text{ levels of brain chemicals} - \varnothing \text{ moods/} \\ \text{sociability}$$

But that, if either the environment or the activity are inappropriate, then that will result in either a high or low extreme of brain chemicals, which themselves bring about unhappiness, minimal and repetitive activity, and organisms that become withdrawn or aggressive.

e.g. Inappropriate environment or activity $= \uparrow\downarrow$ levels of brain chemicals
$$= \text{unhappiness} + \text{aggression}$$

If the terms 'play' and 'play environment' were used to replace the terms 'activity' and 'environment' here, this could be a direct reference to my own theoretical conclusions, of the effects of playing in biased and stimulus deprived environments, which I described in 1988, in the *Leisure Manager*, and in 1996, in *A Question of Quality*, following the earlier theoretical work produced for *PlayTimes* in 1982 (see Chapter 8, Stimulation Theory).

What I proposed then, was that that there was a direct relationship between play and environment, and that playing in adverse environments could increase a child's potential for violent anti-social and/or fantasy driven behaviour – this became known as stimulation theory and introduced the idea that good play environments could compensate for these abnormalities or deficits. Needless to say I did not realise that fluctuations in neurochemicals might be responsible for these aberrations.

Current developments

What makes this so exciting now is that there has been a recent revival of the idea of a relationship between neurochemistry, neuroanatomy and activity and environment, but this time the relationship has been made by a play researcher, Brian Sutton-Smith. In his book, *The Ambiguity of Play*, Sutton-Smith draws a connection between the brain's ability to constantly undergo physical and chemical changes, and the implied latent capacity for plasticity, which would make this possible.

So here we have the human brain, with a relatively infinite capacity for use in infancy, when compared to later life, with the potential for directional, i.e. positive or negative plasticity, which is stimulus dependent.

Given that, from an activity and interactive perspective, play is the most potent characteristic of childhood, then it is reasonable to conclude from the evidence above, that the massive potential of the neonate's brain, is that of a brain waiting to play, to experience that 'ecstasy of variety' as Kent calls it (Sturrock, 1997). And, although the huge cerebral capacity described above is probably only ever partially utilised, its potential acts to underline the crucial importance of appropriate play experiences for children in their early, as well as in their middle and late childhoods.

Plasticity is the brain's reaction to enriching and impoverishing stimuli, where impoverishing stimuli, what I have called 'negative stimulation' (Hughes and Williams, 1982; Hughes, 1988) are responsible for shrinkage or no-growth periods, and enriching stimuli, or positive stimulation, are responsible for growth periods.

Interestingly, in Rosenzweig's *et al.*'s work, impoverishment did not mean bad hygiene, a poor feeding regime or cruelty. Rather it meant a normal, social/nutritional regime, but a comparatively boring one. Whereas an enriched environment only meant that subjects were given access to 'environmental complexity and a training cage'. And it was social access to this cage which caused the 'brain growth transformation'.

Needless to say, the human child might need access to an environment which is more complex and challenging than a running wheel, a maze and a climbing frame, to generate brain growth and an increase in neurochemical activity, but nevertheless the example is there. For rats at least, the addition of these novelties into their lives made a significant difference to the size of their brains and presumably to their capacity to process information, as a result. However, we should also be cognisant of Zuckerman's warning that too much or too little stimulation can also be harmful.

Now, from a playwork perspective the real question that lies behind this short presentation is not about any relationship between play, the play environment and brain activity and growth; I think that case is already proved by the psychopharmacologists.

The question for us is, is it possible that what we do in our practice might have an effect on the level of brain activity and growth of the children we work with? Here I think there is a case for us to answer.

My intuition tells me that most physical and psychological processes operate most effectively under the most natural of conditions. In this context, this would mean that the ranging, personal control, exploration and experimentation, implicit in free play, in a diverse, happy, process dominated play environment would be most likely to create those conditions appropriate for optimum brain growth and neurochemical activity, and result in children whose mood is positive, who are sociable, balanced and considerate. Whilst, alternatively, it would be custodial conditions – where the child's relationship with the play environment is dominated by adult input, is claustrophobic, non-elemental and outcome dominated – which would create conditions resulting in dysphoria, restricted or stereotyped activity, and a child who is unsocial or aggressively anti-social.

I have long feared that current trends risk disabling a generation of children on the alter of ideology. However, what the above connections may indicate is something else I have also feared, and that is that children deprived from an early age of the kind of playful insights which convey personal control, environmental diversity, freedom and a total biological rather than simply a social relationship with life, will be unhappy at best and may end up on the fringes of madness, because of the neurochemical consequences of such deprivation.

Commentary/discussion

Whilst the relationship between plasticity and neurochemical activity, and behaviour and environment, is interesting in its own right, if it can be shown that play behaviour is particularly potent in the process of brain growth, and that the notion of an 'enriched' environment and a good play environment can be seen as synonymous, then the argument for play and for appropriate environmental intervention is strengthened.

Closer scrutiny of Huttenlocher (1992) also sheds light on the process of plasticity and what is called 'synaptogenisis'. Stating that the data suggest that there is a close linkage of plasticity to the process of synapse formation or synaptogenisis, he continues, 'Observations in human infants indicate the existence of a sensitive [or vulnerable] period ... extending over an age span from between ages three and four months to age six or seven years.' This sensitivity or vulnerability is to the process of plasticity, and supports Sutton-Smith's (1997) assertion that 'play's function in the early stages of development may be to assist in the actualisation of brain potential'.

What makes me suggest this, is this. If we assume that sensitivity to plasticity, from birth to age seven, applies to children in general, then there may be a link between play, conducive environments and brain growth. The reason being that, between those age parameters, i.e. birth and six or seven years, children, if able to, will choose to play. That is what children do during childhood. In short what I am proposing is that there is a natural link between Huttenlocher's sensitive period and play. That is, if children play during this sensitive period, brain growth, via the process of plasticity, will be maximised, and if they do not, it will not.

The Rosenzweig et al. work, from 1962 onwards, simply puts another piece in the playwork jigsaw by confirming that environment also plays a part in this equation. What I conclude is that play in a period between birth and middle-childhood, in an environment that is enriched, will promote brain growth and neurochemical activity.

The playing child would not only be benefiting from an enlarged brain, it would also benefit from the 'enriched' nature of the experiences it would be processing, using it. This also supports the link between play and adaptation posited by Sylva (1977) when she says, 'Natural selection would favour the most playful individuals ... for they have acquired more useful information about the potential of the environment and their actions on it.'

However, what, in my opinion, is more important than establishing an embryonic link between play, environment and neurochemical and neurological processes, is the growing evidence of inappropriate environmental impact on brain development. Earlier, I mentioned recent studies by Balbernie (1999) and Perry *et al.* (1995) which also highlight the effects of stress and trauma on low levels of stimulation on brain development.

Other recent evidence, for example, McEwen (1999), demonstrates that stress hormones, resulting from repeated stress, may be responsible for plasticity related brain damage and malformation.

And the relevance of this knowledge to playwork and playworkers? If there is a link between play, the play environment, brain growth and neurochemical activity, then facilitating play in a quality play environment becomes more than just important. If playworkers are able to produce 'enriched' environments that facilitate brain growth through play, then this is a major medical breakthrough, for it may just be that the combination of play and enriched experience might actually alleviate damage and malformation, reversing the impact of stress related brain damage, particularly if the opportunity to play is provided in a context of 'normality' rather than in one of clinical sterility.

Add to this the evolving capacity of playworkers to theorise about the potential of environments to cause abhorrent levels and types of stimuli, and attempt to rectify stimulus bias, irregularity and depletion using environmental modification, and playwork takes a diagnostic and curative stance which is quite new. These are important areas for further model development and research.

In conclusion

Unlike IMEE, which is a more practice based, reflective tool, RAP is a useful and revealing window, deep into the playwork mind, if my own RAP experiences are anything to go by. Working with children at play can yield powerful insights both into ourselves as adults, into the children with whom we work, into the interface between the two, and into the interface between children, playworkers and the play environments we collectively create, and there are very complex and primeval forces at work in each of these contexts.

- Can we be de-humanised by experience? Can where we live, and who we live with de-sensitise us to such an extent that we are incapable of understanding either physical or emotional suffering?

- Is the playworker moving into a position in which s/he can diagnose levels and types of play-deprivation and create the conditions for children to recover from it?
- Is access to play which enables a genetic engagement with our evolutionary pasts, through recapitulation, either possible or even desirable?
- Can the playworker's conclusions about the impact of violence on children at play affect the military/paramilitary view of the appropriateness of conducting war where there are children?
- Can RAP help all of us to reflect on our 'self' as children as a way of informing the behaviour of our 'self' as adults? Helping perhaps to peel away layers of compounded negative justifications, to reveal a clearer and more simple view of what life's journey is about, in much the same way as Grof's COEX system analysis does.
- What signals, if any, is play sending the playworker about the current and future impact of play-deprivation? Certainly, when I devised the extreme positive/negative/Z1/Z2 scenarios in the late 1980s, it felt like there would be an expansion of the Z2 category, with a resulting growth in activity from that quarter. Since then there have been many instances of adults and children fitting a Z2 profile, engaged in random and lethal violence both against adults and increasingly against other children – look for example, at the US.

There is a growing, although not yet conclusive body of evidence, that play is more than an interesting phenomenon. My interpretation is that the evidence clearly identifies play as an absolute life essential for children under, say, ten years of age, and that without exposure to play, and playful engagement with the whole environment, children are at best disabled and at worst, both psychologically and physically disfigured.

The evidence that play can repair damage and enable recovery is also tenuous. The playworker perhaps does not need the 'leap of faith', that others may, because s/he sees the miracle of playing before his or her eyes on a daily basis. Nonetheless, the question is there. Can play repair the impact of play-deprivation? Can it overcome the effects of extreme, erratic and de-humanising experience? I think it can, but how, is another matter altogether. Although having said that, of one thing I am sure, and that is if play has these curative properties, it will be play which is adult-free and naturally-driven rather than contrived, which will be the most effective at doing so.

As we move into the twenty-first century, and as children become the target of increasing social expectations, and as their childhood time is increasingly spoken for by adults, the need for them to have a space which is theirs, in which they can reflect on their lives and interact playfully with their world, increases in urgency by the minute.

As is reflected within these pages, I have always viewed play spaces as sanctuaries, as air-locks, between the adult world and the world of the child. Perhaps that is how they should be viewed. Not as a space in which the 'bums on seats' calculations are made, not as value for money spaces, but as recognition spaces, i.e. spaces which recognise that, as children evolve, they also need to take a breath, take stock and retain some semblance of personal control and direction over their own lives.

Summary of Part III

One of the reviewers of this Book, said Part III was 'all over the place'. You may agree. I have no clever answer to this. Petrie (1996) described *A Question of Quality* as an allegory, and perhaps that is what this book is too. Perhaps at the extreme end of playwork thinking, at the RAP interface, the bridge between imagination and experience is an allegorical space where the type of synthesis we see in Part III is actually created. Allegorical space may actually be where pure play takes place. Where the 'real' world of the adult, and the imagined world of the child become actualised. Perhaps this is Sturrock's metalude?

I wanted Part III to mirror my own RAP journey. To dip into thinking and to consider ideas as they came into my head. To be like the child in the cognitive playground. When I was working on my MA, I decided to try an approach I called 'the process of random search'. It was an attempt at locating by purely random means items, pieces of information, words, anything that grabbed my attention, had some implicit value or meaning, or which interested me. The purpose, to ground my studies in the same kind of methodology a child might use in a play space to locate neophilic attractors, items of interest and so on. Much of Part III is offered in the same vein.

It is intended to be the playwork equivalent of an abstract painting. It should be prefaced, perhaps, with 'What does this mean to you?', rather than, 'This is what this should mean'.

We can forget, although I trust that various sections of evolutionary playwork in its entirety may have reminded the reader, that the child's journey is a jumble of abstract and metaphysical notions, and that too much structure, too much of a fit into how things are at any given time, will not help to prepare the child for the changes that are ahead.

If children are to be enabled to evolve adaptive skills which, if nothing else, is what evolutionary playwork is about, too much certainty, then too much pre-dictability is unhelpful.

From a biological point of view the field of playwork runs the risk of becoming set in its ways. That what it offers children is becoming all too predictable, rather than fantastic, surprising, magic and awesome. For the sake of all our futures' this must be urgently addressed.

Reflections 4

Social events in the play space can be wonderful experiences. But they do high-light the problems caused by different developmental priorities. Driven by their emotions and desperate to conform to their peers' social and cultural norms, older children can get caught up in a spiral of alcohol and excess, which the playworker, whilst not condoning it, may need to supervise in some way – if only to ensure that young people get home safely. Younger children – who, for some, the event may be the first ever – show different priorities for security and neophilic stimulus.

The two parties outlined in this Reflection highlight the differences within the context of a continuum that sees today's adolescents as tomorrow's adults and today's littlies as tomorrow's adolescents.

Reflection: the party

It was the first one. At Christmas. We'd all been excited about it for weeks. A free party for the older kids, with music and refreshments. We'd rushed around the town in the morning buying pounds of bangers and a sack of spuds, decorations, bread and stuff. We were really enthusiastic. It wasn't until we got back that we realised how difficult it was going to be. 'How the hell do you cook a hundred and fifty sausages and bake a sack of spuds in one little oven?' I croaked to no-one in particular. Deb thought of the sausages: 'Hold on,' she said, 'I'll nip home and get my Mum's pan.' Well her Mum must have been a Chef to Lord Kitchener or somebody, 'cause the pan she brought in was about three feet across.

'Ye'll have to take the coffee bar apart to get that on the oven,' William the Raver shouted – everything he said, he always shouted.

Anyway, we did manage. Within a couple of hours the sausages were nearly done, and the bar covered in a light layer of fat which can be obtained in any home, if you have a number of children throwing special pork sausages at three inches of boiling fat from twenty paces – very hygienic!

The spuds were a different problem. Even I could see that basically it was a matter of taking all of the shelves out of the oven and then filling the inside – it was an electric model – up with potatoes. But every time we opened the oven door to see how things were going the whole bloody lot kept falling on the floor. It took us all day to cook those spuds.

Anyway, it was all going great guns. Everyone was eating too much and all that, but it was smashing. That is, until Dave decided that he wouldn't enjoy himself without a punch-up.

What I didn't know, was that some of the older kids had been fortifying themselves with a cocktail of alcoholic takeaways, outside!

He was a smashing kid, but two wine gums and a rum and butter toffee constituted an overdose for him. The first I knew of this was when he was hurtled through the fire door at great speed under the guiding hand of the three parents I'd asked to help as bouncers. 'Somebody's bound to get hurt,' I remember myself thinking.

I was right. Dave did, but only a bit, and he did slurringly apologise to the bouncers for the trouble he'd caused.

Next in line was Karen. A couple of cakes and an illicit swig of cheap Algerian were enough to have her 'yakking' all over the floor. That was hastily dealt with using a bowl under her nose with strict instructions, 'Aim in there from now on.'

Back to the party. The music was up to warp nine by now, and children were engaged in a dance that was reminiscent of pogo-sticking. Unhelpfully, somebody had also rigged up an amazing concoction of watered down cider and syrupy raspberry juice – one cup of that and I knew my cleaning days weren't over yet.

Then, suddenly, Sue and Pat were playing merry Hell, trying to tear one another apart because Terry, our acne'd answer to Valentino, had decided, in a sexual frenzy, to plant a Christmas kiss on Pat's cheek. Unfortunately, he was going out with Sue at the time.

Everything went fine except for one short episode. John and Mike had decided that they wanted to join Alcoholics Anonymous at the earliest possible opportunity, and had consumed a large amount of low-grade liquid between the off-licence and our place.

This only came to my notice when I went outside for a breather.

Mike was laying flat out in the mud which passed as a path to our place in the winter, moaning, 'I'm cold, I'm so cold.'

'I suppose you bloody well would be where you are,' I shouted back sympathetically.

John, on the other hand was much more fun. He had fallen, gigglingly in love with our lamp-post, the one that doesn't work. He was smiling and telling 'Clara', the lamp-post, how much he loved her. Now, I mean, I'm not one to stand in the way of young love, but Clara???

We got Mike home OK. Most of the time it was like carrying John's Clara, he was so stiff!

The last we saw was his body carefully strewn in the hallway of his house, where he swears he woke up next day, and his Mum saying, 'He's a devil, isn't he?'

'Aren't they all?' I said, and went home.

'Well that's the big kids do over,' I thought. 'Tomorrow's the littlies.'

It's wrong to have preferences in these situations I know. The bigger kids are great in their own way. But what with hormones, and emotions, the omnipresent potential for a scrap, and experiments with booze and that, you're always waiting for it to go wrong.

So much was at stake. They'd all put on their 'special' clothes, and for some of them, whose parents hadn't got two pennies to rub together, 'special' meant least frayed, most clean.

They were spotty and shy, and full of bullshit. I loved it. I knew what was happening. I'd been there myself. But the pain was only just under the surface.

'Will he ask me to dance?', 'Will she let me walk her home?', 'Can we make up?', 'Can I get him away from her?'

The tension could be enough to make you feel like a soggy cloth by the end of it all.

But the littlies' party was something else.

All the food and drink was contributed by the kids' Mums and Dads. The older kids came to help – often with their kid sisters and brothers.

We had a magician. We had him every year. He was pretty crap I suppose, but the kids liked him, and so did I, he was so awful.

And we had some great games. Apple ducking, flour cakes, balloon tennis, blind man's buff, pass the parcel, musical chairs. John was resident DJ, always deciding to turn it into the party he never had and making everything chaotic as he randomly changed the rules of traditional games to conform to how he was feeling.

But it didn't matter. It was warm and sweet and gorgeous. The fire and coloured light bulbs and the Christmas tree and decorations made it that way.

The magician did his ham-fisted tricks to the delight of the kids and amusement of the Mums and Dads. John did the music for the games, and I listened for the millionth time to that crackly Woolworths record of covered hits.

More food and orange went down people's clothes than their throats, and in the heat, the steam from the tea pot, and the fag smoke, so un-idealogically sound, the balloons deflated and the paper decorations that we had spent so many hours in making eventually gave up the ghost.

And then it was over. And with the last sandwich, jelly, slice of cake, we said our Christmas goodbyes, our thanks to patient parents, our kisses and hugs to our kids, all clutching little pretty paper presents, we paid and thanked the brother of Houdini, and closed the door, to survey the havoc of two solid days of fun and lunacy.

I looked at Jane, my co-worker, 'Good, wasn't it?'

'Great,' she said, exhausted, and lit a fag.

Given the type of usage, and the numbers using them over the years, Adventure Playgrounds have proved to be very safe places, where accidents of any consequence are very rare indeed. However, just now and again, the combination of lone supervision, mood and materials brings the playworker to the juddering realisation that it is impossible to control every moment, and that sometimes s/he may almost be reduced to prayer.

This reflection also highlights the speed and flexibility that children demonstrate when adults attempt to engage in locomotor games with them.

Reflection: Ali

'You're not right in the head, girl.' I'd just tried a friendly swipe at her and missed. It was one of my more psychological days. 'Shut your row, ten Bob,' she bawled, running at speed onto the bridge. I do wish she wouldn't call me that!

The day before I'd seen Ali at school and the rotten so-and-so had sprayed my 'teachers' clothes with paste. 'I'll get you tomorrow for that,' but as usual she'd just laughed in that deranged way!

She started a wood fight one night when I was otherwise occupied. The idea seemed to be that you got a flat piece of wood – plywood was best – and you skimmed it through the air, in the apparent hope that it would dismember or maim the enemy, whoever they were. The trouble was that Ali, given a catapult, a lump of wood or a half brick, could land a missile across the back of your head with alarming accuracy and force.

The war was apparently progressing satisfactorily as far as Ali was concerned. She was clouting all and sundry, and remaining unscathed herself, that is until Chris came onto the scene. Chris was a beautiful but slow kid, with some learning difficulties. She couldn't have moved any more than one or two steps into the theatre of war before hawk-eye Ali saw her.

Chris must have had a skull like a rhino, for the next time I looked I couldn't believe my eyes. She was standing near the gibbet swing, with a beatific smile on her face, and with the corner of a large flat piece of plywood stuck in her forehead, courtesy of Ali.

I remember thinking how odd it was to see somebody with a foot square piece of wood stuck in her head. I only got the full story later.

'I got her, I got her!' screamed Ali enthusiastically, but I was too busy thinking about Chris to worry.

The next day Ali was at it again. This time I was having none of it, and so when she started to throw things, I ran over, (a) to disarm her, and (b) to remind her of what I had said the previous evening, that we were all very lucky that Chris, hadn't been seriously injured, and that throwing missiles had to stop or she'd have to go. This was not an option I wanted to enforce.

What I didn't see was a rogue piece of wood with a nail in it, which in later playground days would have been rendered safe, and as I ran towards Chris I trod on the nail, and kept running, driving the nail into my foot.

I fell and lifted my foot into the air, the plank and nail still firmly attached to the bottom of my foot. The desire to faint was only slightly ameliorated by the sight of Ali dancing 'round me shouting, 'Ten Bob's trod on a nail, Ten Bob's trod on a nail.' 'Little bastard', I muttered, nearly crying.

As no help was imminent, I had to remove the plank from my foot myself, which was as much as I could do without being sick. Ali had got bored and had cleared off. I limped across the playground with my foot feeling all slick with blood. I closed the playground up as best I could and hopped slowly over to the doctor's surgery nearby. He was getting used to me, I'd been in only a week or so before with a sprained ankle, received during a game of chase. 'Just a little tetanus jab,' he said cheerily. Relieved that not too many Ali's were around, I made my way home for a little rest, before re-opening the playground again.

Reflection: a death in the family

Play spaces, particularly full-time operations, are communities that share the joys and tragedies of their members. However, there are few feelings as desolate for a playworker as those when one of the children dies. The event described in this Reflection completely gutted me. In playwork, as in any form of work involving the young, one has to be braced for it – it happens from time to time. Suicide, accidents, illness – but it's always personal bad news when it happens. This is 'middle of nowhere' territory, a difficult space particularly in this context, where the playworker will sometimes be forced, by events like this, to confront his or her professional and personal demons. Then s/he must remember that whilst playwork can do little about death, it can and does make a significant contribution to the lives of many of the children who experience it.

I stood under a small tree in the drizzle. Cigarette burning as they lowered her into the ground.

She was fourteen, so I suppose you couldn't really call her a kid.

Now she was dead. Leukaemia. Fourteen. Fucking stupid waste.

The kids had wailed and sworn and propped each other up at the realisation that the impossible did happen. And it could happen to them. But most of all they wailed because she had gone, because they loved her.

She was one of those quiet, nice, considerate, attractive people. One of the ones you're always pleased to see. Who ask your advice and who make you feel needed and useful.

She was a part of the crowd, but not a faceless part, and now she wasn't coming back, and, 'Oh shit, what are we going to do?'

Pretty girls sat around, mascara black rivers running down their faces, eyes red from crying. Nothing like the reality of death to bring you crashing from the sometime fantasy that is childhood.

Clumps of boys quietly tried to vent their hurt and found emotions difficult to control.

One of them, whose complexion matched his pasty diet, said he didn't care. More to avoid his pain than to tarnish an icon, but they beat him just the same.

Respect. Respect the dead.

They went in awkward, unsteady groups to see her Mum and Dad and discover that at these times, rational things to say are lost in the fog of grief. They cried a lot, kids, hard as nails, kids who would pulverise an enemy, kids who had never known love, learning a bit about it the only way they might.

And then they drifted back up the hill to quietly discover their feelings and put names to them.

The funeral was a draining event. Lots of them went, going AWOL from school lessons, not even thinking ...

Trying to think what parties and Christmas would be like without her and not able to measure the enormity of the gulf between her and them, now.

Dead. What's that? What's 'dead' mean? Gone where? What's the point in anything?

But like all of these events, it was soon over. Too soon, too final, now she really was no more, now, no longer a possibility, but gone.

For days a bleakness descended over us all.

I remember it from my own time, when, as an eight-year-old, my uncle died of something awful. And one Saturday night we had gone to watch my father in his band playing post-war dance music to transient American ex-D-Day troops, my cousin whose Dad it was who had gone, leaning over the balcony, concentrating on the scene, when she burst out crying as they played *Oh my Papa*. The bleakness of being left without the one who has died.

But like her, as the year wore on, as symbolic play replaced outward emotional display, the pain lessened, grief-lined faces of lonely parents relaxed a fraction as good memories outlived the haunting. Alone, back in my office I asked, 'How many more?' to the poster covered walls. 'All of them,' came the reply.

Chapter 14

In conclusion

Playwork is currently going through a great deal of change. The biggest one being that it is increasingly being seen simply as a description for any work adults do with children after school, rather than as a particular approach to play, driven by particular values. An approach that is trying to ensure that children continue to have access to experiences which have always been available in the past, but which are now increasingly difficult for many to access. Experiences which have great developmental and evolutionary significance.

Being able to play is a human right. And, although the evidence is only building gradually, many are convinced that it is a fundamental human need. Playing in a 'non-adult context' is also essential, and this adult-free experience is particularly important in provision that adult's operate. It enables children to develop a valuable perspective of the adult world untainted by reliance upon, or input from adults. Children who have experience of a non-adult context are more likely to grow up with a healthy scepticism of adult priorities, and as a consequence may be better equipped to enable society to develop and evolve. What into? I have no idea, and in some senses care less. But what I am clear about, at least from my own playwork experience, is that children who have played, even in artificial provision, are enriched and more confident after that experience on the whole, as long as the provision is of high quality.

Playwork is clearly not a socialising mechanism, or a focus for social education. Nor should it be a way of life for children. Access to good quality play provision in which children can experience play types and elements and can do what they are driven to do – sometimes in spite of what their parents or carers might want – for a few hours a day, to ensure that development through play is part of what they can draw from, is all I would make a plea for.

A young life crammed with the pressures of academic or vocational success, with little or no play, is hardly a childhood. That has been stolen or hijacked by the adult agenda. I believe it is imperative that we return childhood and childhood things to our children. If we do not, instead of enabling the development of happy, confident, well adjusted and worldly individuals, we will have contributed to the creation of hopeless and lost adults, still children in many senses, but who because they have not been able to engage with the world, do not see its beauty, but see instead an alien, hostile and frightening place.

Most profound to me is that, when I talk to adults, they remember their childhood and the play in incredible detail. Playing was, for most of them, a hugely significant experience. Now children are increasingly deprived of this experience or of facets of it, and we cannot even guess yet the harm such deprivation might do. Although the play-deprivation data, such as it is, is quite chilling.

We should not forget that not only were we all children, but that much of what we have become was founded in our childhood experience. An absence of play may not only result in none of play's proposed benefits, it also means no play memories, no games to pass on, no playscapes to imagine, no fantastic, hairs-on-your-neck-standing-up feelings when something new and unexpected happens, and no experience of graduated independence, where one could know freedom, but could go home to one's parents or carers afterwards.

I know too well that this is not the definitive evolutionary playwork book; that is a long way off. Writing it, although an interesting personal experience, has been plagued with the frustration of how difficult I have found it to articulate the ideas and experiences of thirty years of playwork experience. The up-side is that evolutionary playwork is only in its embryonic stages. Although it will need to be defended if it is to retain its identity and integrity in a social, political and a professional context that, instead of recognising that it offers its own unique perspective, continually attempts to place playwork within the bounds of inappropriate social policy initiatives like child-care. Playwork's perspective tries to argue that, for reasons of self interest, as well as the love and concern we all have for children, we should work to re-orientate society's priorities more in favour of children's biological needs. We should be rightly alarmed at the continued destruction of the human child's play habitat, its games and its need to range and explore. For the continuation down that path may lead us towards a disaster for our species. Its extinction!

Hopefully the human drive to play will find ways of overcoming the impact of play-deprivation or inadequate or inappropriate space for play. Although if McEwen's (1999) work, and the Huttenlocher (1992), Huttenmoser and Degan-Zimmermann (1995) and Chugani (1998) material to which I referred earlier is any indication, it does not seem to be happening currently and the signs that this will change are not promising for the future either, at least, in theory.

The combined impacts of traffic, parental fears, loss of space and adult incursions into children's playtime mean that many children are playing less. That, and our growing awareness of the devastaing impact of play-deprivation itself bodes ill for current and future generations of children.

If the issues intrinsic to playwork – less play, less time, impoverished environment and the inappropriate impact of adults – are not urgently addressed, the increasing numbers of children affected, unable to adapt, unable to evolve may instead respond biologically to that deficit, violently or through other manifestations of disease, and many countries could be looking at a potential human problem on the catastrophic scale of climate change, AIDS and CJD.

As we needed to play, so we know our children also need to play. We know it intuitively as well as rationally. And yet we do little to provide for it or combat those factors that inhibit it or distort it. We should be careful, for not only might we be becoming blind to what our children depend on, we may be becoming blind to what we are. That may be an indication that we are at last losing the fight to survive as a species, which as a playworker I find sad more than anything. For, at play, more than in any other state, we are truly at one with the universe.

I leave the final word to one of my own sources of inspiration, my friend and fellow playworker the late Frank King:

> We have accepted that children, because they are our future, because they are the future of our society, should be allowed a privileged space, a time in which they can develop themselves.
>
> *International Play Journal* (1996) Vol. 4, Number 3.

Playwork and parenting

Being a parent has always been an awesome responsibility, but it is particularly so now, with so much information to take in; not only information about children's needs but also about the dangers in the environment, the risks or accidents and abductions. Because of this, it is important for parents and carers to get play and playwork into perspective. After all, they can only do so much.

Within the previous pages is a great deal of information about play and playwork, much of it complex and perhaps intimidating to those who are new to it. It needs thinking about, studying and discussing, and most parents will neither have the time nor inclination to do that. My advice, if you are concerned about your child's access to quality play experiences and his or her potential for play-deprivation would be, try to be aware of the potential importance of play and provide for it in any way you can. Take an interest in what your children are doing and perhaps in what they need to do, and be conscious of the environment you are providing for them. For example, try to ensure:

- that they are stimulated to play by ensuring the proximity of interesting, age appropriate materials and objects
- that they have access to the outside world, the garden, the park, or wild areas, so that they can interact with local flora and fauna
- that they have access to music and books in general, and *their* music and books in particular
- that they have the opportunity to engage in proper 'sit-down' style conversations, where they know they are listened to and that their views are valued
- that they meet children from other cultures and play with a sharing and inclusive perspective
- that they have interaction with environments that offer sensory and elemental experiences. You having to do extra washing or clothes drying may indicate that your child is engaging in real interaction, which could impact upon her capacity to survive and develop, and so on.

Think about your own childhood, where you went, what you did, who you did it with, and try to ensure that your child also has access to the best of the ingredients you identify. Try to remember that once they are able to be independent they may not want you tagging along – play is primarily an adult-free experience. If they do ask you along and you have time, go, but resist the temptation to colonise or dominate what happens and be sensitive to the adult-free characteristic of evolutionary play, i.e. that most of the time you should not be there and if you are, ask yourself whose needs are being met – theirs or yours?

Remember, too, that every child is different, that good playwork is about broad brush strokes. Creating a play-friendly space that contains opportunities to get wet, dirty, covered in paint, graze your knee, say words that sound fun, and pretend that you are anything from a Roman soldier to a stick insect, will contribute to your child's development and well-being. Above all, realise that whatever you do, your child is a unique universe in his or her own right whose play should not be a mirror-image of your own. Your children have their own journey to make.

Remember that, however conscientious and knowledgeable you are, you will probably get more wrong than right, which is another good reason for the broad brush approach. Laugh a lot.

Joe, a friend and colleague of mine in Northern Ireland, had been singing the praises of playwork to a relative. The discussion had been about trusting children. He had said, 'Playwork teaches, "If children are playing near water, don't be too protective by hanging onto their coat collars. Stay close, if you are worried, but trust the child to be aware of the dangers and take the necessary precautions."'

The close relative took notice of playwork's wise words. And the next time he took his child to the lake in the park, instead of hanging onto her coat collar, he let her play freely close to the water, trusting her, but at the same time keeping a close eye on her. Obviously not close enough – she fell in!

In a more general sense this amusing story may be an indication that parental over-caution, for all the justified reasons mentioned, may eventually result in children becoming de-skilled; that in the absence of real play experience, children increasingly expect parents and other adults to do their survival thinking for them.

De-skilling

If de-skilling is taking place, how might it be avoided or counteracted? The process of de-skilling may begin at the very start of your child's life, when you are interacting, when s/he is making his or her first tentative attempts to explore, and when s/he is beginning to engage with the wider environment.

How you interact with your child is crucial to the child's skills development. It is also an accurate indicator of whose needs are being met. If you play with the child, is it on the basis of parent facilitating the child's play and the child's development, or is it from the perspective of a big brother or sister who is less interested in facilitating development and more interested in demonstrating their own level of knowledge, skill and expertise? For example, try to avoid answering the questions you ask. Try to avoid asking the child to show you how it would do something and then doing it yourself. This kind of pre-emption is not only frustrating for the child, it suggests that a skills transfer is taking place when it may not be.

Similarly, resist the temptation to show children how to do things when they are playing. First of all, they are playing and consequently do not need to know how to do things. But through playful experimentation and trial and error they will, in time, locate several solutions to whatever problem they are playing with. This will make them more, rather than less, versatile and inventive than they would otherwise have been, and consequently more adaptive. They will not be hampered with the notion of one right answer, but will, instead, go for what they judge is the best of several different options.

If you create an interesting space for your child to play in, try to resist guiding his or her play. The child's own sensory or experiential preferences will enable him or her to make choices appropriate to his or her needs. Certainly talk the child through his or her actions, and share the uniqueness, novelty and first-time-ness of the experience, but be aware that there is a compulsion on the part of many, if not most of us, to manipulate and dominate children's choices, and we should be aware of this. However, this does not mean that choices should never be initiated by the parent/carer. A child may be tired, or afraid, or just uninterested and may only need a nudge to activate his or her attention. The trick is that once attention or interaction has been activated, that we step back and allow whatever play narratives are there to unfold naturally in the child's own time.

Finally, be clear about the importance of intrinsically motivated behaviour in the play process. Children should engage in play because they are personally interested in the novel characteristics of a particular object or space; they should not engage in play because you want them too, or because you or someone else is offering them an inducement. Remember Koestler's statement (1967), that the 'more contaminated an action is with others' motives the less it is play'. What is important about this is that, if a child's play is being contaminated by external motives, not only is it not play, but the child will not benefit from the outcomes play would have normally provided. So subverting the child's motives for your own provides a 'double developmental jeopardy' for the child.

Play types

In general enabling children's engagement in most play types is relatively simple, and only requires time, security, props and permissions. For example, children will be able to engage in symbolic play, fantasy play and imaginative play as long as they feel safe, have some bits and pieces to play with and know that it is OK to do so, i.e. that they will not be laughed at when they take on the identity of a dragon, or talk to an imaginary friend. Locomotor and exploratory play needs space and spatial variety, like mounds or trees, whilst rough and tumble needs an impact absorbent surface and someone to rough and tumble with.

Social, socio-dramatic, dramatic and role play normally need other children too, but props, like dressing up clothes and designated spaces, like a home corner, or a toy shop may also help. Social play is less restricted to specific spaces and more ranging in its content, and may involve a level of communication play in the form of songs, rhymes and jokes. Like the other play types, creative play will need time and security, but it will also need a wide selection of materials, and permissions on your part should include a recognition that destruction and creation are different sides of the same coin. Much of the fun of play is that it can be exciting and messy, and proper space for this needs to be planned in advance. If it is not, the experience could be ruined for the child because it is being limited by your fears that paint will go up the walls, or plasticine will be trodden into the carpet. Needless to say, object play needs objects to play with. These can be as simple as cotton reels and as complex as rubic cubes and puzzles. One of the benefits of this play type is that it enables children to manipulate things and develop their gross and fine motor co-ordination.

Exploratory play needs spaces and materials or spaces to explore. The important thing about this play type is that you need to be sensitive to what kinds of materials and spaces children find interesting – remember neophilia? Mastery play is one of those types that children use at the seaside and in the garden, wherever there is running water or earth to dig in. Perhaps more than any other play type, mastery brings children in touch with the physical nature of the world in which they live.

Deep play is perhaps the most difficult one for adults to facilitate, simply because it involves deliberate risk. However, unless we lock our children up, and we know that this can lead to play-deprivation symptoms, they will engage in deep play somewhere along the line. Help your children to learn to swim, to balance and to climb, to understand when branches or cliff faces are unsafe, and to recognise other hazards like power and railway lines. That way, you can help them to minimise serious injury when they do engage in this play type.

Battery children

I have referred to the term 'battery children' throughout. It is used to describe children who are kept indoors all of the time because their parents are worried that they might be injured by traffic or abducted by strangers. As a parent and grandparent, I do sympathise, but children still have to learn about the world, and the journey will be even more difficult if they have no concept of 'outdoors' or of being responsible for themselves.

The reader may recall the work I cited, by Huttenlocher, which states that between the ages of zero and, say eight years, children have at least twice the brain capacity of those over ten years of age. This over capacity may be what the human brain uses to develop our basic survival and development building blocks when we play. However, this overcapacity is lost after eight years, and unless we have developed these basic building blocks by then, there is no guarantee that they can be developed later. This could put 'battery children' or any children who do not have comprehensive experience of the real world, at a personal disadvantage. That includes children who are driven everywhere by car, as well as those who cannot 'play out'.

Recapitulation

Where you can, ensure that your children have opportunities to engage in recapitulative play. Modern children have intense commercial and educational demands made upon them that may well impact on their physical and psychological well-being. To help them to keep the pressures of the here and now in proportion, try to make it possible for them to engage in 'primitive' or historical narratives. When it is 'safe' to do so, facilitate play with fire, facilitate play in the dark, facilitate dressing up, ritual and story telling.

An essential ingredient for surviving the modern world is having the imagination to keep what it represents in proportion, to not be driven by it alone.

Finally ...

Recognise that your children need to play, that if they do not then they will not be as able to navigate the experiences they encounter in life. That may restrict what they do, who they do it with and where they go. In my opinion, as a playworker, the greatest love we can show to our children is that we love them enough to let them play.

The Ten Newcastle Points

That quality play experiences will help children to:

1 think for themselves and make their own decisions
2 develop their mental and physical abilities and their confidence in them
3 develop an empathy for others
4 develop a set of values that bring benefit to themselves and others
5 test out strategies for survival and development without the stigma of failure
6 resolve the contradictions and inconsistencies that arise as their experience develops
7 be able to communicate their needs, beliefs and desires more clearly
8 have an understanding of the life process as a part of the context for their own identity
9 develop an understanding of the interrelationship of everything with everything else
10 question the relevance, truth, reasons, justice and values behind all information.

Appendix 3

Problem solving

Here are a selection of different problems I have given playwork students to reflect on and analyse, over the years. They can be explored at any level by any level. More than anything they are intended to facilitate the analysis of topics and issues and to encourage and enable playworkers to articulate rationales for their practice. Not only asking, 'What would you do?', but asking 'Why do you do what you do in the way that you do it?' Perhaps a complicated way of saying it, but important. It is not enough to do, as playworkers have intuitively operated for years. Now anyone who works with children should be able, for example, to explain on some level both *how* and *why*, and perhaps even more importantly, *why that way*, and not another way. Our rationales, however embryonic, need to be brought out into the conscious realm, and not hidden as they have been for so long, inside the unconscious realm.

If a problem does not interest or attract you or the group after a few minutes' discussion or thought, move on, until absorption strikes.

The problems range throughout the total spectrum of playwork issues. From explaining complex ideas, to dealing with money, religion, and politics, to inviting comment on 'What makes an environment a play environment?', 'Wha is the role of the playworker?', Developing play projects in a variety of contexts, supervised provision and fixed equipment, children's communication and behaviour and equal opportunities policies, and so on, a real mixed bag. If you want to suggest amendments or improvements, or even alternatives to certain problems, or if you want to offer problems where you feel none exists (if we do what you suggest we will acknowledge you accordingly) please let us know.

Have fun . . .

The importance of play and playwork

Exercise 1 (With acknowledgements to Stephen Renee)

The Worm Exercise. As you move through the environment you operate, you notice on several occasions a child meticulously cutting up worms into 10 mm pieces. What do you do, when, and why?

Exercise 2

You are attending a public meeting as a concerned resident/parent. The meeting has been called to discuss the lack of provision for children in the area. The meeting although impassioned is good humoured, until a member of the meeting with a reputation for being 'HARD' states that play, 'WHATEVER IT IS' is made to appear more important than it is by a load of mammy pamby liberals.

How would you react and what would you say?

Exercise 3

A community group wants to explore the issue of play. Design a short training course which would raise their awareness of the importance of play and how quality provision should reflect this.

Exercise 4

At last we have managed to raise a large amount of capital and revenue. Some people want to spend it on six modern fixed equipment play areas, others want to develop an open-access, staffed play area. What arguments – educational, financial, effectiveness, etc. – can I bring to bear to enable adults to make a 'good' decision on which form of provision is most appropriate?

Exercise 5

A national focus to bring the 'importance of play' to the notice of a more comprehensive audience has just been launched. What would you put on the agenda for this campaign, and why?

Exercise 6

At the end of your talk on the need for play provision in a busy, built-up area, a local 'hostile' Councillor says, 'We didn't need any of this when we were young. These days children have everything done for them.' What is your considered response?

Exercise 7

You attend a public meeting to discuss the creation of a playground for local children. During the proceedings you say that play is important in the process of human development. Somebody asks you what you mean. What do you say?

Exercise 8

You are discussing play provision policy with elected members and officers of the local authority. Play, children and play provision all seem low priorities on their agenda. Give five brief points which you hope will change this.

Exercise 9

You are involved in facilitating learning for a group of volunteer playworkers whose schemes are of the school holiday only variety. In expressing their ideas for this coming summer most of them describe programmes which seem highly organised and inflexible for the children who will attend. You are expected to comment. What do you say and why?

Exercise 10

The workers on our project fall into two camps. Some prefer mainly to offer the kids a programme of activities, while the others feel that the choice should be the child's. Who is right and why?

Exercise 11

I think involving children in designing or running the project is an intrusion by adult concepts into their playtime and childhood.
   What do you think and why?

Exercise 12

To build the structures we need to erect poles, and to do that we need to close the project. The kids say that they'd rather not have the structures than have the playground closed. What do you say and why?

Exercise 13

Feelings are split. Some of the team feel that paint, paper and brushes should only be available when their use can be properly supervised. The others feel that materials should be available the whole time and that any resultant mess is normal for this 'type' of project. What do you feel and why?

Exercise 14

Gary is ten. He is angry, aggressive and unhappy. His social and communication skills are minimal and he's just started to come to your project. Your value base is that access to play opportunities are a human right and that each child should be treated as a valued individual. How do you demonstrate this to Gary?

Exercise 15

Not only do the children love fire/water-play, it is vital to their elemental awareness. However, quite a few parents do not like the mess and danger associated with them.

How do you deal with this dilemma?

Exercise 16

Craig came to the office to tell me that he and some of his mates had 'done a warehouse last night' to get some money for the play project. What should I do and why?

Exercise 17

We want to give the children access to painting and to the techniques of painting. Some of the team think we should employ an art teacher to instruct children, others say 'bring in an artist and just let her work – the kids will learn by being with her'.

What do you think and why?

Exercise 18

How we work with children is decided by the values we hold. What values do you believe would help to guide how we work with children?

Exercise 19

One sign of a 'good' play project might be the number of children using it. Another might be their 'happy' demeanour. Describe six other criteria that would be met by 'good' play provision.

Exercise 20

I want to build a camp but the programme only offers cookery and computer games today. I thought this place was here to meet my needs, what should I do?

Exercise 21

Quality in play provision implies that something is 'good'. What is it that has to be good, and why will it benefit children in some way?

Special issues

Exercise 22

The play project you are about to develop is in an area in which the predominant culture believes in gender separation.

How would you expect to approach this problem in your first year?

Exercise 23

I work as a Play Development Officer on an isolated play project in an area which has serious sectarian/racist overtones.

Please outline up to five external support mechanisms which might help me to continue my work and at the same time minimise the real threat to myself?

Exercise 24

Some of the children attending your local playcentre have been spraying slogans of an extreme nature on the external walls of the Centre. Although you feel that children should have access to the widest spectrum of opinion in order to facilitate 'informed choices', you are concerned about what this might develop into. What do you do and why?

Exercise 25

Parvina comes from a very devout Muslin family that believes that women should dress 'modestly'. Last week, in the hot weather, the playworkers, some male, some female, turned up in shorts and very revealing tops. Parvina complained.

What should the playworkers' response have been and why?

Exercise 26

You are busy, you are stressed, you have got a lot on. You are leaving the office in a tearing hurry to get to an important meeting. Outside, propped against the wall is a ten-year-old girl you vaguely recognise. In her left hand is a can of lighter fuel. She has a sore on one of her nostrils where she has been using the gas. What do you do and why?

Exercise 27

A playworker on your patch is concerned that parents are stopping their daughters using the local playground. The reason for this appears to be mostly rumours relating to sex, drug use and overt sexist attitudes relating to the girls, by their parents. How do you deal with this?

Exercise 28

My name is Sakine, I am a twenty-one-year-old female playworker on an estate known for racial harassment. Although the adult population is set in its ways, the children are great, although the effects of the adult culture shows through their play behaviour. What can I do to facilitate thought about this

a   With the children?
b   With the adolescent and adult?

Exercise 29

As a Play Development Officer you know you will be overworked, underpaid and stressed. What strategies would you adopt to ensure personal and professional survival?

Exercise 30

You have already asked Rosemary, who is twelve, big and strong, three times, not to smoke on the playground.

This time you have asked her to leave and she has said, 'You make me.' What's your next step and why?

Exercise 31

You notice a group of older (12–14 years) boys/girls making lewd remarks about one of the project's female/male workers, every time they walk past. How do you react to this and why?

Exercise 32

The other day Osman's dad came onto the playground and started to hit him for not being at church.

What should a playworker's strategy be in situations like this and why?

Exercise 33

It is winter and very cold. Your arrival at the project is greeted by the same sister and brother who have been there at opening time for the past week or so. Although they look healthy, they are cold and badly dressed for the weather. They also seem hungry. What do you do, and why?

Exercise 34

The project's Management Committee want a smoking ban imposed on the playground. As many of the older kids smoke you know that a ban will be counter productive. What can you do to make the Management Committee aware of this and perhaps pursue a more appropriate course of action?

Exercise 35

Hooshang and Agneya are both twelve years old. Today they came onto the project obviously under the influence of something, but they did not smell of alcohol. What intervention, if any, would you make, and why?

Stimulus bias and stimulus deprivation

Exercise 36

Siobhan was born on the estate, she is now twelve years old. The local open spaces are littered with burnt-out cars, and the only play area is totally vandalised. Many parents are unemployed and local young people gain excitement from joy-riding and shop lifting.

a   How would you attempt to rectify the experiential imbalance in her life?
b   By what outcomes would you measure your success or failure?

Exercise 37

When Kylie hit you with a half brick she explained her actions as freely-chosen, personally-directed and intrinsically-motivated. How do you explain this apparent deviation from the normal benefits attributed to play?

Exercise 38

Jean-Yves is twelve years old. His parents are professional people, who are materially and economically secure. For years his father has physically and psychologically abused him with lies, ignoring him and with periodic beatings. His mother knows but is too afraid to intervene. Your job is to give Jean-Yves access to appropriate play experiences. What do you provide and why do you judge it will work?

Exercise 39

A short while ago a new crowd of kids came onto the project. They had not been there more than a couple of minutes before they started to throw things around. My co-worker asked them to stop and one of them, the leader – told her to 'fuck off'.

What should I do now and why?

Exercise 40

Eva is a bully. Today she dropped a football onto Tagbo's face whilst she held him down with her feet. Tagbo was obviously terrified. What intervention, if any, should I make, and why?

Exercise 41

You observe two children you know to have suffered abuse, and deprivation, calling another kid from some local travellers 'a Gyppo' and 'tramp'. How would you deal with this sensitive issue and why?

Exercise 42

In the heat of the moment a white, wheelchair bound boy calls another child 'a black git'. How would you deal with this and why?

Exercise 43

Gita's parents are wealthy. She is ten years old. She lives in a large house in its own grounds. She has two brothers and a sister. Their parents do not let them mix with local children, and they go to a private boarding school miles away.

How might this context affect Gita's play and the perspectives she gains from it?

Exercise 44

One of the few strictly enforced rules at our project is 'no stone throwing'. Recently Gary, a rather big and violent fourteen year old was asked three times to stop throwing stones. On the third occasion he turned around and threw a stone at me. It missed.

What should I do now and why?

Exercise 45

Tracy's play is restricted to the house and immediate area. Her parents are alcoholic and violent. She has frequently become the target for their aggression throughout her life. She is twelve years old. She has been systematically tortured on occasions. She is confused, angry and alone. Forecast Tracy's behaviour and feelings in five years if this pattern continues. Give your reasons.

Exercise 46

Zehui lived in what was the industrial heartland of the West. She is seven years old. The whole area has been suffering terrible economic decline for six years. Where she now lives is an area of dereliction, unemployment and car crime with an unspoken code of non-grassing. Zehui plays in the streets, vandalises empty properties and has recently started drinking. You have been awarded a huge budget to make appropriate play provision for Zehui and her friends. What would you provide, how and, most importantly, why?

Exercise 47

Ian, who is seven years old, lives on the eighth floor of a high rise block with his unemployed and disabled father. The block is slowly being evacuated for demolition. This situation has existed for six years. Ian's only playmates are dolls, video cartoons and computer games.

a   What effect will this environment have on Ian's behaviour?
b   What kind of play environment could address his needs?

Exercise 48

Duke is a five-year-old boy who plays a lot on his own. His mother is very affectionate to him but his father communicates very little. Duke loves to light fires and often uses dead animals in his play. Although he is not anti-social, he is not really interested in being with other children or in doing what they do either. Forecast Duke's behaviour in ten years if this pattern continues. Give your reasons.

Exercise 49

Sacha dreams of dressing up, of having pets and playmates, of parties, of fun and laughter, but instead she spends her playtime in a bare room left alone for hours on end. How might she spend her time, what will be the consequences of this experience and why?

Exercise 50

Ishmael is from a Muslim background. He has lived on the border of a predominantly Catholic area all his life. He is eight years old. Five years ago a bloody civil conflict broke out between the Muslim and Catholic communities, bringing to a head ancient sectarian/racial hatreds, and culminating in abductions, executions, bombings and drive-by shootings.

From the perspective of the potential for play-deprivation, what affect might this have had on Ishmael's behaviour and perceptions, and what as a playworker would you provide to address his situation?

The playworker and the play environment

Exercise 51

Identify ten essential criteria for being a good playworker.

Exercise 52

You are on the selection panel to choose two playworkers for a local adventure playground. Devise four questions for interviewees that would enable you to identify the 'right people for the job'.

Exercise 53

Recently I was asked what my job is. I said that it was to 'play with the kids'. Do you agree and why?

Exercise 54

One older playworker I know said you could tell the quality of the project by what she called the 'approach ratios'. That is, a high child-to-playworker approach level and a low playworker-to-child ratio. What do you think and why?

Exercise 55

The playwork menu arranges play experiences in four distinct categories – concepts, elements, identity and senses. Taking each category in turn, wordstorm popular play experiences into the various categories. Explaining why they belong there.

Exercise 56

'Children should be encouraged to tidy up after themselves.' How does this fit within a playwork philosophy of 'facilitating behaviour which is freely chosen, personally directed and intrinsically motivated'?

Exercise 57

Mel has been the Assistant Playworker for about six months. Today, Parveen has begun to talk to him in confidence about her uncle's sexual abuse of her. As a <u>playworker</u>, how should Mel react to this disclosure?

Exercise 58

A playworker perceives the children as biological, as well as social entities. How might this affect the style and content of any intervention s/he makes?

Exercise 59

When children are happily doing their own thing, what level of contact should a playworker have with them, and what form should it take?

Exercise 60

Bring to mind a specific incident of children's behaviour which you found difficult and record it, or describe it in some way on chart paper.

When the behaviour was actually taking place, what was:

i   your perception of the child(ren), what did you feel and why did you feel that way?

ii   the child's perception of you, what was s/he feeling and why was s/he feeling that way?

iii   your perceptions of the play space, what things did you have to consider and what were your priorities?

iv   the child(ren)'s perception of the play space, what were their needs and was the play space fulfilling them?

v   your reaction to the behaviour, what did you do and why?

vi   the child's perception of your reaction – did your action do something useful and positive, or did it reinforce or confirm a particular view of the world for the child?

Exercise 61

There are fifteen distinct play types. Discuss the materials, props and environmental conditions you would need to facilitate each one.

Exercise 62

The level of cleanliness and hygiene of any play project is a measure of the worker's respect for the kids. What other factors also give out this message of valuation to them, and why is this so?

Exercise 63

A 'good' play-enabling environment contains essential 'physical' and 'qualitative' criteria. In your view, what would they be?

Exercise 64

You have been asked to arrange a holiday for children from an inner-city area. Money is no object, within reason. Where would you take them and why?

Exercise 65

What indicators would tell me that the qualitative criteria I have devised in the development of a play site are the right ones?

Exercise 66

In his Theory of Loose Parts, Nicholson states that, 'Children love to interact with . . .'

a   What do the children you work with love to interact with?
b   Write a list of twenty loose parts you judge should be available and discuss why.
c   Nicholson suggests that children need to interact with fire, gases and so on. How can this be done?

Evaluating and assessing children's play needs

Exercise 67

The kids came over and said, 'This is a brilliant playground.' If the children said that about your project, what in particular would they be saying about it and why?

Exercise 68

You have been asked by your boss to assess the play needs of the children living in a particular housing development, and to suggest possible provision ideas to him or her. In the absence of any guidance,

a   how would you address the problem of assessing play needs?
b   how would you match provision to these needs once assessed?

Exercise 69

Your patch contains an adventure playground, two holiday playschemes and four fixed equipment play sites. It is your job to evaluate their effectiveness. What criteria would you use to do this and why?

Please give your response in two forms:

a   in the context of play as development/survival
b   in common sense, easy access language.

Exercise 70

The Khan's have one ten-year-old daughter and two sons, one eight years old and one six. One son, Parvez, is wheelchair bound, the other Murza, is blind.

What steps would you take to ensure that each of the Khan children have equal access to the play opportunities you provide?

Exercise 71

You have been appointed as the senior worker on a new play project whose characteristics have yet to be defined. Your manager says that she wants the project to be a response to the play needs of the local children.

Without asking the children themselves, how would you:

a   assess their play needs?
and
b   what responses would you suggest to these needs and why?

Strategy, policy and design

Exercise 72

UNESCO will give your organisation a rolling budget of £250K over three years to create, manage and evaluate a play project to bring the children of a divided community together, on receipt of a convincing developmental strategy. What do you think that strategy should include?

Exercise 73

You are going to work at a different project which has been established for over ten years and is in a state of decline. All you know about the project is that it is 'heavy', male dominated and displays an obsession with sport, particularly football and pool. The area is populated by people from a culture little understood by you.

As the new senior worker, outline the four-part strategy you would employ at the project during the early part of your term there.

Exercise 74

You are the senior worker on the project. For the past few weeks the time keeping of one of the other workers has fallen well below par and is affecting the performance of the team and the general ambience of the project.

What is your strategy for dealing with this?

Exercise 75

You want to create an evolutionary play space. What will be your main considerations and why?

Exercise 76

A community group you work with wants to develop a small play area on their estate. They are currently looking at catalogues from fixed equipment manufacturers and they have already raised over half the money they need. You have persuaded them to wait and to participate in a design exercise with you. What design criteria for a 'good' but 'realistic' play environment would you invite them to explore at this stage?

Exercise 77

On our project a lot of the outside area is taken up by 'boys' games' like football. Suggest three ways in which an outside area can be more fairly utilised to cater for needs other than ball games.

Exercise 78

You have been appointed as the senior worker on a brand new play project. Management has asked for your ideas in relation to the landscaping and design of the outside area, which is approximately $100\,m^2$ in size.

List and sketch your ideas of what you feel would be most relevant, paying particular attention to providing opportunities for the expression of the major play types.

Exercise 79

Tomorrow you have to talk to members of the local Recreation Committee about the development of one ingredient of a play policy.

You know they are interested in establishing a number of unstaffed, equipped play areas of the swings, slides and climbing frame type. You want them to put more thought into the process. Make a list of the development criteria you would regard as important in this context and list beside each item a physical provision response and the reasons why you would choose it.

Exercise 80

Kylie wants to do deep play, Desmond symbolic play, Tanvir creative play, and Gill and Itoku, rough and tumble. How would you facilitate these within the play environment you operate?

Useful playwork addresses

Organisations and individuals who can offer advice, training and/or research in Evolutionary Playwork:

PlayEducation/Bob Hughes – played@dial.pipex.com
Jess Milne – 07944 874821, jess@superlife.com
Marianne Mannello – marianne.mannello@talk21.com
Hackney Play Association – 168 Pitfield Street, London N1 8JP, 020 7729 6396
Mike Conway (See Hackney Play Association)
Sandra Melville, PLAYLINK, The Co-op Centre, Unit 5 Upper, 11 Mowll Street, London SW9 6BG
PlayWales, Baltic House, Mount Stuart Square, Cardiff, 029 2048 6060
     mail@playwales.org.uk
Doug Cole and Jo Jones – d.cole@cardiff.gov.uk
Stephen Rennie – S.Rennie@lmu.ac.uk
Gordon Sturrock, The Play Practice, 41 Rudloe Road, London SW12 0DR
Steven Chown, Play Development Officer, Leeds City Council, Under 8's Service, 9th Floor West, Merrion House, Leeds LS2 8DT, 0113 247 4990 steven.chown@leeds.gov.uk
Cath Gordon – gin88@dial.pipex.com
Barnet Play Association – BarnetPlayAssociation@compuserve.com
Perry Else – Perry.ludemos@virgin.net
Mel Potter – mel@celyddon.org

Bibliography

Abernethy, W.D. (1977) *Playleadership*. London: NPFA

Abernethy, W.D. (1984) in *Playwork: Bases, Methods and Objectives. Proceedings of PlayEd '84*. Bolton: PlayEducation/Bolton MBC

Allport, G.W. (1954) *The Nature of Prejudice*. Cambridge, MA: Addison-Wesley

Amir, Y. (1969) 'Contact Hypothesis in Ethnic Relations', *Psychological Bulletin*, 71, 319–42

Arendt, H. (1958) *The Human Condition*. Chicago: University of Chicago Press

Austin, R. (1986) 'Playground Culture in Northern Ireland', *Junior Education*, November

Balbernie, R. (1999) 'Infant Mental Health', *Young Minds Magazine*, 39

Baldwin, J.D. (1982) 'The Nature–Nurture Error Again', *The Behaviour and Brain Sciences*, 5, 155–6

Ball, D.J. and King, K.L. (1991) 'Playground Injuries: A Scientific Appraisal of Popular Concerns', *J. Roy. Soc. Health*, August, 134–7

Bar-On, D. (1993) 'Children as Unintentional Transmitters of Undisclosable Life Events', in Stiftung für Kinder (ed.), *Children, War and Prosecution*. Osnabruck: Stiftung für Kinder, UNICEF

Bateson, G. (1955) 'A Theory of Play and Fantasy', *Psychiatric Research Reports*, 2, 39–51

Bateson, P.P.G. and Hinde, R.A. (1976) *Growing Points in Ethology*. Cambridge: Cambridge University Press

Bateson, P. and Martin, P. (1999) *Design for Life*. London: Cape

Battram, A. (1997) 'Designing Possibility Space', *PlayEd '97*, Ely: PlayEducation

BBC (1998) 'Beyond a Joke'. Horizon

Belfrage, S. (1987) *The Crack*. London: Grafton Books

Bennett, E.L., Diamond, M.C., Krech, D. and Rosenzweig, M.R. (1964) 'Chemical and Anatomical Plasticity of Brain', *Science*, 146, Oct.

Bexton, W.H., Heron, W. and Scott, T.H. (1954) 'Effects of Decreasing Variation in the Sensory Environment', *Canadian Journal of Psychology*, 8, 2

Boden, M.A. (1979) *Piaget*. Brighton: The Harvester Press Ltd

Bonel, P. and Lindon, J. (1996) *Good Practice in Playwork*. Cheltenham: Stanley Thornes

Bruce, T. (1994) 'Play, the Universe and Everything', in Moyles, J.R. (ed.), *The Excellence of Play*. Buckingham; Philadelphia: Open University Press

Bruner, J.S. (1972) 'Nature and Uses of Immaturity', *American Psychologist*, 27, 8

Bruner J.S. (1974) 'Child's Play', *New Scientist*, 62, 126

Bruner, J.S. (1976) 'Introduction', *Play: Its Role in Development and Evolution*. New York: Penguin

Bruner, J.S., Jolly, A. and Sylva, K. (1976) *Play: Its Role in Development and Evolution*. New York: Penguin

Burman, S. (1986) 'The Context of Childhood in South Africa: An Introduction', in Burman, S. and Reynolds, P. (eds), *Growing Up in a Divided Society*. Johannesburg: Ravan Press

Cairns, E. (1987) 'Society as Child Abuser: Northern Ireland', in Rogers, W.S., Hervey, D. and Ash, E. (eds), *Child Abuse and Neglect. Facing the Challenge*. Milton Keynes: The Open University

Children Act (1989) *Guidance and Regulations*. Vol. 2, Chapter 6.

Chilton-Pearce, J. (1980) *Magical Child*. New York: Bantam Books

Chugani, H. (1998) *BBC News*, 20th April.

Cobb, E. (1993) *The Ecology of Imagination in Childhood*. Dallas: Spring Publications

Connolly, K. (1973) 'Factors Influencing the Learning of Manual Skills by Young Children', in Hinde, R.A. and Stevenson-Hinde J.G. (eds), *Constraints on Learning: Limitations and Predispositions*. London: Academic Press

Convention on the Rights of the Child, United Nations, September 1990

Conway, M. (1996) 'Puddles – a workshop', *PlayEd '96*. Ely: PlayEducation

Cooper, R. (1996) *The Evolving Mind*. Birmingham: Windhorse Publications

Cosco, N. (1999) Personal communication.

Darwin, C. (1859) *On the Origin of the Species*. Oxford: Oxford University Press

Dawkins, R. (1989) *The Selfish Gene*. Oxford: Oxford University Press

Duncan, M.R. (1977) 'The Cultural Ramifications of Recreation in Belfast, North Ireland', in Stevens, P. (ed.), *Studies in the Anthropology of Play*. West Point, N.Y.: Leisure Press

Edelman, G. (1992) *Bright Air, Brilliant Fire*. London: Penguin Books

Eibl-Eibesfeldt, I. (1967) 'Concepts of Ethology and their Significance in the Study of Human Behaviour', in Stevenson, W.W. and Rheingold, H.L. (eds), *Early Behaviour: Comparative and Developmental Approaches*. New York: Wiley

Eibl-Eibesfeldt, I. (1970) *Ethology: The Biology of Behaviour*. New York: Holt, Rinehart and Winston

Einon, D.F., Morgan, M.J. and Kibbler, C.C. (1978) 'Brief Period of Socialisation and Later Behaviour in the Rat', *Developmental Psychobiology*, 11, 3

Einon, D. (1985) *Creative Play*. Harmondsworth: Penguin

Else, P. and Sturrock, G. (1998) 'The Playground as Therapeutic Space: Playwork as Healing', in *Play in a Changing Society: Research, Design, Application*, the Proceedings of the IPA/USA Triennial National Conference. Longmont, CO: IPA

Erikson, E.H. (1963) *Childhood and Society*. New York: W.W. Norton

Evan, D. and Zarate, O. (1999) *Introducing Evolutionary Psychology*. Cambridge: Icon

Fagan, R. (1974) 'Modelling How and Why play works', in Bruner, J.S., Jolly, A. and Sylva, K. (eds), *Play, Its Role in Development and Evolution*. London: Penguin Books

Fagan, R.M. (1978) 'Evolutionary Biological Models of Animal Play Behaviour', in Burghardt, G.M. and Bekoff, M. (eds), *Development of Behaviour*. New York: Garland Press

Furedi, F. (1999) 'Why Are We Afraid For Our Children?', in *Proceedings of PLAYLINK/Portsmouth City Council Conference*. Portsmouth: PLAYLINK

Feitelson, D. (1977) 'Cross-Cultural Studies of Representational Play', in Tizard, B. and Harvey, D. (eds), *Biology of Play*. London: William Heinemann Medical Books Ltd

Ferchmin, P.A. and Eterovic, V.A. (1979) 'Mechanisms of Brain Growth by Environmental Stimulation', *Science*, 205, 3

Fraser, M. (1974) *Children in Conflict*. Harmondsworth: Penguin

Freud, S. (1918) *Totems and Taboo*. New York: New Republic

Frost, J.L. and Jacobs, P.J. (1995) 'play-deprivation: A Factor in Juvenile Violence', *Dimensions*, 3, 3.

Garbarino, J. (1993) 'Challenges We Face in Understanding Children and War: A Personal Essay', *Child Abuse and Neglect*, 17, 787–93

Garbarino, J. and Kostelny, K. (1997) 'What Children Can Tell Us From Living in a War Zone', in Osofsky, J.D. (ed.), *Children in a Violent Society*. New York: The Guilford Press

Garvey, C. (1977) *Play*. London: Fontana/Open Books Original

Geertz, C. (1972) 'Deep Play: a Description of a Balinese Cockfight', *Daedalus*, 101

Geertz, C. (1973) *The Interpretation of Cultures*. New York: Basic Books

Goleman, D. (1995) *Emotional Intelligence*. London: Bloomsbury Publishing Plc

Gordon, C. (1999) 'Riskogenics: An Exploration of Risk', *PlayEd '99*. Ely: PlayEducation

Gould, S.J. (1996) *Full House: The Spread of Excellence from Plato to Darwin*. New York: Harmony Books

Grof, S. (1975) *Realms of the Human Unconscious*. New York: The Viking Press

Groos, K. (1898) *The Play of Animals*. New York: Appleton

Gruber, H.E. (1974) *Darwin on Man*. New York: Dutton

Gunner, M. (1998) 'Stress and Brain Development'. Talk delivered to Michigan Association of Infant Mental Health. 22nd Annual Conference

Hall, G.S. (1904) *Adolescence: its Psychology and its Relations to Physiology, Anthropology, Sociology, Sex, Crime, Religion and Education*. Vol. 1. New York: Appleton

Handscomb, B. (1999) 'Who is Judging Who? Part One', *PlayEd '99*. Ely: PlayEducation

Hardin, R. (1995) *One for All*. Princeton, New Jersey: Princeton University Press

Harlow, H.F. and Harlow, M.K. (1962) 'The Effect of Rearing Conditions on Behaviour', *Bulletin of the Menninger Clinic*, 26, 213–24

Harlow, H.F. and Suomi, S.J. (1971) 'Social Recovery by Isolation-Reared Monkeys'. *Proc. Nat. Acad. Sci. USA*, 68, 7, 1534–8

Hart, R. (1979) *Children's Experience of Place*. New York: Irvington

Hart, R. (1999) Personal Communication. 24 September

Heron, W. (1957) 'The Pathology of Boredom', *Scientific American*, 196

Hickey, E.W. (1991) *Serial Murderers and their Victims*. Pacific Grove, CA: Brooks/Publishing Co.

Hodgkin, R.A. (1985) *Play and Exploring*. London: Methuen

Hughes, B. (1984) 'Play a Definition by Synthesis', in *Play Provision and Play Needs*. Lancaster: PlayEducation

Hughes, B. (1988) 'Play and the Environment', *Leisure Manager*, 6, 1

Hughes, B. (1993) 'A Child's World: Risk, Reality and Learning', *PlayLinks*, Feb.

Hughes, B. (1995) 'Editorial', *International Play Journal*, 3, 2

Hughes, B. (1996a) *A Playworker's Taxonomy of Play Types*. London: PLAYLINK

Hughes, B. (1996b) *Play Environments: A Question of Quality*. London: PLAYLINK

Hughes, B. (1997a) 'Playwork in Extremis: One of Many Applications of Playwork's Values, Methods and Worth', in *Proceedings of The World of Play, The Changing Nature of Children's Play and Playwork*, San Antonio, TX: University of the Incarnate Word

Hughes, B. (1997b) 'Towards a Technology of Playwork', in *Proceedings of PLAYLINK/Portsmouth City Council Conference*. Portsmouth: PLAYLINK

Hughes, B. (1998) 'Playwork in Extremis – The RAP Approach', in *Proceedings of Childhood and Youth Studies: Towards an Interdisciplinary Framework*. Cambridge: Anglia Polytechnic University and DfEE

Hughes, B. (1999a) 'Does Playwork Have a Neurological Rationale?', in *The Proceedings of PlayEducation '99 Part One*. Ely: PlayEducation

Hughes, B. (1999b) *Games Not Names*. Belfast: PlayBoard

Hughes, B. (1999c) 'Uncensoring Play – Towards an Evolutionary Perspective for Facilitating Recapitulation', in the *Proceedings of the 14th IPA World Conference, Lisbon, Portugal*. IPA: Lisbon

Hughes, B. (2000) 'A Dark and Evil Cul-De-Sac: Has Children's Play in Urban Belfast Been Adulterated by the Troubles?' MA Dissertation. Cambridge: Anglia Polytechnic University

Hughes, B. and Williams, H. (1982) 'Talking About Play 1–5', *Play Times*, London: N.P.F.A.

Hutt, C. (1979) 'Exploration and Play', in Sutton-Smith, B. (ed.), *Play and Learning*. New York: Gardener Press

Hutt, S.J., Tyler, S., Hutt, C. and Christopherson, H. (1989) *Play, Exploration and Learning*. London: Routledge

Huttenlocher, P.R. (1990) 'Morphometric Study of Human Cerebral Cortex Development', *Neuropsychologia*, 28, 6

Huttenlocher, P.R. (1992) 'Neural Plasticity', in Asbury, McKhann and McDonald (eds), *Diseases of the Nervous System*, 1, 63–71

Huttenmoser, M. and Degan-Zimmermann, D. (1995) *Lebenstraume für Kinder*. Zurich: Swiss Science Foundation

International Play Journal (1996) Vol. 4 Number 3

Jennings, S. (1995) 'Playing for Real', *International Play Journal*, 3, 2, 132–41

Jones, S. (1993) *The Language of the Genes*. London: Flamingo

King, F.M. (1987) 'Play Environment's Criteria', Paper, Merseyside Playwork Training Project

King, F.M. (1988) 'Informed Choices'. Liverpool: PlayEducation Meeting

King, F.M. (1988) *Bristol Play Policy*. Bristol City Council: Leisure Services

Koestler, A. (1967) *The Ghost in the Machine*. London: Hutchinson

Kotulak, R. (1996) *Inside the Brain*. Kansas City: Andrews and McNeel

Loizos, C. (1967) 'Play Behaviour in Higher Primates: a Review', in Morris, D. (ed.), *Primate Ethology*. Chicago: Aldine Press

Lorenz, K. (1972) 'Psychology and Phylogeny', in *Studies in Animal and Human Behaviour*. Cambridge, MA: Harvard University Press

Lyons, H.A. (1974) 'Terrorist Bombing and the Psychological Sequelae', *Journal of the Irish Medical Association*, 67, 15

Machel, Grac'a (1996) *Impact of Armed Conflict on Children*. United Nations Department for Policy Co-ordination and Sustainable Development (DPCSD), August 1996

McEwen, B.S. (1999) 'Stress and Hippocampal Plasticity', *Annual Review of the Neurosciences*, 22, 105–22

McFarland, D.J. (1973) Discussion of Connolly's (1973) contribution

McGrath, A. and Wilson, R. (1985) 'Factors Which Influence the Prevalence and Variation of Psychological Problems in Children in Northern Ireland'. Unpublished paper: Annual Conference, The Development Society, Belfast

McKee, M. (1986) 'Playwork', *PlayEd '86*. Ely: PlayEducation

McKinney, W.T., Young, L.D., Suomi, S.J. and Davis, J.M. (1973) 'Chlorpromazine Treatment of Disturbed Monkeys', *Arch. Gen. Psychiatry*, 29, Oct.

Meares, R. (1993) *The Metaphor of Play*. London: Jason Aronson Inc.

Melville, S. (1996) Personal Communication

Melville, S. (2000) Personal Communication

Milne, J. (1997) 'Play Structures', *PlayEd '97*. Ely: PlayEducation

Miller, S. (1973) 'Ends, Means and Galumphing: Some Leitmotifs of Play', *American Anthropologist*, 75, 87–98

Moore, R.C. (1986) *Childhood's Domain*. London: Croom Helm

Morris, D. (1964) 'The Response of Animals to a Restricted Environment', *Symposium of the Zoological Society of London*, 13, 99

Morris, D. (ed.) (1967) *Primate Ethology*. Weidenfeld & Nicolson

Murphy, D. (1978) *A Place Apart*. London: Penguin Books

National Centres for Playwork Education and Training (1995) Values Guide – National Vocational Qualifications in Playwork

Neumann, E.A. (1971) The elements of play. Unpublished doctoral dissertation. University of Illinois

Nicholson, S. (1971) 'How Not to Cheat Children: The Theory of Loose Parts', *Landscape Architecture*, Oct.

Novak, M.A. and Harlow, H.F. (1975) 'Social Recovery of Monkeys Isolated for the First Year of Life: 1. Rehabilitation and Therapy', *Developmental Psychology*, 11, 4

Ogden, T. (1993) *In One's Bones – The Clinical Genius of Winnicott*, Goldman, D. (ed.), New York: Aronson

Orr, D.W. (1993) 'Love It or Lose It: The coming Biophilia Revolution', in Kellert, S.R. and Wilson, E.O. (eds), *The Biophilia Hypothesis*. Washington, DC: Island Press

Palmer, K. (1994) http://dialog.net:85/homepage

Palmer, K. (1994) *Steps to the Threshold of the Social. Part 3: Anti-Category Theory*. Copyright 1994 Kent D. Palmer

Palmer, S. and Major, B. (1987) 'Adventure Playgrounds – Survive and Thrive', *PlayEd '87*. Ely: PlayEducation

Parkinson, C. (1987) *Children's Range Behaviour*. Birmingham: PlayBoard

Patrick, G.T.W. (1914) 'The Psychology of Play', *Journal of Genetic Psychology*, 21, 469–84

Pearce, J.C. (1977) *Magical Child*. New York: Bantam

Perry, B.D. (1994) 'Neurobiological Sequelae of Childhood Trauma: Post Traumatic Stress Disorders in Children', in Murberg, M. (ed.), *Catecholamines in Post-Traumatic Stress Disorder: Emerging Concepts*. Washington, DC: American Psychiatric Association

Perry, B.D. (1995) 'Childhood Trauma. The Neurobiology of Adaptation and Use-Dependent Development of the Brain. How States Become Traits', *Infant Mental Health Journal*, 16, 4

Perry, B.D., Arvinte, A., Marcellus, J. and Pollard, R. (1996) 'Syncope, Bradycardia, Cataplexy and Paralysis: Sensitisation of an Opiod-Mediated Dissociative Response Following Childhood Trauma', *Journal of the American Academy of Child and Adolescent Psychiatry*.

Petrie, P. (1996) Personal Communication.

Piaget, J. (1951) *Play, Dreams and Imitation in Childhood*. New York: W.W. Norton

Pinker, S. (1998) *How the Mind Works*. Harmondsworth: Penguin

PlayBoard (1990) *Play Without Frontiers*. Belfast: PlayBoard (NI)

PLAYLINK (1992) *Open Access Play and the Children Act*. London: PLAYLINK

PLAYLINK (1997) *Risk and Safety in Play: the Law and Practice for Adventure Play-grounds*. London: Routledge

Reaney, M.J. (1916) *The Psychology of the Organized Game*. Cambridge: Cambridge University Press

Rennie, S. (1997) *The Roots of Consensus*. M.A. Dissertation, Leeds Metropolitan University

Rennie, S. (1999) 'The Isms of Playwork', *PlayEd '99*. Ely: PlayEducation

Rosenzweig, M.R., Krech, D., Bennett, E.L. and Diamond, M.C. (1962) 'Effects of Environmental Complexity and Training on Brain Chemistry and Anatomy', *Journal of Comparative and Physiological Psychology*, 55, 4, 429–37

Rosenzweig, M.R. (1971) 'Effects of Environments on Development of Brain and of Behaviour', in Tobach, E., Aronson, L.R. and Shaw, E. (eds), *The Bio-Psychology of Development*. New York: Academic Press

Rosenzweig, M.R., Bennett, E.L. and Diamond, M.C. (1972) 'Brain Changes in Response to Experience', *Scientific American*, Feb

Rowe, J. (1986) 'The Green Play Concept', *PlayEd '86*. Ely: PlayEducation

Ruse, M. (1979) *Sociobiology – Sense or Nonsense*. Boston: Reidel

Schlosberg, H. (1947) 'The Concept of Play', *Psych. Rev.*, 54, 229–31

Schwartzman, H.B. (1978) *Transformations – The Anthropology of Children's Play*. London: Plenum Press

Shepard, P. (1982) *Nature and Madness*. San Francisco: Sierra Club

Simpson, M.J.A. (1976) 'The Study of Animal Play', in Bateson, P.P.G. and Hinde, R.A. (eds), *Growing Points in Ethology*. Cambridge: Cambridge University Press

Singer, J.L. (1973) *The Child's World of Make-Believe*. New York: Academic Press

Smith, P.K. (1978) 'Play is Only One Way to Learn', *New Society*, July.

Smith, P.K. (1982) 'Does Play Matter? Functional and Evolutionary Aspects of Animal and Human Play', *The Behavioural and Brain Sciences*, 5

Smith, P.K. (1994) 'Play Training: An Overview', in Hellendoorn, J., van der Kooij, R. and Sutton-Smith, B. (eds), *Play and Intervention*. Albany: State University of New York Press

Smith, P.K., Cowie, H. and Blades, M. (1998) *Understanding Children's Development*. Oxford: Blackwell Publishers

Smyth, M. (1998) *Half the Battle*. Derry Londonderry: INCORE

Sobel, D. (1993) *Children's Special Places: Exploring the Role of Forts, Dens and Bush Houses in middle-childhood*. Tucson: Zephyr Press

Spencer, H. (1896) *Principles of Psychology*. Vol. 2, Part 2 (3rd edn). New York: Appleton

Steinbeck, J. (1935) *To A God Unknown*. London: Heinemann

Sturrock, G. (1989) 'Shamanism', *PlayEd '89*. Ely: PlayEducation

Sturrock, G. (1997) Personal Communication

Sturrock, G. and Hughes, B. (1998) 'Definition of Sectarianism', in Hughes, B. *Games Not Names*. Belfast: PlayBoard

Sturrock, G. (1999) Personal Communication

Suomi, S.J. and Harlow, H.F. (1971) 'Monkeys Without Play', in *Play*, a *Natural History Magazine Special Supplement*, December

Sutton-Smith, B. (ed.) (1979) *Play and Learning*. New York: Gardener Press, Inc.

Sutton-Smith, B. (1997) *The Ambiguity of Play*. Cambridge, MA: Harvard University Press

Sylva, K. (1977) 'Play and Learning', in Tizard, B. and Harvey, D. (eds), *Biology of Play*. London: Heinemann

Talbot, J. and Frost, V.L. (1989) 'Magical Playscapes', *Childhood Education*, 66, 1, 11–19

Taylor, C., Bonel, P. and Bagnall-Oakley, R. (1999) 'The Good Enough Playworker and the Facilitating Environment', in *The Proceedings of PlayEducation '99 Part One*. Ely: PlayEducation

The Children Act (1989) *Guidance and Regulations*, Vol. 2, Chapter 6. Section A

Thomashow, M. (1995) *Ecological Identity*. Cambridge, MA: MIT Press

Tobin, J. (1997) 'A Second Chance for Christian', *The Detroit News*, 9th February

Towards A Safer Adventure Playground. (1980) London: NPFA

Tsukamoto, I. (1997) 'Playing, Praying and Painting', *PlayEd '97*. Ely: PlayEducation

Vachss, A.H. and Bakal, Y. (1979) *The Lifestyle Violent Juvenile: The Secure Treatment Approach*. Lexington, MA: Lexington Books/D.C. Heath

Vandenberg, B. (1978) 'Play and Development from an Ethological Perspective', *American Psychologist*, 724–36

van Hooff, J.A.R.A.M. (1972) 'A Comparative Approach to the Phylogeny of Laughter and Smiling', in Hinde, R.A. (ed.), *Non-verbal Communication*. Cambridge: Cambridge University Press

Vygotsky, L.S. (1978) *Mind in Society*. Cole, M., John-Steiner, V., Scribner, S. and Souberman, E. (eds) Cambridge: Harvard University Press

Wilber, K. (1996) *Up from Eden*. Wheaton, IL: Quest Books

Wilcox, B.L. and Naimark, H. (1991) 'The Rights of the Child, Progress Towards Human Dignity', *American Psychologist*, 46, 1, 49

Wilson, E.O. (1975) *Sociobiology*. Cambridge: Harvard University Press

Wilson, E.O. (1992) *The Diversity of Life*. London: Penguin Books

Winnicott, D.W. (1992) *Playing and Reality*. London: Routledge

Wood, D.J., Bruner, J.S. and Ross, G. (1976) 'The Role of Tutoring in Problem Solving', *Journal of Child Psychology and Psychiatry*, 17, 89–100

Woolcott, J. (1987) 'Activity – Exploration or Entertainment?' *PlayEd '87*. Ely: PlayEducation

Zuckerman, M. (1969) 'Theoretical Formulations: 1', in Zubek, J.P. (ed.), *Sensory Deprivation: Fifteen Years of Research*. New York: Appleton-Century-Crofts

Zuckerman, M. (1984) 'Sensation Seeking: A Comparative Approach to a Human Trait', *The Behaviour and Brain Sciences*, 7

Index